D1525688

THIS BOOK WILL SHOW YOU HOW TO:

- Remove Derogatory Information That Reflects Negative on Your Credit Reports.

- Re-establish or Build First Time Credit.

- Obtain Visa and Mastercards with Interest Rates as Low as 10% Annually.

- Get Visa and Mastercards Even if You Presently Have a Bad Credit History.

- Develop and Maintain Sole and Separate Credit (as a Woman).

- Choose a Bank That's Right for You.

- Get Signature Loans and Other "No Questions Asked" Lines of Credit.

- Overcome the Hurdles of Being Self-Employed When Applying for Credit.

- Pay Some of Your Creditors Late Without Having Your Delinquency Reported.

- Consolidate Your Bills and Get Out of Debt.

- Make Money with Credit.

Plus Much Much More!

THE
WORLD
OF
CREDIT

DAVID B. TRIEMERT

Papermate Publishing Company

Long Beach, California

THE WORLD OF CREDIT

Published By
Papermate Publishing Company

All Rights Reserved

For information address:
Papermate Publishing Company
4320 Atlantic Avenue
Suite 4-A
Long Beach, CA 90807

Printed In The U.S.A.

DEDICATION

To the millions of normal everyday American Consumers who've never quite understood the "ins" and "outs" of our credit system - may all things be made clear.

To all of you who feel you've been short changed in your world of credit - it's time you got your money's worth.

To the entrepreneur who's success in life has been hindered by a lack of Start-Up or Operating Capital - may you one day own the Bank!

FOREWORD

For this book, written by David Triemert, I typed the final draft, edited, crossed some "t"s and dotted a few "i"s, being careful to retain David's folksy, homespun style.

This book is largely autobiographical. David is your typical "high school dropout makes good" type of entrepreneur. Now, at the tender age of twenty-six, he has worked one half of his life to support himself. He has finally become quite successful, and writing seems to be his forte.

Having known David and to work with him has been an experience. Our friendship has blossomed into maturity. David has helped me in the growth of my own company as well; he has a natural insight into solving business problems.

I'm quite sure you'll enjoy reading this book. It's certainly unique, and it contains something of value for practically everyone. There must be a world of people out there who should read The World of Credit.

Ed Deveny,
Deveny Technical

ACKNOWLEDGMENTS

First of all I would like to recognize and give credit to my dear friend Debbie Fruh as the source of inspiration which gave birth to my writing career.

To my family who shared the journey through the world of credit with me, both good times and bad, especially my mother Ellen Triemert. She was my first creditor and the one who has demonstrated the most belief in me through her unconditional actions and unconditional love. In return I hope to debt service her as I would a 30-year mortgage in the years to come.

Also I'd like to thank all my creditors, business associates and friends for their trust and support they've shared with me over the years.

Many people were involved in the preparation of this work. A special "Thank You" goes out to Lucio Ortiz, Arlene Phillips, Deborah White, Catrina Morrill, Ed Hernandez, and Francie Rozycki.

Finally, I would like to recognize Ed Deveny for helping me transform this dream into a reality. His contribution has been the frosting on my cake.

David B. Triemert

THE
WORLD
OF
CREDIT

DAVID B. TRIEMERT

Papermate Publishing Company

Long Beach, California

TABLE OF CONTENTS

Preface

Chapter

Appendix

PREFACE

Welcome to the World of Credit.

For the last eight years, I've been actively involved in the credit industry. In writing this book, I've dedicated myself to share every bit of credit information I have come to learn from experience over the past. I've challenged myself to let my hair down (so to speak) and shoot straight from the hip in writing this book. After reading this material, I'm convinced that any questions you may have held regarding consumer credit will be fully answered. I believe the general public is entitled to being well informed on how this credit system of ours works, who the key players are and furthermore, how to play the game.

Our credit system is very large and complex. It took me years of practice and research to untie all the knots in it. In writing this book, I can honestly say that the contents have been gathered through hard-core credit experiences. I, personally, have done very well in building credit and I have also done a fine job of ruining my credit, too! I've been on both sides of the coin. Not only have I spent a small fortune on all these experiences but I've also done very well in the Credit Consulting Business. I've helped many others establish or re-establish their credit.

My motivation to write on the credit system came to me while being a consultant in the industry. One of my previous books, The Art of Building Credit, was written as a "do-it-yourself" manual. It was sold to our callers who could not afford our services in the office. It contained 150 pages of good credit-building information but was limited to just building credit, whereas this book covers almost every aspect of consumer credit known.

Shortly after The Art of Building Credit was completed, one of my associates challenged me to write another book on the credit system which would be affordable to all, could be purchased almost anywhere books are sold in the U.S., would answer every question one could conceivably have concerning consumer credit, and would be easy to read and comprehend.

I accepted the challenge!

I decided to write one more book: A *one-size-fits-all* credit book; a credit book that would satisfy the needs of men and women, young, middle-aged, retired, student; self-employed, divorced, bankrupt, and even the already established. Yes, I even have some information of value to the person with Gold Plated Credit.

I named this book <u>The World of Credit</u> for a couple of reasons. The first is that we in America, in the 1980's, 1990's and beyond, live and will continue to live in a world that operates on and revolves around credit and there's no reason to believe it's going to change. The only changes I've seen in this crazy world of credit are in the attitudes of the people who have always paid cash in place of plastic or another form of credit. The American people have come to realize that just one major credit card is vital in our present lives. The second reason I named this book The World of Credit is because the word "World," meaning "big," properly describes the size and caliber of these institutions behind all this credit, from the lenders and merchants, right down to the credit reporting agencies themselves. These are billion-dollar corporations I'm talking about. Since this book is to be sold nationally, it was written in such a way that all the practices and principles it contains will work and hold true regardless of which state you may live in. Some states, however, have different lending regulations that they are subject to but I'll be sure and outline any variations when they apply.

In closing this introduction, let me just say that your past credit experience is *history*. If your past has been positive, carry it forward into the future; however, if your past has been negative, let today be your birthday and start over. You don't have to live in subjugation to bad credit if you don't want to. This book will show you how to remove all derogatory credit information from your reports in most every instance.

I hope you find this book to be worth its weight in gold, and, once again, I personally welcome you to The World of Credit.

CHAPTER 1

WHAT'S CREDIT

What's credit? The word credit is derived from the Latin word "credere" which means - belief! Credibility, or your "Credit" "Ability" - your ability to be granted credit and pay back on time as agreed, is what credit is really all about. Most people see credit as a thing; to me, credit is an action. It's a motion word, an ongoing process which never seems to stop. To some people, credit is a fresh, crisp and lively experience, especially to the young person buying his or her first new car on credit terms or the newlyweds who are about to move into their first home and start making mortgage payments, building some equity for the future.

On the other hand, credit can be dull, frustrating or boring to someone who's over-burdened with bills or for those who suffer from a bad credit experience. Credit for the people in these situations can be sheer torture! Personally, I've worn both hats.

I can remember my first credit transaction. With a co-signer, I borrowed $800.00 from my credit union to purchase a home stereo. It seemed like so much fun - just sign on the dotted line and away you go. Well then, the first payment came due and that kind of put a damper on things, but it was still exciting to know that someone actually trusted me enough to give me money in exchange for my written agreement stating that I'd pay it back on time as agreed along with some interest as a profit to the lender.

Before my first credit transaction on the stereo had been paid off, I made another credit purchase on a $300.00 car stereo. I applied through a finance company and was approved for that deal without a co-signer. I thought, "What fun! This is truly marvelous!" Over the next twelve months I bought a gold pocket watch on credit for $300.00, a motorcycle for $1,000.00 and then some furniture for $500.00. I ordered five or six magazine subscriptions, joined a dozen book and record clubs, borrowed another $4,000.00 for a down payment on my first home and then another $300.00 to replace the pocket watch I had lost but was still paying for. Everything was fine and dandy, all payments were being made on time as agreed.

Then came a major challenge in life: borrow $500.00 on my signature alone, no collateral, no co-signer, just me, on my signature alone. Well my bank approved the loan! I was walking in tall cotton. I was so proud of my accomplishment that I paid off the $500.00 in thirty days and then asked for $2000.00 a few weeks later and was approved on it, too. A few months later summer rolled around. I decided I didn't really care for the job I was in so I quit. I took the summer off. Somehow I rationalized that - hey, I'm only 19, I've been working full time for six years now, I deserve a break; besides that, who wants to cook steaks eight hours a day on a 600° broiler in a 100° restaurant kitchen? Not once did I realize that my creditors wouldn't take the summer off with me. It never dawned on me that the bills would keep coming in, vacation or not!

It didn't take much time for the bills to pile up, the phone began to ring with unpleasant creditors on the other end asking when I was going to make good on the account with them. I didn't work for three months. It seems like 90 days is the borderline in which creditors turn into connoisseurs of causing pain, pressure and discomfort.

Some of my accounts were turned over to collection agencies. These people are "masters" at making you sweat! They have a knack for making you downright miserable! I've often thought that the people who work for these collection agencies must have been abused or battered as children. They can be ruthless people! Don't ever tell one of these people you "intend" to pay a bill because "intentions" don't pay bills! That's what I've been told anyway.

When I tallied up all my bills, I found myself over $18,000.00 in debt at age 19. I decided it would be to my best interest to get a job. Nothing is difficult when you have the proper motivation.

However, paying back all this debt was a challenge when I looked at what I was paying for. The motorcycle was smashed up, the second pocket watch had been stolen, as well as the car stereo. The home stereo was sold at a fraction of its cost to a friend. The house I bought ended up being turned over to my brother. The furniture was later traded for a motorcycle which was later impounded, never to be seen again, and my credit was ruined!

What's credit? Well, it's nothing to play around with or abuse. Credit is a tool. It can make or break you.

Consumer debt (stereos, motorcycles, boats, furniture, clothes, etc.) will wipe you out in no time at all if you don't have a handle on your spending.

On the other hand, credit can actually save you money. It allows you to purchase necessities when they're on sale but too short on funds to pay cash for them. Credit can put you into the home of your dreams providing you can afford the monthly payments. Credit enables you to buy merchandise at distressed prices, to be enjoyed by you, or to be resold for a cash profit.

Many credit cards offer what's called a "grace" or "float" period. This is where you make a charge and then pay for it in full before the billing due date. There's no interest or finance charge if the full amount is paid in full each month. However, the lenders for Visa, MC, American Express, etc. still profit from the 2%-7% service fee that they charge the merchants.

Credit is good for those who learn to harness it whereas it's bad for those who are harnessed by it. Credit is a tool, not a toy! Probably the worst thing that can happen to you when you fail to pay your bills on time as agreed is that it will usually follow you for seven years on your credit files. Yes, it also ruins your reputation with personal bankers and small independent merchants where you deal directly with the owner, unlike big department stores where there's no personal relationship established. However, your inability or irresponsibility whichever causes you to pay your bills late or not at all, results in the worst part that most negative credit experiences remain on your credit reports and haunt you for *seven years* from the date they were reported to the Credit Reporting Bureau.

Your credit reports act as your silent partner, your shadow; they follow you everywhere you go, even, in some cases, if you move out of state. Your credit reports are an outer reflection of the inner person as far as your habits and attitudes towards paying your debtors is concerned. To let a lousy $50.00 doctor bill go unpaid and get turned over as a collection account tells other prospective creditors that you're irresponsible in your credit transactions and, furthermore, these new prospective creditors to which you apply for new credit will almost always deny you credit privileges if they see that just a $50.00 doctor bill has gone unpaid or unsettled in a case where it's being disputed by you, the consumer. Why would they want to loan you $500.00 or $5,000.00 if you had problems with a measly $50.00 doctor bill? If you can't handle a $50.00 medical expense, how will your manner of payment be in paying 48 monthly installments of $250.00 on a new car? I'm not chewing anyone out here. I'm just saying hey - put yourself in the lender's position. They want to see your track record, how have you paid your bills in the past? Personally, I don't care how you've paid your bills in the past. Furthermore, how you pay your bills in the future won't have much impact on me or my future either. I'm only saying that it's time we all wake up to this crazy world of credit we live in.

This book was written for "you" - not for me! Yes, it's going to be a great financial blessing, but that is not my motive for writing this book. My main drive in putting all this information and experience into book form that anyone can read and understand, is to fulfill what I've come to recognize as a vital need in America today. Some of you people need to learn how to establish first-time credit. Many of you need to repair derogatory credit. Some need to expand their credit lines and banking relationships, others need to learn to "place value" on their credit once they have it before they mess it up like I did. There are a lot more needs in mind that I hope to fulfill in writing this book, but my main desire once again is basically to give consumers a fair shake at learning this important information about our credit system, how it works and how it can work for you or against you.

I look at credit as a game - and it's not always a fair game - but you should know all the principals and rules that govern and control this game. You can win at this game just like any other. This game involves a *winner*, many times a *loser*, and a *strategy*. This game awards winners with new and higher credit lines and better terms and interest rates and on the flip side, this game chastises or penalizes losers in that they are forced to borrow at very high rates of interest and unfavorable credit terms, that is, if they can even get credit at all.

Whether you've been a winner or a loser in this game before, whether by choice or situation, I believe this book can still be a gold mine to anyone who follows its principles, regardless of which of the two categories you fall into. If you already have some good credit history behind you, then this book can show you how to get better terms and interest rates on credit cards and bank loans. I'll show you how to talk with bankers, how to negotiate interest rates and terms, how to pay some bills late when you "absolutely must" and not have it reflect on your credit reports, how to protect your credit once you have it and a host of other valuable credit practices.

If you've been a loser in this world of credit in the past, whether it was due to neglect on your part, a billing dispute with a creditor or a situation that was just unavoidable, this book will teach you how to turn your failure into success. You don't have to be subject to your past if you don't want to be. You don't have to let your past haunt your future. You can stand up and take control of the situation. You can become a winner again in this world of credit. The game is not over until you die.

If you've ever had the priceless opportunity to deal with a collection agency you probably have the illusion that your credit is ruined for life! Well, it's just not true, not if you won't settle for and accept it as so. If you have good credit, cherish it, protect it, pay on time and read this entire book. If you have derogatory credit, stick around and I'll show you how to take care of that, too.

I attended a seminar in Phoenix, Arizona a few months ago and upon arrival, as I was checking into the hotel, the reservationist at the front desk insisted on seeing a major credit card. It was like going through customs and being asked for a passport. I couldn't believe it!

Try renting a car without a major credit card; it's pretty tough to do. You almost always end up renting a *wreck*!

Having at least one major credit card is *vital*. Cashing checks, renting carpet cleaners, even renting an apartment or office space. Almost always a major credit card is necessary. The reason? Well, there are several reasons actually. One is that merchants, whether it be Ace Rents It, Hyatt Regency, or Hertz Rent-a-Car, have come to realize that anyone who has at least one major credit card is not a total deadbeat, anyway. This person renting the car or hotel room must be somewhat responsible if he has a Visa or American Express card. Any total flake can carry a few hundred dollars cash in his pocket. Think about it. If you were Hertz Rent-A-Car, would you trust a $15,000.00 automobile to a person who didn't show at least a minimum amount of responsibility? What if he gives you a $100.00 cash deposit to rent one of your cars for the weekend and the car comes back in shambles? What if there are dents, scratches, cigarette burns in the seats, empty beer bottles on the floor, weeds and dirt jammed up in the wheel wells and bumpers?

Hey - this actually happens. This is not an imagined horror story. A friend of mine used to work for one of these car rental companies, and until he shared some of his company's experiences with me, I could never understand why you simply had to have a major credit card to rent a descent car. But now, I can see their justification for such a practice.

How about the hotel owner? He provides a nice clean room for you to sleep in and after you check out, the maid's heart skips a beat when she opens the door to clean your room. The beds are torn up, the mirror is broken, the TV has orange juice dripping out of the bottom of it, all the bath towels are missing and there's a clubhouse sandwich carelessly disassembled on the carpet next to one of the beds. Upon further investigation, it's found that there's an unpaid bar and restaurant tab at the front desk, $40.00 worth of long-distance phone calls and two movies that weren't covered with the $70.00 in cash you paid for the room with, when you checked in last night. And where are you? Probably on a jet at 35,000 feet or 100 miles down the road, moving on to your next destination. I know this is an extreme example but you get the picture, lots of people walk out of hotels without paying a restaurant tab or telephone bill.

How about the merchant who accepts your check for $100.00 worth of groceries? Suppose he doesn't subscribe to the services of CheckMate or TeleCheck, or a check system where he would be guaranteed payment by one of those companies should your check bounce. Why should he accept your check without a major credit card as a second form of identification?

Why is a major credit card requested? Well, the first reason is that you show at least some degree of responsibility and stability.

Deadbeats or flakes don't usually carry Visa and Mastercard. Reason number two? Well, it goes like this. I'm not an attorney, I don't practice law and I question the legality of this practice - but upon receiving a check from you, the cashier writes your Visa or Mastercard account number on the back of your check. Now, presuming the merchant does not subscribe to the services of a check guarantee company, should the merchant find the check is returned due to "insufficient funds" or "account closed" or "stop payment," then the other avenue of recourse is to attempt collecting the amount of the check from the bank who issued your credit card. The merchant may try to force the bank card issuer to make good on the check!

The car rental companies use a similar practice in that if you drop the car off with excessive cleaning and maintenance work to be done or damage of some sort, they don't fill in the final balance until the car has been refueled and checked over as far as physical appearance is concerned.

The hotel? Well, when you sign that credit card slip, it's like a blank check to them. If you leave without checking out at the front desk, bar and restaurant tabs or any other charges for incidentals will be added to your bill before they send it to the bank for payment.

Each and every day, we move more and more away from a "cash society" and on into a "credit society." That's why I can honestly say that everyone will need at least some credit at some time or another in the future.

They may even try to do away with cash altogether eventually. You wouldn't even see your paycheck anymore. It would be deposited into your savings or checking account automatically, and to disburse funds you would either write a check or be issued a debit card. A debit card is like a credit card but the only difference is that there isn't a monthly billing because the money comes right out of your savings account. You present the debit card just like a credit card when making a purchase but the purchase is subject to your having enough funds in your account to cover the purchase. If the funds aren't there, then your purchase is denied just like a purchase is denied when a merchant calls in for approval on a credit card purchase and you're over your limit.

Debit cards are available and being used today but I don't like them. Actually, I'd much rather pay cash for everything but that's not always possible. I still like the looks of the $100.00 bill, especially when you have 5 or 10 of them in your pocket. Paper even feels better than plastic - it smells better and sometimes (but not always) it spends better. I've yet to meet up with a mugger who insists on a major credit card over cash. I guess it's safe to say "Don't leave home without it."

Credit comes in two basic forms: *secured* and *unsecured*. There have been thousands of different credit packages designed by lenders over the years to attract new business but they all boil down to being either a secured or unsecured form of credit. For me, I don't mind using a new car I'm going to purchase as collateral on that particular loan. Nor do I mind putting a mortgage note, secured by a Deed of Trust, as collateral against the home I'm going to purchase. These are secured forms of credit. The lender has some collateral he can use should you default on the loan, but I can't find any rhyme or reason in using a car or home or boat as collateral against a personal loan obtained through my bank.

I've always liked getting personal loans on my signature and on my signature alone! I hate dragging co-signers into the bank with me to co-guarantee a loan.

To me, on personal loans and lines of credit I perceive these as unsecured loans. What good is this type of loan if you need a co-signer or collateral? Personal loans are not personal if a co-signer is needed to complete the loan. It's then a joint loan or a two-party loan. A personal loan is not personal if it's approval is contingent upon sufficient collateral; it just doesn't seem like a "personal" loan that way. Maybe I'm somewhat backward in my thinking this way; I'm sure that many bank loan officers would say that I am, but, on the other hand, maybe it's because of having this type of attitude that I've done as well as I have with personal loans. At the present time, I'm only 26 years old, and I've already successfully received over 50 personal loans and lines of credit that didn't require collateral or a co-signer, the highest loan being $15,000.00! Many of these were from private parties but some were from commercial lenders as well. In most cases, I'll borrow money from a friend or associate before I'll ask a bank for a loan. I'd much rather have a friend make money off me than a group of board members and investors who own the bank. However, a banker is a good source to have in your hip pocket if and when you can use his money to prosper and move ahead in life.

What's credit? I believe that credit is not truly genuine, honest-to-goodness credit unless it's <u>unsecured</u>! What fun is there in getting a loan if it requires a co-signer or collateral? If a person or a bank acts like they trust and value my relationship with them but ask for co-signers or collateral, then that makes me question how much they really "DO" trust me. Whenever someone asks me for collateral or a co-signer, I immediately get this look on my face like they just asked to sleep with my wife! Although I'm not married, they unmistakenly get the message. It never fails! They never ask that question a second time!

I guess I was just brought up on the principle of trusting and being trusted. As long as you know you're gonna pay back the loan with interest, regardless of any situation or circumstance, if you know in your heart that you're gonna pay it back, then why should you, the reader, have to put up collateral and/or co-signers on personal loans and lines of credit? If you display this kind of trust, this attitude, belief and commitment, why shouldn't you be able to get unsecured signature loans like I do? Why wouldn't a lender or a personal friend or relative loan you some money if you projected an image like this? If they knew beyond the shadow of any doubt that they'd get their money back, plus interest - WHY WOULDN'T THEY?

What's credit? Well, beyond the trust factor and the credit history and the manner of payment and the belief level, credit is a habit - it's an attitude, and real honest-to-goodness, down-to-earth, genuine credit is credit granted on an unsecured basis - no strings attached!

There are three "C"s in credit; I'll cover them briefly just so you're familiar with them. The first "C" is "character". Some questions a lender will need to answer for himself are: What type of person are you? How do you conduct your affairs? Do you bounce checks or change jobs or residences every year? Are you solid or are you flaky? Do you pay on time as agreed?

The second "C" is "collateral" (but I don't buy that program on personal loans).

The third "C" is "capacity". Can you afford to make another monthly payment? Do you have enough cash left over after paying all your other bills to make this new credit card payment or this new car payment, etc.? This "C" is based upon your income to debt ratio.

The income to debt ratio is used by most lenders but some have different limits as to how high your ratio can be and still be approved for a particular credit line. The way to figure out what your income to debt ratio is: Add up all your monthly payments and expenses you now have and match that up to your monthly take-home pay. If you take home $1,000.00 per month and your monthly payments and expenses are (let's say for the sake of argument) $800.00 per month, you would have an 80:20 ratio, that is, an 80% debt to a 20% spendable income ratio. Most lenders want a minimum of 35% spendable income in order to grant you a line of credit. This is just a ratio. Keep in mind that this is not an "absolute." I've received loans when there were more horses in the barn than I could afford to feed, so to speak.

Let's move on and talk about Credit Reporting Bureaus or Credit Reporting Agencies (CRAs) as I like to call them.

CHAPTER 2

CREDIT REPORTING AGENCIES (CRAs)

Years ago, a merchant or lender would use the telephone and call your other creditors for credit references on you, but today, for the most part, it's all done by computer. When you apply for credit at Sears, for example, or your local car dealer, the person checking your application for credit (providing they subscribe to a major Credit Reporting Agency), just punches your name, address, social security number and date of birth into their computer, (which is linked up to the Credit Reporting Agency), and then the computer spits out every credit transaction they have recorded on you over the last seven to ten years. This report will usually show your employer and your former address as well.

A credit report is begun on you when you first apply for credit. The information stated on a credit application is recorded at the Credit Reporting Agency (CRA). Chances are very good that more than one CRA has recorded some credit information on you. There are approximately 2,100 CRAs across the nation. Many of these will be offices of the five major firms. The five major CRAs starting with the largest first, is TRW. The next largest is Trans Union Credit Information Company (TU). Third in the order is Credit Bureau, Inc. (CBI), fourth is Chiltons Creditmatic System, and fifth is Associated Credit Services, Inc. (ACS), formerly known as the Pinger System.

Just to give you an idea on the size of these CRAs, I can tell you that TRW has over 150 million consumer credit reports on file, Trans Union has over 140 million credit reports on file and CBI, Chiltons and ACS combined hold well over 200 million credit reports on file. In Southern California, where I live, the three major CRAs that supply most of the credit information in this part of the country, are TRW, Trans Union and CBI. In Northern California the major CRAs are TRW and CBI. In New York, the major CRAs are TRW and CBI, and in Texas, the major CRAs are Chiltons and Associated Credit Services. Each state will vary. You will find the corporate office addresses of the five major CRAs listed in the back of this book plus the state file coverage of each. Business credit ratings are supplied by either Dun and Bradstreet or by Standard and Poors. You can use the five major CRAs' state file coverage listings and the other list of Major U.S. Credit Bureaus by State, both found in the appendix, as a reference for finding who has a report on you. One would also be wise to call a few merchants or lenders in your local trade area and simply ask them who they subscribe to for credit reports. Most of these merchants and lenders will give you the same answers. Most will give you at least one name of the five major CRAs, if not two or three names.

Once you have the names of the major reporters in your local trade area, you'll want to get a copy of your credit file from each of them, even if you never had any credit before. I went to my local CRA when I was 17 just to see what a credit report looked like and it just happened to have a bunch of derogatory credit information on my name and address. Remember, I was only 17 at the time. I wasn't even old enough to have legally binding credit, but when my report was pulled off the computer, it stated that I had several unpaid credit card accounts that were turned over to a firm for collection. Yes - the name was exactly the same as mine but the social security number and the date of birth were different. Even though it wasn't MY bad credit on there, do you suppose a lender would check to make sure the social security number on the report matched up with the one I had given him, had I been applying for credit? Chances are he wouldn't bother. He'd probably see all those negative credit entries on my report and say, "Rejected. Next!"

This happens every day, folks. My last name is very uncommon. Since I'm in the business of correcting derogatory credit reports, I see this happen all the time. Credit reports can really get sloppy when I'm dealing with a Jones or Smith or Johnson or Peterson. Common names like these can really be a mess. Another big area for error on the reporter's behalf is when a junior or senior is involved. Many times a man and his son's credit reports will get mixed up.

For instance, I've seen where a junior defaulted on two student loans and it came up on senior's report. Of course, it's not accurate, but when senior applies for a new car loan and junior's student loans show up on his report, senior won't be approved until the matter is resolved. Of course, it can be removed, but it's inconvenient and uncalled for. CRAs have proven to be very sloppy in the service they provide. All they seem to need is a name and address (or even a similarity will suffice many times) and they slap it on the report. If they were to match up social security numbers or dates of birth, a lot of this inaccurate reporting would be avoided. The same holds true if they would use Jr. and Sr. as a means of determining who's who.

Some of this derogatory reporting is the fault of the merchant. They make mistakes too, I've seen it happen alot. And then they have the nerve to drag their feet when you ask them to correct their records. They act like they are doing you a painstaking "favor" by getting their slop off your credit report.

Probably the most classical error in credit reporting I've ever seen was with one of my clients. This lady came into the office for our services because she and her husband had just been denied credit to purchase a mobile home. She swore she and her spouse had clean credit. Their combined income was sufficient to make such as purchase. We pulled all of her credit reports and found that they were clean; she had one 30-day late payment but that's no reason for denial. We pulled her husband's reports. One of his showed a $3,500.00 collection account for a credit card in favor of one of the larger banks. After a thorough investigation, we found that this credit card had belonged to her first husband but it showed up on her second husband's report! How this happened I have no idea. He had no association whatsoever with that account. The last name of each husband was as different as night and day but the bottom line is that this negative entry showed up on her second husband's report and caused them the inconvenience and embarrassment of being denied credit - plus they paid us a fee on top of that to have the matter resolved.

A good friend of mine related a story to me the other day concerning her roommate who applied for credit on the purchase of a piano but was denied. After questioning the reason for denial, it was found that this gal "supposedly" had a lien filed against a property she "supposedly" owned in Florida. But the fact of the matter is that she's never even been to Florida and she certainly doesn't own any real estate there!

In another case involving an associate of mine, this person has "gold plated" credit. Well, he does but his reports didn't reflect it. He received a pre-approved Visa card opportunity in the mail. He signed the agreement and then received a letter of denial. He couldn't figure out what in the world was going on. One day he's "pre-approved" and the next day he's denied credit with the same lender. Well, we pulled his reports; Trans Union and CBI were loaded with derogatory credit information. It just so happened he was denied rental on an apartment just a few days later. It has all since been corrected, but look at the inconvenience this person was put through. Like my client stated, he had no idea how these reports could get so "botched up". His TRW was as clean as a whistle but his TU and CBI were a mess. The person at the rental firm saw all the negatives on TU and never bothered to even consider why TRW was so clean. Well, my associate asked me to call the man renting the apartments and educate him on credit reporting systems and their errors. He was then approved for renting the apartment but what a hassle!

Recently, another friend of mine called my office. She was in tears. She was suppose to go on vacation in a few days. She went to her credit union to borrow $1,000.00. She had borrowed money there before and paid it back on time as agreed; she had good credit with them. In processing her application though, a TRW was pulled and a Texaco charge account with a $1,300.00 outstanding balance showed up on her report. She was denied the loan. After calling the Texaco billing department on this account, it was found that a guy she once dated had listed her as his spouse and signed her name on the credit card application. Here is a clear case of forgery and fraud; there's no way they can stick her with having *contractual liability* on this account but the worst part is that she was denied the loan and it messed up her plans for the vacation. With this example the CRA is not at fault. They only reported the information supplied to them by the oil company, but it's still their report showing a derogatory credit entry. Whether a negative entry on your credit report actually belongs to you or not, it still constitutes sufficient cause for denial. Credit Reporting Agencies are in the business of collecting information on consumers and selling it to merchants and lenders who want to check your past credit experience. The more dirt the CRAs can dig up on us, the more valuable their service becomes.

You'll also find that most CRAs just happen to be in the bill collecting business or are sleeping under the same sheets with a company who's in the collection business. It's a most vicious circle. The lenders and merchants pound us with some of the slickest advertisements man has ever been exposed to and then the CRAs come in and sweep up all the dirt.

In the beginning of this chapter, I said that regardless of your credit experience to date, find out who the CRAs are in your area and get a copy of your report. If they don't have one on you, start one! When you receive your reports, check each detail on them to be sure everything is accurate and up to date. More on correcting credit reports in the next chapter.

I don't want to create a bunch of fear or panic when I strongly recommend that you, the reader, pull all of your reports regardless of your past experience; I'm only saying that it's best to make sure that your reports are correct and up to date now, than to be faced with the possibility of having derogatory remarks come up the next time you apply for credit.

Credit reports cost between $5.00 and $8.00 each. They can be obtained for free if you have been denied credit in the last 30 days. Some state laws allow 45 days. If there are two or three major reporters in your area, the one who supplies your creditor with the report where they based a denial, this CRA must give you the credit report at no charge. The other two would be able to charge up to $8.00 for their report on you.

Husband and wife have separate reports. Joint credit will usually reflect on both reports. Some of the husband's sole and separate accounts may even show up on the wife's report. This is most common in the Community Property States such as California. Non-community Property States will generally separate the husbands credit from the wife's unless it is a *joint account*.

There are two ways to receive a copy of your report. No, actually, there are three. The third way is by having a prospective creditor give you a copy of the report he pulls on you when you apply for credit with him. He's not supposed to do this although I've seen it done. The other two ways to receive a copy of your credit report are by mail or in person. Getting a copy in person is by far the best way because you'll be sure to get it and you can make any necessary changes right there on the spot! To get a copy by mail, simply call them first to see what the charge is (providing they didn't supply your report to a lender who turned you down for credit in the last 30 days or so) and then write them a letter giving your full name, Jr., Sr., etc., your maiden name if you are married, your present address, previous address, social security number, date of birth, and a check or money order for the cost of each report. Sign and mail your request. Once you receive ALL of your major credit reports, you now have what I call your "credit profile."

Note: Credit Reporting Agencies only gather information supplied to them by creditors. They also pay a staff to scan public records for bankruptcies, liens and judgments. IT'S YOUR RESPONSIBILITY TO MAKE CERTAIN THAT YOUR CREDIT REPORTS ARE ACCURATE. You have to take it on yourself to make sure that all the information contained in the credit profile is accurate. Credit Reporting Agencies just gather and store information and produce credit reports for their subscribers based on the data they have recorded on you. Furthermore, I highly recommend that you do a "credit check-up" at least once a year just like you would an annual physical and make sure your reports are accurate. Don't leave this up to the CRAs because they won't do it; they can't do it; they're swamped with consumer disputes and credit report requests as it is!

Each CRA is separate. TRW, for example, has offices nationwide which are linked together, but they don't exchange information with the other reporters. They keep their information to themselves. Now there are credit reporting services that mortgage companies and landlords use. These outfits subscribe to the major CRAs and produce what's called a Standard Factual Credit Report using information obtained from one or more of the CRAs. On big money deals like new home loan mortgages, the lender will usually pull reports from two or more major CRAs themselves or they will have a credit report service do it for them.

I said earlier that the major CRA's have offices nation wide and are linked together among themselves. But it's interesting to note that they won't know your from New York or Texas unless you tell them. Alot of people come to California seeking new beginnings. Since some are wise enough not to use their old address if they've encountered some problems there, they start out with fresh credit again. The CRA's computers are not set up as of yet to scan all 50 states, but eventually they will be. Right now, for the most part they only search the files of the state you reside in. If a person moves to another state and has good credit where he comes from, he can then request for the CRAs in the new state to order his files from the previous state, and have that information added to his reports in most cases.

CRAs themselves do not give credit ratings or make decisions concerning credit application approvals. Credit approval is strictly up to each individual lender based on the information the CRA supplies them with. CRAs strictly collect and store information supplied to them by your creditors. Many creditors will report your manner of payment each month; others will report every three, six or twelve months. Many banks won't report an installment loan until it's been paid in full, at which time they supply the CRA with the manner of payment and satisfaction of the loan.

Some smaller merchants and lenders won't report at all. It doesn't pay for them to report. Mortgage companies don't usually report your manner of payment, even American Express doesn't supply the CRAs with your manner of payment. Oil companies don't usually report either. If your Shell Oil card is turned over to a collection agency to satisfy payment, then, yes, it will probably show up then as a collection account. Yet there are a few collection agencies who don't always report either. Keep in mind that each CRA has a different base of customers who subscribe to their service.

Sears, for example, may subscribe to TRW and Trans Union (for credit reports to process applications and to report monthly payment activity on their customers) but not CBI. Ward's, on the other hand, may subscribe to Trans Union and CBI but not to TRW. Some major credit grantors will report your credit activity to all the major CRAs in your area. Each merchant and lender has his own procedures. You can tell who is reporting to which report simply by examining all your credit reports once you have them.

Pulling copies of your credit reports is fun, that is, if you have decent credit. After you receive your entire profile, you'll probably see some things on there you forgot all about and you may not find some things you may have expected to be on there. Also, you, will probably find something that's either outdated, inaccurate or not even yours on at least one of your reports.

Note: Should one of the major CRAs in your area be TRW, they've introduced a new service called TRW Credentials. To join this service is strictly up to you. It can be beneficial, or it could be damaging for you over the years to come. I'm sure the other major CRAs will come out with a similar program but, once again, the decision to subscribe to this service is strictly up to you.

To start with, the present fee to join this service is $30.00. Along with your credit report you can add a Consumer Financial Profile to be submitted along with your credit report to participating creditors checking your application. TRW states that this can replace the need for filling out long, complicated credit applications; you can even apply for credit over the phone using your Credentials card. It's about the same size and looks like a credit card. It contains your name and membership number on the bottom of the card. The people who engage in credit fraud will love this idea. With the Consumer Financial Profile form you fill out, you list all your assets and liabilities. Here's where a crook can list a bunch of un-verifiable assets to make himself look really solid like his $100,000 face-value life insurance policy, the 20-unit apartment building he owns free and clear and the $50,000.00 worth of gold bullion he has in his safe deposit box, etc. As a member of this service, they also provide a service at no extra charge which protects all of your credit cards in case of loss or theft and they will even provide for change of address for all your credit cards should you move.

Well, the nice features here that I can see is that you can avoid filling out long credit applications; I despise those things! And you can receive free credit reports whenever you wish during your membership. If you personally pull a report on yourself more than four times a year, then this service might be of value to you from a "cost per credit report" stand point.

About filling out the Consumer Financial Profile, well it does give you a chance to put your best foot forward by listing all your assets. But, then, a Court of Law can get a copy of this if you are ever sued, and have access to everything you own. It can be good or bad to join this service; I guess it all depends on your point of view. As I said earlier the decision to join this service is strictly up to you.

I'd also like to add that TRW has come out with another new service called WATCH. For $15.00 per year, TRW will notify you if any negative remarks get added to your report during your membership. Sounds like a good idea to me providing that they don't take three months to notify the consumer of a negative remark having been reported.

My conclusion on our credit system as a whole in America is that we do have the greatest credit system on earth. However, when we the people must pay the price for the CRA's incompetence and or just plain sloppiness, then I personally find alot to be desired. There's always room for improvement, a task the CRA's are slow to tackle when it comes to serving us consumers efficiently and effectively.

CHAPTER 3

REMOVING DEROGATORY CREDIT INFORMATION

In the back of this book you will find a reproduced copy of the Fair Credit Reporting Act Law. All Credit Reporting Agencies are regulated by the Federal Trade Commission. Also, there may be additional State laws that the Credit Reporting Agencies in your State must adhere to. To find out if there are any additional laws that pertain to the CRAs in your State, there are two sources you can contact for a copy of those laws. The first source is the Attorney General of your State, found under Government Offices in your phone book; or, if you know an attorney, you can ask to see his Code of Civil Procedures book and look under the title of Credit Reporting Agencies. These laws are fairly simple to read and understand. Although the CRAs are supposed to operate within these laws, I must say that often times they don't . For example, let's take a look at what a segment of the FCRA laws state:

611. Procedure in case of disputed accuracy

(a) If the completeness or accuracy of any item of information contained in the file is disputed by a consumer, and such dispute is directly conveyed to the consumer reporting agency by the consumer, the consumer reporting agency shall within a reasonable period of time re-investigate and record the current status of that information unless it has reasonable grounds to believe that the dispute by the consumer is frivolous or irrelevant. If after such a re-investigation such information is found to be inaccurate or can no longer be verified, the consumer reporting agency shall promptly delete such information. The presence of contradictory information in the consumer's file does not in and of itself constitute reasonable grounds for believing the dispute is frivolous or irrelevant.

Now, as to the "completeness or accuracy" of an item on your report, when it's disputed, the CRA must investigate the dispute within a "reasonable period of time." To me, a reasonable period of time is 10 to 15 business days; however, in California, the law says 30 days is a reasonable period of time. After this time period has lapsed, the CRA is supposed to remove the item of dispute if the creditor or source that supplied the CRA with that information hasn't responded. I've seen TRW, Trans Union Credit and Credit Bureau, Inc. go 60 to 90 days before deleting disputed information and in a few cases even longer.

There have even been cases where some CRAs have been sued and were ordered by the Court to pay for damages done to a consumer's reputation for not deleting derogatory credit information from the consumer's credit report.

Although it can be difficult and time consuming in getting the CRAs to remove derogatory credit information, that's not to say it can't be done though, because it can. It just takes some time and effort. These CRAs are very large corporations. They seem to be caught in a state of frustration and confusion. The left hand has no idea what the right hand is doing and vice versa. For years the CRAs have been on the gravy train but now, it's become utter chaos! One of the major CRA's has made up a form letter at the time of this writing that they send to consumers whose requests to investigate derogatory credit information are believed to be frivolous. For awhile there, it seemed that everyone's request to investigate and verify credit information was frivolous. It seemed like a convenient way for them to tell us consumers in a nice way to go stick it!

I know they have a very heavy work load and I'm sure the pressure in the investigative department must be great - even worse, they don't make a dime on investigating consumer disputes. How effective would you be on your job if you didn't earn a red cent for doing it?

One would think that these CRAs would increase their investigative staff to serve the public better but that doesn't seem to be the case. I know this would increase the company's payroll but it might just as well increase the CRA employees' morale and, in turn, provide you and I with a more efficient and accurate credit reporting service.

Some of you may be asking what I mean by *derogatory* credit information. Derogatory means anything that "belittles." A 30-day late payment six years ago is derogatory from my point of view. Even a late payment one year ago is derogatory in my opinion. Any negative or incorrect information is derogatory. I remember when I first learned how these credit reporting systems worked. I was shocked to find that all credit information stays on your report for seven years, and ten years for a bankruptcy, or until the governing statute of limitations expires, whichever is the longer period. Get this: paid tax liens are normally removed after seven years from the date they are paid in full! This means you could make full restitution on a six year old tax lien and then it would remain on your report for another seven years; lawsuits, judgments and collection accounts are removed after seven years. It seems that this system is somewhat counterproductive. With the way these laws have been written, it basically says you're a fool to pay off anything because it will just start the seven years all over again.

I'm saying that if you have an "unpaid" collection account which is six years old, it will fall off your report in one more year if you don't pay it, but if you do pay it, your report will read "Paid Collection" for another seven years from the date you pay it, and a "Paid Collection" account or "Judgment Satisfied" doesn't do your report a whole lot of good. It still reflects that you were "once" turned over to a collection agency.

As the system has it - unpaid tax liens remain on your report until they are satisfied. Once they are paid, they will remain on your report as a "satisfied tax lien" for seven years but it can be removed once paid by using the FCRA laws. Just ask them to prove that it's yours.

Unpaid collection accounts, suits judgments, or any other adverse information which, from the date of entry, antedate the report by more than seven years, must be removed.

It's weird! A $50.00 collection account is held against you for seven years, but a "driving while under the influence of alcohol" ticket is only held on your driving record for three years where I come from. Doesn't this appear to be backwards? I feel that your negative credit history should be removed after three years while the DUI should stay on your driving report for seven years. One $50.00 collection account or even a $500.00 collection account won't kill anyone. But one drunk driver can kill a lot of people; even one death is too many. It seems that the big money people behind these large institutions and the high power people in government are more concerned with dumping black marks onto our credit reports than they are about us killing their loved ones while intoxicated behind the wheel. It just doesn't seem right. I believe we need to look at what we have here and make some changes. It's terrible that we are punished "twice as long" for a non-criminal act than we are for a crime that takes thousands of lives each year on our roads and highways.

In our office, anything that's paid and over one year old is derogatory! Even bankruptcy! You can only file bankruptcy every seven years, according to law. To remove it from your reports prior to the ten year date that it would normally come off, doesn't allow you to file again before the seven years are up, but many people are led to believe that their credit is ruined for ten years. Some people still believe the myth that by filing a bankruptcy, any merchant in town will give them credit because they can't file for bankruptcy again for another seven years.

This is the furthest from the truth. When your credit reports reflect a bankruptcy, no one wants to do business with you - they brush you off at the door. Filing a bankruptcy petition doesn't make you into a preferred customer like the myth leads us to believe. If you're a multi-million dollar corporation, a bankruptcy against some of your creditors can sometimes insure future credit with a couple of your other present creditors, but a personal bankruptcy has the exact opposite effect.

What I'm saying here is that I don't believe there's anything wrong with "challenging" anything that's been on your credit report over one year, is paid, and/or is incorrect. The way to

remove derogatory credit information from your credit report is to
challenge the Credit Report Agencies to investigate and verify a
credit entry which you dispute.

A reason for your dispute might be any of the following:

- This is not my account - please verify and remove.
- This is my ex-husband's or ex-wife's account; please remove from my report.
- I don't recall ever being (30-60-90) days late on this account - please investigate and correct.
- Your report shows this account went to a collection agency; please show me what it was for and when. I don't agree with this.
- I don't believe this is my judgment; please verify.
- This is my son's account; remove from my report at once.
- This account was paid on time as agreed; why does it show as a negative entry on my report? Please correct.

Be specific in describing your dispute. These disputes are just samples - be more specific.

Each of you will have your own reasons to dispute the derogatory entries on your reports. When you dispute an entry, the CRA is required to investigate the matter in dispute with the source which provided the information. In turn, the source who supplied the information must go back and look up the account in dispute and, then, answer the CRA with information concerning the account status within a reasonable period of time or else the CRA must delete the items from your report. What happens in most cases is that the supplier of the information won't answer the request to furnish accurate or updated information and the negative entry will be removed or corrected. Either that or someone will fumble the ball (your dispute gets lost in the shuffle and must be removed). What happens is they're caught in a *legal technicality* and the item must be corrected or removed.

When a merchant gets a request to verify whether or not you were 30 days late on your car payment three years ago, rather than pay someone $5.00 to $7.00 an hour to see if in fact you were 30 days late on a payment three years ago, the request will end up in the trash many times and go unanswered. In turn, the derogatory remark must be deleted. In some cases a business that you've dealt with will be out of business or under new ownership and will not bother to verify whether or not you paid a few days late. They are too busy conducting their everyday business activities. For some creditors, finding information about your account for over a year ago is like looking for a needle in a haystack. If they can't find it or don't look for it, the CRA must delete the negative entry.

Many times a merchant will report a late payment when in fact it was paid on time. If you don't dispute it, it remains as shown on your reports. Don't let them slop up your reports. You have to fight back.

Lawsuits, judgments, liens, and bankruptcies are all recorded in public records. Here, the CRAs pay college students a minimum wage to scan the public records at the County Court House to record judgments and things of that nature. By the same token, the CRAs must pay these college students to dig up items that we, the consumer's, dispute. The overall effect is poor on their part. Searching public records is a real pain, especially for a lousy four bucks an hour. Many times these records are un-verifiable and, once again, the item must be removed from your credit report.

I remember when I first started out in the Credit Repair business. I was told how easy it was to remove derogatory credit information from credit reports. Well, the CRAs pulled a "fast one" on me. I disputed the accuracy of a few items on my report and about six weeks later, I received an updated report but nothing had changed. I then got wise to them. I asked them to supply me with the name of the person who did the investigation, the person they spoke with at the source who supplied the information, the address and phone number of the source, the date the investigation took place, and what their findings were in the investigation. Note: They have to tell you who they spoke to and what information was supplied to them by the source. They will often lie to you saying they investigated your dispute when in fact they didn't.

They may try to weasel out of investigating your dispute by doing nothing for 30 days or so and then sending you an updated report showing you the results of their investigation. The result is that they may not have even investigated your dispute. This is just another nice way to say stick it!

As far as the CRA making a claim that your request is frivolous, here, too, they have to give you a specific reason why they believe this to be true. The FCRA states: The presence of contradictory information in the consumer's file does not in and of itself constitute reasonable grounds for believing the dispute is frivolous or irrelevant.   Don't let them pull a fast one on you. When you're through reading this book, you'll be well informed as to what your consumer rights are.

When I'm working with a new client, the first thing I do is scan all of his or her reports. I mark any derogatory credit information on them. Next, I ask the client to explain in detail what happened in each incident. Each credit report comes with a form to dispute the accuracy contained in the report. I never dispute more than five negative entries at one time. To dispute every derogatory entry on a report when it shows over five negative entries could constitute reasonable grounds for believing the request to investigate is frivolous.

After the client has written each reason of dispute, I have him or her sign the dispute form and then I make three copies on the copy machine. We then send the original copy to the CRA. After 35 to 45 days, if they've not responded in the form of an updated report, send them another letter stating they received your request to investigate some items on your report. I also enclose a copy of the original dispute.   The letter I write will look something like this:

Dear Sir:

Over five weeks ago I sent you a letter requesting that you investigate these accounts with Dillinger Savings and Loan and The Bank of Jessie James. You received my request on (date) and I have not heard a word from you. What seems to be the hold up?

Will you please respond?

Patiently waiting,
Danny Dolittle

I make three copies of this letter, also, sending them the original. Now, if they don't respond in two weeks, I send them another letter which looks something like this:

Dear Sir:

Oven seven weeks ago, I sent you a letter asking that you investigate these accounts with Dillinger Savings and Loan and The Bank of Jessie James but you didn't respond. Two weeks ago, I sent you another letter asking you to take action on this matter and still I've not heard from you. My patience concerning this matter is running thin. Please respond; I'd hate to have to take a day off work to come into your office and handle this in person. Respond in five business days or I will be forced to file a complaint with the Federal Trade Commission. Act immediately, please.

Danny Dolittle

Once again, I make three copies of this and send them the original along with a copy of everything else I've sent them prior to this letter.   The envelope they receive keeps getting bigger and bigger; your case is building. Wait a couple of more weeks if you've not received an updated report, then do it again. The next letter would look something like this: (NOTE: DO NOT COPY THESE SAMPLE LETTERS; USE YOUR OWN WORDS BUT USE THIS SAME APPROACH.) If you copy these letters word for word, they'll say "Aw, heck, this guy read The World of Credit," and throw your request in the trash. Lawsuits will result because of it against the CRAs I'm sure, but be yourself and use your own words. Don't use abrasive language or make any threats you can't back up. Be stronger in each letter but in a fairly nice way. Now, here is what your next letter should reflect:

Dear Sir:

I don't know what in the world you're doing with my request to investigate these accounts on my credit report. I had to file a complaint with the F.T.C. regarding your company's performance. I'm sure you'll be hearing from them shortly. Enclosed are copies of all my letters I've sent you over the last nine weeks. I expect that you would want to resolve this matter at once.

If I don't get a response from you within the next five business days, I will come down to your office and resolve this matter in person.

Please respond.

Danny Dolittle

Note: I'm taking this to the furthest extreme. In most cases your disputes will be investigated and corrected within 60 days, but it can drag out longer in isolated cases. If you feel your case should be turned over to an attorney, I can only recommend that this be done at your own discretion. Personally, I have never sued anyone; as for all my clients, they haven't needed to, either, in dealing with CRAs. I have, however, read several case histories in which consumers had successfully sued and were awarded up to $10,000.00 due to derogatory credit reporting by the CRA.

Note, I found that a simple phone call to the CRA (a few days after their time to investigate has lapsed) will work wonders too, sometimes better than writing and sending letters. Anytime I call they say "it's in the mail".

About filing a complaint with the Federal Trade Commission. You can get a complaint form from your regional F.T.C. office which is found under the United States Government Offices listing in your telephone directory. You would call and ask for them to send you a complaint form. It's a simple one page form. List the name and address of the company you're complaining about. List your name and address; you can remain anonymous if you choose. Then you'll briefly state your complaint. Keep it simple. Just state that you requested that some items on your report be investigated, mention all the follow-up letters you sent and the amount of time which had elapsed. Sign the form, date it, and send the original back to the F.T.C. You may also want to file a complaint with the Attorney General's Office of your state.

Now, Christ will probably return before the F.T.C. gets this matter resolved, but it still looks and sounds good. No business wants any government organization snooping around in their business affairs, analyzing modes of operation, etc. It does help but I don't believe this is the solution. In most cases, the CRAs will respond within 60 days. It does help, though, to file these complaints when time frames get rather lengthy.

If your case is one of those rare incidents where time frames get up around the 90 day mark, get a tape recorder and go down to visit the Credit Reporting Agency. Ask for the supervisor while your tape recorder is on. Be sure the supervisor sees that every word he says is going on tape. State your case, demand an updated report on the spot! I really don't believe you'll have to go this far with it but the tape recorder is a great tool should you need to use this method. It works great when dealing with bureaucrats, especially the I.R.S. when you have a dispute in your tax bill with them.

Now, in most cases, the CRA will respond within 60 days and remember that if an entry still shows as derogatory on the *updated report*, be sure and write them for the facts on the investigation as laid out earlier in this chapter.

Should they supply you with the facts, you can still write or call the source directly and ask them to give you the exact details on the derogatory entry. With one of my clients we pulled out four oil company collection accounts with a simple phone call to each. A key phrase to keep in mind here is that <u>if you squeak long enough, someone's gonna oil ya.</u>

In each credit report the CRAs state that, *in the event the disputed item has not been resolved to your satisfaction after the investigation has been completed, you can add what's called a Statement of Explanation to each entry on each report by supplying them with a written explanation.*

The FCRA Law states:

611 (b) If the re-investigation does not resolve the dispute, the consumer may file a brief statement setting forth the nature of the dispute. The consumer reporting agency may limit such statements to not more than one hundred

words if it provides the consumer with assistance in writing a clear summary of the dispute.

(c) Whenever a statement of a dispute is filed, unless there is reasonable grounds to believe that it is frivolous or irrelevant, the consumer reporting agency shall, in any subsequent consumer report containing the information in question, clearly note that it is disputed by the consumer and provide either the consumer's statement or a clear and accurate codification or summary thereof.

Once again, it costs the CRAs a lot of money to pay employees to add this information to the computer. What will happen, sometimes, is that the CRA will just wash their hands of the situation and delete the entire entry and be done with it altogether rather than add it to your report.

I've yet to write a letter of explanation for any of our clients. The derogatory entries usually come off the first time disputed and for the ones that don't, we just continue to pursue the matter as outlined in this chapter until it is corrected or changed to our client's satisfaction.

It takes some effort and patience to have derogatory credit information removed from reports but it is possible. It can be done and is being done all across America. You, too, can do it providing you're willing to do the work that's necessary to achieve such a result. I feel it's much easier to clean up a credit report than it would be to go without credit privileges, especially in the 1980s and even more so in the 1990s. If you don't have the time or the patience to do it yourself, you can hire a credit repair service to clean up your reports.

Now, let's recap the procedures used in disputing derogatory credit information:

1. Order ALL of your credit reports.
2. Scan each report and mark each derogatory entry. Be sure your name, address, social security number, date of birth, employer, etc. are all listed correctly. Make certain that your Jr. or Sr. or II, III, or IV follows your name if you are one.
3. Start disputing the derogatory information. If you have over five entries to dispute on any one report, send out the

first set of disputes and wait 30 days to send out the next set, regardless of whether or not you received an updated report on the first set.

4.   Make three photocopies of each dispute form for your files.

5.   Always send the original copy to the CRA.

6.   Wait approximately 30 to 40 days before expecting an updated report or before sending out the second set of disputes should you have over five derogatory entries.

7.   After 40 to 45 days have elapsed without receiving an updated report, it's then time to send a letter or to call each CRA as outlined earlier in this chapter. (See sample letters.)

8.   When your updated reports come in, match them up with the information you disputed, making sure all changes have been made. In the event an entry was not changed, re-dispute it a second time.

9.   If the CRA cannot resolve a disputed entry after it's been re-investigated, ask the CRA for the details of their investigation, getting the name, address and telephone number of the source, the date of investigation and the person at the source they spoke with, what was said, etc., and then contact the source yourself. If they don't remove the derogatory entry, then either write a letter of explanation to be included in your credit report or, if you feel you have a strong case against them, consult a competent attorney about starting a lawsuit.

10. Just for the sake of it, file a complaint with the F.T.C. if you're unsatisfied with the quality of the CRA's service. If enough of us complain, maybe then we can force these large companies to renew their commitment to abide by the Fair Credit Reporting Act laws more than they do.

CHAPTER 4

CREDIT REPAIR CLINICS

The Federal Trade Commission warns consumers to *beware* of any business that claims in its advertisements that it can *erase* bad credit from consumer credit reports. Well, I'll endorse the F.T.C.'s warning. Almost every month, I sign up a new client who has been ripped off by a person or business promising to erase bad credit. Personally, we don't promise to erase bad credit. We assist our clients in removing derogatory credit from their reports using the FCRA laws. Entries that are over the governing statute of limitations, incorrect, unable to be verified or unmistakenly belong to someone else are removed because of a legal technicality. We operate our office according to the F.T.C. regulations and guidelines. I feel we provide a much needed service in an honest, affordable clean-cut manner.

The Credit Reporting Agencies, however, don't share this same feeling. Credit Repair Clinics cause the CRAs to clean up their act and it costs them millions of dollars each year in investigative work and updated reports. I have a heart the size of Texas but my skin is an inch thick when I search for love to send the CRAs.

I'm very displeased with the service for which we pay these CRAs. Yes, you are paying for this service, even if your a "cash" paying consumer. It's built into the cost of the merchandise whether you pay for your purchases by cash or credit card. It's a part of the "operating expense" which is paid by the profits on the can of paint you bought at Wards last week. Maybe you didn't buy a can of paint from Wards last week, but somebody did; they'll just get you somewhere else is all. The fact is that you and I are paying a premium price for these credit reporting services.

Perhaps the writing of this book will cause enough public attention to what's going on and some changes will be made. We need a credit reporting system that lives by the laws of the FCRA as stated in FCRA Section 602 where it states that CRAs are to exercise their "grave" responsibility as to fairness, impartiality and respect for the consumer's right to privacy. It goes on in the next section to talk about confidentiality, "accuracy," relevancy and proper utilization of such information in accordance with the requirements of this title. Furthermore, 60 to 90 days is not a reasonable period of time for them to correct and update your report. Thirty days is more than reasonable.

Well, back to my clients who've been ripped off by hit and run credit erasers.

Two of my latest clients had once paid $1,000.00 to have their reports cleaned up. The first guy gave the money to a fellow worker who he's never seen since, and the second guy gave $1,000.00 to a real estate agent who said he had a friend working in the CRA who had access to deleting credit information from their computer. Well, nothing happened; his reports stayed the same. He did recover $500.00 of his money from the real estate agent but he never did get the other $500.00 that supposedly went to some guy who worked in the CRA.

Don't fall for this type of system. It's foolish to even think that these CRAs would allow access to just any employee who could punch the DELETE button on the computer. Yes, I'm certain that some employees of CRAs have done things of this nature in the past, but to pay someone who knows someone who can do it is rather dumb. Even if there really is such a person you or someone else knows who can actually do this, they probably won't be doing it very long, they'll be issued a "pink slip" and there's also a hefty fine that goes along with this kind of activity.

If you should hire a Credit Repair Service, be sure it's a reputable firm. For one thing, they should be licensed and bonded. They should project a professional business image and, most of all, they should guarantee their work. One would be wise to call their local Better Business Bureau and see if there have been any complaints filed against the company. It also helps to ask close friends you can trust if they know of anyone who specializes in this field, preferably a friend who has had their reports cleaned up successfully. Take all necessary precautions. Many of these companies will fulfill their end of the agreement to your satisfaction but you must be patient. It takes time to cure these credit disputes.

As for those advertisements to clean up derogatory credit in the national tabloids, I cannot comment based on any personal experience with them. However, if I were to hire a Credit Repair Service, I would want to do business with them in person, locally.

The fee structure for each Credit Repair Service may vary. Some will charge a flat rate "per report" "per person" ranging from $125.00 to $175.00. Others will charge on a "per entry" "per report" basis. The fee per entry can vary between $30.00 and $50.00. We work on the per entry basis. An entry consists of all the derogatory remarks that follow any one merchant's or lender's name. On a TRW report, it would look like this:

Bank of America   (account number)   30 (2) 60 (1) 90 ( )

In this example, Bank of America has reported 2 (30 Day) lates, and 1 (60 Day) late. Bank of America would be one account which equals one entry.

A lien is one entry; a judgment, a collection account, a charge-off, all are single entries. We don't consider the correction of name spellings, social security number corrections or employer or previous addresses as entries though - these are free of charge because they need to be correct in order to correct the report.

Just be careful in selecting a Credit Repair Service if you plan to have someone else do your reports for you. There are a lot of good services out there but just like any other field, we have some bad apples among our profession, too.

CHAPTER 5

COLLECTION AGENCIES AND UNPAID ACCOUNTS

For as long as I can remember, I've always been an Entrepreneur. One of my earlier business ventures just happened to be a collection agency. I still laugh when I think about what I did back then. I formed a collection agency called T-N-T Collections, Inc. I was so excited in the start-up phase, designing letterhead, envelopes, business cards and form letters. It was fun; I had great expectations about its success. Well, to keep a long story short, when it came time to develop accounts and get on the phone to start hounding my clients' delinquent accounts, I lost every ounce of motivation I once had in the start-up phase. I decided to scrap this venture altogether. There was no way I could muster up the guts to harass people over the phone about collection accounts. Just a few months prior to my becoming a professional collector, I had been harassed by bill collectors on accounts I once owed. There was absolutely no way I was gonna bug people with nasty letters and phone calls.

I'd always been a likable person and I wanted to stay that way. My impression based on my experience with bill collectors was that they woke up each day and ate a handful of "mean pills" for breakfast. They seemed as if they woke up on the wrong side of the bed each day. My inner voice said - here's a sure-fire way to become an alcoholic and develop ulcers. Who wants to get all bent out of shape each day over a stupid profession? I often wondered if these people would be as demanding at home as they were in the office. I can just imagine some guy coming home from work after eight or ten hours of bill collecting and saying to his wife, "Honey, it's ten minutes to eight; I want my pot roast reheated and on the table in front of me by 8 o'clock or you're in serious trouble!" Who could live with someone like that? Who could live with themselves being like that? I wonder how many bill collectors take their lives each year? What's the rate of suicide among bill collectors? What's the rate of divorce among them? To me, divorce is sometimes worse than suicide. Either way, I didn't want any part of it.

I've put a lot of ventures on the shelf, some of which I've later taken off to achieve a good level of success, but this collection agency venture was buried once and for all, never to experience life again, EVER!

A few weeks ago a lady came into my office for assistance in building credit. She cut me a check for $125.00 and it bounced. I ran it through my account a second time and it bounced again. I waited a couple of weeks and called her bank but the check was still not good. I waited a few more weeks and it was still not good. Now I could have pulled a commonly known trick of calling her bank, asking to verify funds, give the name and account number and say the check was in the amount of $75.00 instead of $125.00. Had there been $75.00 in there, I could have pulled $50.00 out of my pocket, deposited it in her account and then cashed my check for $125.00, but I decided it would be best to just leave it alone. So instead, I just sent her the check back with a note saying, "If you ever need our service in the future, please feel free to call on me, I'll be more than happy to help you with your credit needs." I don't expect to ever hear from her again. Although I was able to forgive and forget, Telecredit or Instacheck, one of those check guarantee companies will record this transaction as a *non-sufficient funds* entry on their computers and use it against her for the next 18 months.

Also, I could have filed suit against her and been awarded a judgment in my favor of three times the amount of the check, or $375.00. That would be a piece of cake, but my heart would never let me do it. Had my collection agency ever gotten off the ground, I really doubt it would have gone very far. I'm just not the right type of person for that job. It takes a special breed to become a successful bill collector. I think you have to be dropped on your head when you're a baby. Maybe bill collecting is a good vehicle to use for getting back at the world, I just don't know. I have no idea whatever gave me the idea that I'd enjoy bill collecting or that I'd be successful at it.

Well, anyway, bill collectors supposedly fulfill an important role in our society. They collect millions of dollars each year on delinquent accounts that may otherwise have gone unpaid, for large and small companies alike. Many of the larger corporations that extend credit have an in-house collection department. These collectors are usually employees of the corporation and work on a salary. This type of collector is more controlled and somewhat mild compared to an outside independent collection agency. Large companies like Ward's and Sears restrict their collection employees a little more than the independent collection agencies. Even though you may be the subject of a collection account, Ward's doesn't want you going around bad mouthing their stores because it can be bad for business, but the jerk who works for Strong Arms Collection Agency could not care less what you think or say about him. All he's concerned with is that you pay your bill so he gets a paycheck.

I have a classical true story I want to share with you. When I rang up all that debt I talked about in Chapter 1, the next job I took was at a bar and restaurant. There was one bill collector who hounded me at home every week just like clock work. He had a one-of-a-kind voice and a very limited vocabulary and, come to think of it, he also had a problem with alcohol. He was the guy who came in every night and got his fix. He was the guy I had known from someplace, but I couldn't match his voice to a face I'd remember. One night, while sitting at the bar, counting how many dinners we had served, it hit me like a ton of bricks - he was the same obnoxious jerk who hounded me over a small unpaid telephone bill each week. Sure enough, I asked the bartender who the guy at the end of the bar was and what he did for a living and, yep, it was him alright! He was the owner of the collection agency that had my phone bill as one of his accounts. He used an alias at work but it was him. He changed names upon arriving and leaving his office, but that voice went everywhere he did.

Well, now that I knew it was him calling me every week, but he didn't know I knew it was him, I decided to have a little fun and make him "earn" his money. I never did pay him, though, I sent the payment to the phone company. Whether he got any of that money, I don't know, but I did have some fun with the guy. He was a whiner - complained about everything it seemed. I got a kick out of watching him entertain out at the bar every night. If I'm not mistaken, he would drink Johnny Walker "Red" on the rocks and lots of it. I firmly believe that old Johnny was this guy's "out", his escape from that rotten profession he was in.

In paying a collection account you'll want to take some caution. First of all, you'll want to see if that collection account appears on any of your credit reports. If it does it's always best to make arrangements with the collection agency to remove the negative entry from your reports when payment in full is made on the account, but each collection agency will have their own policy towards such a practice. Some collection agencies will do it and others won't. (Some will say they "can't" take it off, but that's like saying they "can't" call you at home).

Based on my experience in the credit repair office, I found that the collection agencies who remove entries upon receiving full payment on an account do a much better service and collect more money for their clients than the hard-to-deal-with agencies. I found that the best way to get someone to do something you want them to do is to make them want to do it. A hard-to-deal-with bill collector makes you want to hang up on him; we all are somewhat rebellious by nature. Now on the other hand, a bill collector who calls and says, "I can pull this negative entry off your credit reports if you can make some kind of arrangement to satisfy this outstanding bill. Do we have a deal?" That type of approach (in my opinion) is much more effective in collecting bills versus being rude and nasty over the phone. Many bill collectors try to get under your skin but the overall effect is negative and counter-productive.

It's foolish that a collection agency will put ego and old dusty company policies ahead of profit. If I were the owner of a collection agency, I'd want my accounts to come in and pay off, which, in turn, I'd remove the negative entry from their reports so they could get some more credit to mess up again so that I could have them as an account again. Collection agencies make money on accounts collected, not on ruining credit reports. I guess one of the joys in collecting delinquent accounts is in having the power of putting the "screws" to someone's credit report. Big Deal! I get up and go to the office each day to earn a living versus going in to satisfy an ego or to carry a chip on my shoulder another day forward in life. What a rotten profession to be in!

Be sure to make any possible arrangements to have negative entries removed upon payment in full on that account. It's best to request a letter to this effect.   Personally, if I were to ever meet up with one of these guys again, they'd be hard pressed in getting me to pay off an account unless they removed it from my report altogether. "Paid Collection" looks just as bad as "Collection Account" in most cases.

When an account is turned over to one of those screwballs for collection, you can safely bet that they'll try and get full payment out of you which you may not have. Arrange a payment plan, get it in writing also but really push for having the derogatory entry removed.

Some collectors will even discount the bill for fast payment. You may be able to pay $300.00 cash to satisfy a $500.00 bill. Be sure and get a "paid in full" receipt. Creditors usually turn accounts over to collectors at 50% of their face value. Others will say - give us 50% of whatever you collect. With large discounts like these, there's always room for negotiations. Anything's negotiable!

Never make payments on a collection account with your personal checking account because they may record your account number and pull a fast one on you. With your account number and the bank's name, they can call your bank around the normal payday periods: Fridays, the 1st, 5th, 15th or 22nd day of the month - and then slap a lien on your account. It happened to me once. My loan on the smashed motorcycle went to collection before the insurance company paid if off, but, in the meantime, I had sent a $200.00 check to the collection company to shut them up for awhile. Shortly after I put my paycheck of $600.00 in checking to cover my rent and some other bills, this collection company put a freeze of $500.00 on my account. I didn't know it, though, and I was out writing checks paying bills, the checks came marching home! Don't ever pay collection accounts with a check written on your personal account. If you do, then don't deposit anymore funds in that account other than to cover the check and keep the account active.

Most bill collectors will tell you to send them post-dated checks. If you owe $300.00 and agree to pay them $100.00 a month for three months, they will usually try this method. Take caution in this; they'll deposit the checks whether they're good or not, just to make some more money on you.

One collection firm for a large oil company, a name everyone would recognize, called one of my clients and asked to verify a credit card number on his Visa. The client thought nothing of it at the time but later received a notice that his Visa account had been closed because it was way over the limit. The collection company made a half dozen charges of $49.50 on our client's account and turned them in for payment to satisfy the collection account. The Visa card had a $50.00 floor limit on it meaning anyone accepting that Visa for charges over $50.00 must call the bank who issued the card to get an authorization number. Any charges under $50.00 are guaranteed payment automatically. Where did the collection firm get our client's Visa card account number from? Right off his credit report, of course! Collection agencies can pull your report any ol' time they want to!

It's these kinds of practices that leave a bad taste in my mouth with collection agencies. My client has a very strong case for a lawsuit if he were to pursue this matter further. The collection company did not call our client to authorize this transaction, rather they just called to verify his Visa card account number, creating false representation.

In the back of this book you will find a reproduction of the Fair Debt Collection Laws. Be sure and review them if you're the subject of a collection account. Know your rights. Bill collectors lay awake at night conniving new methods to get their greedy little paws on your money. The Repo Man is in the same family tree but he usually snatches your car in the middle of the night versus your cash; more on him later.

Remember, professional collectors aren't saints either. I've had professional collectors come to me for credit repair and counseling. Chances are very good that the person pouring the coals to you about your delinquent doctor bill just might be trying to catch up on late payments of his own. Don't let these people rain on your parade. Put them in the proper perspective.

A young man came into my office a month ago in utter panic. He was late on all of his credit card payments. He wanted me to help him file for bankruptcy (which I don't provide as a service) because he was led to believe that he would be "jailed" for not paying his bills. When I added up all of his bills his total indebtedness was just over $1,200.00 and his back payments amounted to $350.00. Here's a case where a collection agency almost drove a person to file for bankruptcy for fear of being put in jail.

How many other people do collectors force to panic? I recall reading a newspaper article recently about a young man who jumped from the top of an eight story building to his death. It was found that he was over-burdened with debt and the article went on to state that a lot of unpaid debt is usually a part of a suicide victim's profile.

Don't let them get under your skin. Read the laws that pertain to Fair Debt Collection and use these laws in your favor if you should need to. That same section is complete with Government agencies to complain to if you're mistreated.

Note: If you have any unpaid collection accounts and you write to the CRA disputing the accuracy of the account - you may find that you just poked a sleeping tiger with a stick. Often times it will only re-activate their collection efforts all over again.

CHAPTER 6

REPO MAN

A few months ago I saw a movie called "The Repo Man." The movie left a lot to be desired, but many of the repo methods used in the film were the same as those used in real life.

This chapter is based on real life experience: my own. I personally had a car repossessed just a few months after moving to California from Minneapolis.

I was a contractor back there and in mid-January, I got a bug to move to a warmer climate. On the day I left, in mid-January, it was 80 below zero (allowing for the wind-chill factor). I had been out shoveling snow off roofs as a means of income to pay my bills. Contracting there is a feast in the summertime but a famine sets in every winter. Everything freezes over and there's little work to be found in contracting.

When I arrived in California, I had $20.00 in my pocket. I stayed with friends of mine, put some ads in a few small papers, and in about three weeks the phone started to ring and the work rolled in.

I was behind one payment when I had left Minnesota; it was up to two payments when I started working again. Thirty more days slipped by, and my car was repossessed. It just so happens that I had about $2,000.00 in cash on hand the day they picked it up. Being a couple of payments behind is not always a cause for banks to place a repo order, but I think what triggered them to take this action was that I left town without giving them prior notice . I'm sure they felt I had skipped town and wouldn't pay the back payments or any future payments.

It happens when you least expect it. My roommate asked to use my car to run an errand early one morning. I threw him the keys; a couple of seconds later he returned and asked where I had parked the car. I thought someone had stolen it. I called the Police Department to see if it had been impounded but they didn't have any record of it being towed. My inner voice said "call the bank;" they confirmed that it had been repossessed.

The Repo Man is a talented little Devil, he usually works during the wee early morning hours. I never used to make any sense out of seeing a tow truck pulling a new car which didn't appear to be smashed up, and particularly in the middle of the night. I could understand such an action at that hour had the car just been in an accident. But to see a nice clean, wrinkle-free car being towed at 3:00 or 4:00 a.m. was a bit strange to me. Some repo professionals will drive cars away but I believe the usual method is to hook the car up to a wrecker and tow it.

People who are expecting a visit from the Repo Man will sometimes try to outsmart him, but the Repo Man is pretty wise. He sweeps the streets of your neighborhood looking for your car if it's not in your driveway. Locked garage doors and subterranean parking places won't always stop a determined Repo Man; all he needs to do is "think" he knows where it is and it can be considered repossessed.

Automatic garage door openers operate on radio signals, and by taking the back off a remote control, the frequency can be monkeyed with to open most any garage door.

While living in Minneapolis, I did some construction work for a Repo Man. He was about 40 years old and had a hard time getting around. He walked with a cane, each step he took seemed to cause him discomfort.

He was very interesting to talk with, he shared a lot of Repo stories with me. It was most definitely an exciting and adventurous, but dangerous, profession. He had been shot at and wounded on three different occasions while repossessing cars.

He told me about the time he was out in front of a house in the early morning, just about to drive a Lincoln Continental away when the owner stepped out of his front door, rapidly blowing off six rounds from what sounded like a cannon, knocking out every window in the car. I asked what he did then? He said, "I drove away!" I asked if he weren't scared? He said, "Naw, the guy was out of bullets and the car was running, what's to be scared of?"

He's one of those kind of guys you look at and ask yourself if he's all there or not. Being a Repo Man sounds kind of fun to me until the gunfire starts.

If your car is about to be repossessed, well, I don't know what to tell you. These guys are slick! And not only in taking the car, but in locating it as well. Repo Men are excellent "skip tracers" when a person has moved to a new address, whether it is across town or across the country.

To start with, they may send a piece of junk mail to your house with the words "Forwarding Address Requested" in the top left hand corner of the envelope. When the Post Office delivers the letter, and it finds your address has been changed, the Postal Service forwards the letter to your new address and, then, notifies the sender of the forwarding address, being most people file a change of address when they move.

Another way they will find you is by calling your old phone number to get the new number. The first three digits tell what part of town you're in. Then it's just a matter of looking in the proper cross-reference directory. They can even use your credit card number in a much sneakier way. They can call the credit company billing department and rudely ask, "Where's my bill?" The representative will ask the account number of the bill in question. "It's 3471-0770-1234; what address are you sending it to? Are you still sending it to (subject's old address)?" "No, sir, we sent it to 365 Main Street, Apt. 5, on June 30th." "Oh, I'm sorry, let me check with our apartment manager and see if he may have received it. Thank you. Good-bye." Now they have your new address and it's repo time.

The more talented Repo Men and professional collectors will use some methods much more sophisticated to locate you. They will often use the Credit Reporting Bureaus to find your change of address.

The Post Office has an office which can locate people. There is also an office that the Armed Services has to locate people who are in or recently joined the Service.

Driver's License Bureaus can locate people, too. They have, in each state, an office that will, for just a few dollars, give the driving record of any person plus that person's present address, even if they moved out of state.

In most cases, if someone wants to find you bad enough, they will.

I had a client come in awhile back who wanted counseling about his present credit situation. In reviewing his reports, I found a repo on his TRW which was about a year old. I asked him to explain what had happened to get his car repossessed and he fumbled around for a few seconds and then blurted out, "I still have the car." I said, "You still have the car? That's incredible!" I was amazed! He went on to say that he moved to a different address and fell behind on his payments. He didn't really try to dodge the Repo Man; he just never contacted the bank.

I couldn't believe it. This guy drove around in a bank-ordered-repo for over a year and they never caught up to him. Had he planned to outsmart the Repo Man, he probably would have lost it in less than a month.

I guess this shouldn't come as any big surprise though. I was attending a real estate investors alumni meeting where the man putting on the meeting talked about a vacant house he had spotted. It looked to be a nice two or three bedroom home in a quiet neighborhood. The grass and shrubbery were overgrown and the paint had started to peal. It looked as if it were a bank repo. He did a title search on it and found the owner's name; it was a bank-owned repo, R.E.O., (real estate owned0. He contacted the bank to make an offer and they said it wasn't their property. He thought, boy, that's strange. He did some more research, chain of title, etc. and kept coming up with the same conclusion that the bank was the legal owner. He made several calls to the bank over a period of time but kept getting the same response - that they didn't own the home. Over a year passed by until a phone call to the bank president initiated an investigation into the matter, only to find that they actually did own the home.

After hearing this, I thought to myself - I'd sure like to be in a position to lose track of an $80,000.00 asset and not even know it. It just goes to show that Repo Men and R.E.O. departments make mistakes, too.

As it goes with a bill collector's efforts and practices, so goes it with the Repo Man in that many times they will use *illegal* tactics to recover automobiles. I've heard alot of case stories where repo men have used very shady means to snatch a car. If you have been the subject of what looks to be a raw deal, contact an attorney or legal aid and review your case with them. You may be able to recoup some money for the actual damages caused.

CHAPTER 7

WHAT TO DO WHEN DEBTS PILE UP

What should one do when debts pile up? Well, I guess the first step to take would be to panic. I mean really panic, turn it on full blast for a day or two and then develop a creative solution to your problem, and then never worry or panic about your bills again. The next thing to do is to call your creditors and explain your situation. I know this is hard to do sometimes and the creditor realizes it's hard for you to do, but they'll usually cooperate with you in lowering your payments or something of that nature. Don't wait to call your creditors after your account has been turned over to collections; call them as soon as you see the problem develop. A creditor with any brains at all would rather receive partial payment than no payment at all.

The mistake most people make is that they wait for their creditors to start calling them. It may be too late then. They seem to get madder with each day that passes without you calling. Many times, providing you call them as soon as the problem develops, a creditor, let's say a department store, will tell you to stop charging until the final balance has been satisfied. But if you wait 30 or 60 days for them to call, then chances are very good that they'll close your account and turn it over for collection while the bill is still fresh.

Most creditors will deal with you but it's up to you to initiate the first phone call. It's better to have a creditor stop you from charging, and eventually reinstate your account than it is to have your account closed at grantor's request. Accounts closed at grantor's request have a negative effect on your credit reports.

When debts pile up, most people will stir and worry, many will suffer from sleepless nights, tension, upset stomach and racked nerves. The first solution that comes to mind is bankruptcy. Some will carry it beyond that to suicide. Don't get yourself all worked up about it. Far too many people "flip out" when a financial tragedy sets in.

Put things in their proper perspective. In the first place, the sheriff won't come and take you away. Secondly, it's only temporary, this won't go on forever; it will soon be solved. Thirdly, this experience will make you become a much bigger, better and wiser person. And fourthly, in every adversity, there's a seed of equal or greater benefit, and something good can happen because of this!

I remember one time when I didn't have $10,000.00 to pay off a note when it was due. I called the guy and set up a meeting to talk with him. The meeting went much smoother than I would have ever imagined. At the end of the meeting, I said, "You know, Mr. Creditor, I wish I owed you $100,000.00 instead of just $10,000.00 because I'd have to develop a way to pay you that $100,000.00 back; and once I knew how to earn $100,000.00, then I'd be able to make another $100,000.00 to keep for myself." He laughed, and said, "I wish you owed me $100,000.00, too."

Ever since I was about five years old, I have been "all ears" when I heard someone talking about success. I never was a true believer in luck. As I grew up, and to this day, I still spend at least a few hours a day listening to success stories of people who, when faced with a problem, turned the problem into a *challenge* and made millions off of stupid ideas they never would have thought of had they first not created a problem to solve.

I've studied the lives and success stories of over 200 millionaires, and in each real life, modern day story, every single one of them had come across great financial challenges in their lives. I could fill an entire book just writing stories about financial challenges that successful people have encountered in their endeavors.

I could fill a book on "my experiences" alone. Let me give you some names of great people who have conquered what seemed to be a financial mountain to them at the time.

Walt Disney is my favorite. It's been said that he filed bankruptcy three times. Disneyland in California was first drawn up on a paper napkin. From that it was turned into concrete buildings, paved roads, a giant parking lot and a host of rides and attractions that people come to visit from all over the world. Do you suppose he was ever short of cash or late on some payments? How about Disney World in Florida or the Disney attraction in Japan. Do you think he ever encountered some financial challenges along the way?

J. C. Penney was an old man, flat broke and millions in debt on top of that before he was successful with his first store in Montana, with a string of them to follow throughout the country. Can you imagine being millions in debt at the age most men are getting ready to retire?

Colonel Sanders had a nice little empire going until the state ran it over with a new highway. The Colonel took what money he had saved up and set out on the road selling his great chicken recipe. He didn't sleep in hotels, folks; he slept in the back seat of his car at truck stops. The Colonel would never have built the largest restaurant franchise in the world if the state hadn't messed up his finances. The list goes on and on.

Me? I've been lower than low concerning finances many times before I got mad enough to make some changes in my attitude that would affect my life-style. It doesn't seem that long ago that a five dollar bill gave me the same amount of relief that a $500.00 paycheck gives some other people I know. Getting my hands on five dollars was like payday to me.

I believe that God gives us financial challenges in our lives to make us bigger and better people. I believe that the Creator of the universe gives us dreams and the ability to achieve them, but we somehow fail to consult our inner voice. I believe that this Creator gives us a million different ways to overcome the burden of debt and I further believe He'll show us how to become financially free, but we're much too busy striving and worrying to hear that inner voice.

If your debts have piled up or do pile up in the future, and you share the same beliefs I just stated, then, instead of blaming the Almighty, try thanking Him because, although this situation of being over-burdened and in debt is the pits, it's usually His way of saying He has a bigger, better way, one of which is, you won't be crushed by debt. He goes on to say that He wants you to use some of this new money you're gonna earn to help some other people in one form or another. All I'm really saying is that there is truly a blessing behind every problem, a rainbow following every storm; just don't get all bent out of shape when your debts pile up - if they do.

Everyone at sometime in his or her life has some degree of financial challenges to deal with at least once. Ask yourself if this *problem* will break you, or will you break it? The *problem* doesn't care. It doesn't care if you solve it or if you stew and worry over it. One way or another, the *problem* realizes that its position is only temporary.

It's just a matter of how you're gonna solve it, but the *problem* doesn't care how you solve it; it just knows it will be solved. The *problem's* replacement is the *solution.* The *solution* offers many creative avenues to take. The *solution* says you can file bankruptcy or get a debt consolidation loan or make arrangements to pay partial payments or not pay at all. The *solution* doesn't care which avenue you take either; the *solution* is only here to complement the *problem.*

In every problem there's at least a dozen solutions. There's usually many things you can do to turn your situation in a more positive direction.

When clients come to our office for debt consultation, some of what we do to help them is to make a list of all their creditors and amounts owed. It's important to know exactly what it is they're up against. Sometimes, it's just a matter of making arrangements with a few creditors to get a 30 or 60 day extension.

One of our more recent clients needed only 60 days to get back on her feet. She had close to 20 different accounts, and all were coming due in just a few days.

When she first called our office, I'd learned that she had remained in the panic stage over two weeks, much too long to be in panic. She had lost her job but found a new one shortly after. Her income was barely enough to cover her monthly payments. At best, providing her car didn't break down, she was left with $25.00 a week to live on. She could stand to have lost a few pounds but her major problem was all her bills were coming due about two weeks before she'd receive her first paycheck from the new job.

Since her first priority would be to keep current on all her payments, we decided it would be best for her to get a loan to consolidate all her credit card payments. She borrowed $3,000.00 from a finance company. With the proceeds, we paid off all but three of her charge cards and made two advance payments on all of her other bills, including rent. The payment on the new loan was about $100.00 a month, less than her combined payments on all of the charge cards we paid off. When all the smoke settled, she was now in debt a year longer than she would have been hadn't she gotten the new loan. But we saved her credit, she was paid two months in advance on all her other payments and, best of all, she could get a good night's sleep once again. We got her out of her stage of panic. The extra year's worth of interest she will have to pay on the new loan is cheap compared to the price she was paying for her mental health. She then decided to get a part-time job to give her more money to live on.

When debts pile up, there's always a solution to be found. The first priority in almost any case is to protect your credit as much as possible. A lot of people want to run out and file bankruptcy when their finances turn sour. Nine times out of ten I strongly urge clients to stay away from bankruptcy. Bankruptcy is a last resort solution; your rights to file bankruptcy should be reserved for that moment when your faced with "no way out" but to file. There's almost always another way out other than bankruptcy.

When debts pile up, it's often necessary to look for ways to cut out any spending for the "unnecessary niceties" of life like cable TV, movies, sporting events, hobbies, etc. I don't like being deprived of the things I enjoy most either but if I must cut back on some of life's fun things to save my credit, I will. I realize in advance that it's only temporary. I've been to people's homes where they complain about having too many bills as they lay on the couch watching a pay cable movie on a $600.00 color TV.

I had a friend who owned two cars, one of which he didn't use, and two motorcycles, one of which he never drove. He often complained about bills: Had he sold this extra car and motorcycle, he would have had plenty of money to pay his bills and a few bucks left over for entertainment.

I remember one time, selling my one and only means of transportation so that I could pay some bills that were pressing. I knew I'd only be out of transportation for a short time. To me, paying those bills were more important than having a vehicle to drive. I walked to work and back, three miles each way. Not only did I need the exercise, but I found myself coming up with creative solutions to some other challenges I had to deal with concerning my business.

If you, the reader, have debts piling up, find some things you are not using and sell them to relieve some of your debt. A good rule of thumb to follow is: If you have an item which you haven't used in the last six months and don't plan to use in the next three month's, sell it!

I know a guy who has $40,000.00 to $50,000.00 in "high tension" debt. He also has a million dollars worth of used business equipment in his back room. I recommended he sell some of the equipment to relieve that debt, but he said the discount would be too great to make the sacrifice. He's right next to having a heart attack but the financial loss seems to be more important than his physical and mental health. I told him that with the time he's spending worrying about that debt, he could easily use that time to recapture the loss on the discounted sale of some business equipment in three to four months, using his now clear, worry-free, creative mind.

People are afraid to let go of somethings that inevitably hold them back. It's very difficult getting to second base if you don't take your foot off first. Nobody wants to lose status or prestige, and no one wants to go backwards in life, but I'm amazed at the number of people I've seen go down with a sinking ship, only to lose something they probably could have sold to begin with. If you feel your car is going to get repossessed, sell it before it does, and not only will you pay the debt off but you just might have enough money left over to buy a less expensive automobile that will serve your purpose until you can afford a newer car later.

Don't let your pride get in the way. Pride will cause you to fight it and you'll probably eat up any equity you have in it with repossession and legal fees. You'll end up with an "involuntary repo" on your credit report and absolutely no cash out of the transaction.

I'm amazed at the large number of people who lose their homes due to foreclosure. Some of these homes have substantial equity factors in them. I will say that some people really are unaware of what to do in a foreclosure situation but common sense would tell them to discount the home 10% to 15% of its value and sell it before it's taken back by the lender. I will admit that the real estate market goes into a slump sometimes when interest rates are high. But there's always a market for real estate when there's a good deal to be had. There is almost always a buyer to be found for discounted real estate property.

One of my clients was faced with foreclosure not long ago. His payments were $400.00 a month and he was three months ($1200.00) behind when the bank threatened to foreclose. He spent countless hours worrying about it. I discussed the problem with him and came up with four creative solutions.

The first solution was to sell one of his many vehicles he had and use the proceeds to pay the back payments; he didn't like that idea. Solution number two was to use the $20,000.00 equity in that property to trade as a down payment discounted to $10,000.00 on a new piece of property; he didn't care for that idea either. Solution number three was to forget about the matter completely for 90 days (he had 90 more days to make up the back payments before the bank would take it back); and use that time to create enough new accounts in his business to make the $2,400.00 he would now need to catch up on the payments. He wasn't crazy about that idea either.

In my final gust of words, I said OK, then. If none of these solutions appeal to you, then stop worrying about this entire matter once and for all and get on with your life because your worry won't change anything! Plan on renting a home when the bank comes to get this one, and start using your now worry-free, creative mind to develop ways to enhance your life-style in the future.

Some people actually think that their "worry" will change the problem but the problem doesn't have any ears, it doesn't hear your worry; it doesn't have eyes, therefore, it can't see your tears. It's just a problem that knows it will be solved one way or another.

I remember being involved in a business that was failing. I thought my worry would change the problem but it didn't. Not only was I worried, but I became frustrated, filled with fear, lost a lot of sleep, and later suffered from what I believed was an ulcer. My stomach felt like it was on fire! I became immobilized in my actions toward resolving this major problem in my life. After being overcome by inertia, I said, "That's it; I'm done with this mess." I got mad! I turned that fire in my stomach into a "burning desire" to become "rich"! I started putting things in their proper perspective. I realized that it was only a business that I could later replace with a new business should this one fail. I realized that I could not control everything that went on in the world outside of me, but that I could control everything that went on "inside" of me.

I went for walks, every morning upon rising and every night before retiring. I used this wonderful computer between my two ears to create a motion picture in my mind of each problem being successfully resolved. I broke out in laughter a few times just from the imagined joy of conquering each problem. I replayed this movie in my mind's eye many times before the problems actually did get resolved but it seems as if the moment I changed my attitude and outlook, the much needed solutions began to surface. Sales gradually increased, the right people came into play at just the right moment and everything ended up working out just fine. It was then I realized how many fears that I've created, but how few of them actually came true! Don't allow your mind to run wild, carelessly creating fears that will never come true.

Earlier in this chapter, it may have sounded like I was telling you to just give up all faith and throw in the towel when faced with a problem that's bigger than you but that was just to say don't "marry" your problem or it will eat you up! Don't marry your problems. Problems, financial problems and most other problems are outside of you. You're still a uniquely created, magnificent human being. You are not your problems and your problems are not you. You might be a part of the problem or the cause of a problem, but "you" are not the "problem."

When debts pile up, it's because of something you "once" did or because of something that "once" happened to you to make your debts pile up. Something you "once" did, even if it was yesterday or this morning, or something that "once" happened is now a thing of the past, but you still remain; you still "are." You are not your problems and your problems are not you. Learn to separate yourself, your wonderful, magnificent self from the world outside of you.

It's quite obvious that when a problem occurs, like debts piling up, something needs to be changed. Maybe you need more income or maybe it's just to decrease your spending a little bit. Many people believe that just making more money will cure their financial difficulties. But this theory won't hold water in most instances. I've seen people who make six-digit incomes get behind on their payments. You may wonder how a person earning $100,000.00 per year can run short on spendable income but they do; it happens every day; they just spend more than they make is all.

A young millionaire friend of mine asked me to find him a good buy on a home with a view in BelAir. I thought, "No problem. How much do you want to put down and what do you want your monthly payments to be?" He said he had $250,000.00 to put down and he wanted his payments to be under $7,000.00 per month. Seven thousand dollars a month for a house payment? Two thousand dollars a month I could see, but $7,000.00 a month for a house payment? I told him "no problem; I'm sure I can find you a fairly comfortable home with a view with payments under $7,000.00 a month!" I later found out that the monthly payment on his Mercedes was $800.00 per month. No problem.

Do you see my point? Big wage earners buy big ticket items that come with big monthly payments and, yes, of course, they face big problems when they get over-indebted or the source of their income dries up.

In most cases, to increase your income is not the complete answer to your financial problems because you'll just spend whatever more you earn. The real answer to your problem is in controlling how much you spend. It's not usually your income that gets you in trouble financially: It's your expenditures that cause the problem.

I hate budgets. I can't stand limitations of any kind. I have found that I have to make money faster than I can spend it and sometimes that can be a challenge. If you work for someone else and receive an hourly wage, then it may be a good idea to design a workable budget and limit yourself accordingly, whereas if you work on commission or have your own business, you can usually drum up new business to increase your income if you have a couple of months of excessive spending. In either case, just watch what you SPEND and you'll be OK. I get a kick out of people who play Santa Claus on Christmas and spend the rest of the year working like a dog to pay it off. Watch what you SPEND your money on. There is nothing wrong with giving, but, if what you give comes back to haunt you, then I'd question the real necessity of that which you gave.

If you ever find yourself with more bills than you have money for, stop charging on your credit cards; put them away or cut most of them up, hanging on to one or two to maintain some open credit accounts though. Many times people will cut up all their credit cards only to have to re-apply in the future.

Stop buying on impulse; leave your credit cards and checkbook at home when you're out mall walking. Sleep on it a few days before making any large purchases. In most cases, you'll find that you really didn't need that new dress or that new riding-type lawn mower with the chrome wheels and in-dash stereo system.

Don't let this chapter discourage you from increasing your income; I'm all for earning additional income. Just watch what you spend it on and put some aside in a reserve account to cover any excessive spending, or to cover your bills for a few months in the event of a job loss.

CHAPTER 8

DEBT CONSOLIDATION

Shall I *consolidate* or shall I not? If you do, take the same precautions you would in choosing a credit repair service. Although many companies claim to help solve your debt problems, some of these firms will only create new ones for you.

Woe be to those who turn their money over to an "it's-in-the-mail Debt Consolidation Company." These firms end up taking extensive Caribbean vacations at your expense; you must be careful in choosing a reputable consolidation company. Scores of people have been burned by what I like to call "Congratulations" companies. "Congratulations, you're our next sucker." This is not funny. If there's a business opportunity that has a free lunch to offer, it is the Congratulations business HANDS DOWN!

With a Credit Repair Service, you might put $150.00 - $200.00 in a deposit account, but with the Congratulations company you might be giving them $200.00 per week for six to eight weeks before they go Bahamas.

In deciding which consolidation company to do business with, I recommend that you first call Consumer Credit Counselors. They have over 200 offices in 44 states; best of all, they are a non-profit organization and the fees they charge are very minimal. I highly recommend that you contact them prior to any consolidation firm. I'm sure there are some companies out there that provide a clean-cut, honest service, but you cannot afford to find out which one it is if you're already having a problem paying your bills. Plus, these firms can charge anywhere from 15 to 35%

of the funds you give them to pay your bills, as their fee. The idea here is to get out of debt versus creating another expenditure, an expensive one at that.

Consumer Credit Counselors (CCC) are supported by contributions from the business community. When you contact them you'll be mailed a standard budget form to list all your debts and income. You must complete this form before they can analyze your financial situation. To start with they'll look for areas to trim your expenses, possibly enough to cover all your debts depending on your own individual situation. If after trimming the fat from your life-style, you still come up short on funds to cover your debts, CCC may then recommend a debt management program. Providing you and your creditors approve, CCC will design a game plan in which everyone will be satisfied, often times asking creditors for extensions or to lower or even drop the interest or finance charges altogether so that you can get back on your feet and the creditors can get at least the principle balance paid back to them.

Providing all parties involved approve of this plan, CCC will require that you pay them a set amount each month, which they will administer accordingly to your various creditors. You must also agree not to take on any more debt until this matter has been resolved; you'll probably find it difficult to get credit when you're in a situation like this anyway.

All counseling sessions are free, however there is a small minimal fee to cover some of the costs of the debt management programs. In a hardship case there is no fee at all. How can you beat a deal like this? They won't absorb 15 to 35% of the money as a profit to them. This is not a form of bankruptcy. Many Congratulations companies will reel you in on something called a Debt Relief Program or a Debt Reorganization Plan which is usually just a toned-down phrase for Chapter 13 Bankruptcy.

Bankruptcy of any kind is a very negative entry to have on your credit reports. You don't want to go this route and in most cases you won't have to. Avoid filing a Chapter 13 at all costs - it's just not good, folks; there's usually an alternate route to follow.

Some businesses will advertise that they make consolidation loans. Consolidation loans can often be helpful but you really need to watch what you're doing. Some of the biggest crimes known to mankind have been committed with paper and ink.

Many times in the fine print of a loan agreement, your house will be attached as collateral. Be very careful what you get yourself into. You could wind up living on Skid Row in a cardboard shack.

Consolidation loans are best used when they're applied for when all your payments are "current." You're then in a much better position to entertain the possibilities of a consolidation loan because your mind is clear and generally more open to spotting any unfavorable terms or conditions of the loan such as using your home as collateral.

A loan such as this can also have many benefits to it. Normally, the interest rates on credit cards are pretty steep, 21% on some Visa cards. If you have several credit cards with high interest rates, it's sometimes wise to get one big loan at a lower interest rate to pay off all your high interest rate accounts. Once again, be careful with anything that looks like a good deal because it could have hidden costs that would eat up any savings on lower interest rates. It could actually end up costing more than you thought you were saving.

If your bills are backing up and you need more information on debt consolidation or if you're considering whether or not to get a consolidation loan, call the Consumer Credit Counselors and talk your situation over with them first. They could save you a of lot trouble and perhaps some money too. Look in the Appendix for the address of the CCC office nearest you.

CHAPTER 9

MANAGING YOUR CREDIT

In managing the credit you now have or plan to get in the near future, there are some "red flags" you'll want to be sure and watch for. These red flags are advanced warning signals that you could be getting in over your head and not even know it. Become familiar with these credit *check-points* just so you'll recognize some of the events that take place prior to credit taking a turn for the worse. You don't want all of your hard-earned credit to start running backwards on you. Credit is much too precious for that. Engrave these safety principles on the front of your mind so as to avoid credit problems in the future.

First of all, if you run out of money before payday, you're probably already in trouble and don't know it. Secondly, if you juggle bills or rob Peter to pay Paul, there could be a problem being created that you need to examine. A trap I once fell into was in using cash advance features from Visa and Mastercard to pay my everyday living expenses. The heart of this problem is very clear, income. I didn't even have enough income for rent.

If you find yourself charging more on your accounts than the amount you pay on those balances each month, a storm could be brewing. If you find yourself accepting pre-approved credit card promotions being sent to you when things are already a little tight, this could cause a major problem. If you receive late notices on any of your bills or if you find yourself paying the late fee on your rent or home mortgage payment, then there could be danger. If you find yourself racing to the bank and making a deposit to cover checks, chances are very good that you're getting over-extended.

All credit accounts have limits on them which were once based on your income and ability to pay. As you obtain more and more accounts, your indebtedness usually increases and you find yourself paying out more than what's coming in or at least trying to anyway. What we need to do is set our own "<u>personal credit limits</u>" that will allow us enough money to pay all our bills and living expenses, plus tuck a few bucks away. You can raise your personal limit as your income increases but you must also allow for the rise in the cost of living each year.

·I trust that you're capable of figuring out what your own personal credit limit should be. Once you've arrived at a dollar amount it's then your responsibility to stay within your limit. Discipline your spending habits so that your habits work for you versus you working for your habits.

Managing credit is quite simple providing you set some personal credit limits and stay inside them.

CHAPTER 10

BANKRUPTCY (B-K)

Bankruptcy filings come in three basic forms: Chapter 13, 11, and 7.

The Chapter 13 is a debt reorganization plan which, when filed, takes effect immediately, and all collection efforts or foreclosure proceedings must cease. Once the 13 has been filed, the court allows the person filing it a certain amount of time to draw up a repayment plan of his delinquent accounts. In order to file, you must have a regular source of income. With that amount in mind, whatever it is, you must demonstrate your ability to make your normal monthly payments and make up any back payments within a three year period of time, and up to five years with the Court's permission. This plan is then submitted to the Bankruptcy Court for approval. When approved, you would then start paying your monthly payments to the bankruptcy trustee, who, in turn, pays your creditors and acts as a mediator between you and your creditors over any questions they may have. You would remain under this plan as long as you continued to pay the trustee and providing you do not take on any more debt.

The cost to file a 13 is $60.00 and there is also a 10% fee of your total payments which is the trustee's fee; if you have an attorney represent you, his fees are additional. You retain all your assets providing you complete the plan. If you voluntarily quit paying the trustee, the Chapter 13 will be dismissed. Should you become ill or laid off while on this plan, the trustee may possibly grant an extension if you ask.

This is a good plan to use in most cases where your home is in foreclosure providing you can either make up the missed payments, obtain new financing or make a quick sale and pay off the defaulted mortgage before the lender takes the house back. Although this can be a great tool in the right situation, I'd still recommend that you seek to find other alternatives.

I don't like the idea of filing for bankruptcy. Creditors don't like to see these come up on credit reports either. They treat you as if you have a deadly disease.

Creditors don't care to even speak with you when your reports reflect a bankruptcy. I will admit that as the B-K seasons with time, some secured creditors will overlook it somewhat if you're really solid in all of the other areas of qualifying for credit - like length of time at residence and work, net worth, and ability to pay the payments on this new piece of credit. Even though as time goes on and the B-K starts losing its power, the fact still remains in the back of their minds that you once filed bankruptcy.

As for Chapter 7, this really looks like you burned some creditors. Chapter 7 simply means the Court appoints a trustee to round up all your assets, (less some exemptions) sell them at auction for whatever they can and the proceeds go to pay off all your bills. A Chapter 7 wipes the slate clean but leaves a stain on your credit reports for ten years. Chapter 7 is the "last resort;" you really don't want to do this unless it's the only way out. Personally, I've been in a position to file a 7 many times but I never did because I felt that even though my debts would have been dismissed by law, morally I'd still owe the money. I feel that anyone who ever found me worthy enough to lend money to was worthy of getting paid back! Maybe not on time as agreed but paid back as soon as possible, with interest!

Avoid a bankruptcy at all costs; they're quite costly and counterproductive. If you are forced to file a 7 and your case is fairly simple, then I'd recommend that you use your local legal service clinic to help you file. The cost to file at present is $90.00. An attorney would charge you anywheres from $500 - $1,200 for the same service your local legal clinic can provide for free.

Should you ever feel your financial situation is insolvent, don't go running off to a bankruptcy attorney for a quick fix. I've talked with clients who've been told by an attorney that the only way out was bankruptcy, but, after careful review of their situation, we found alternate routes to take and avoided it. Some attorneys are flaky, too. Their recommendation for you to file a B-K just might be coming from their pocketbook versus their heart or conscious mind. Not all attorney's have their client's best interest at heart all of the time.

Before seeking the advice of an attorney concerning your financial affairs, I'd first contact the Consumer Credit Counselors.

Beware of the "want-to-be-lawyers" who engage in coffee shop talk concerning bankruptcy. Many people are fast to recommend filing a B-K. If you listen to and follow their instructions, you may be in for a rude awakening. If someone ever recommends that you file, ask if they ever filed before; most will say no. It's hard to give away something you don't have, it's hard to describe what Hawaii is like if you have never been there, and it's foolish to recommend bankruptcy if you never filed, and it's downright stupid to take someone's advice to file a B-K if they never experienced it themselves.

If you've filed a B-K in the past or if you should be forced to file one in the future, don't forget to separate your actions from the wonderful human being you are. Banks experience a form of bankruptcy now and then, too. It's called being "insolvent." At the time of this writing, there are over 1,300 lending institutions on the Fed's Watch List or "Hot Sheet" as I like to call it. Of this list of 1,300, fully 160 lending institutions will be forced to close their doors in 1986 because they're insolvent; they're bankrupt! The FDIC has to come in and bail them out! In 1985, 125 lending institutions went belly-up and I'm sure that 1987 will be an interesting year also.

Banks are not perfect, either; don't let those expensive TV commercials fool you when they say that "We're 5 Billion Dollars Strong!" They don't mention the $4.9 billion in weaknesses (liabilities) on the other side of the balance sheet.

Avoid filing a bankruptcy at all costs, it really puts the screws to your credit reports.

Alot of people believe that when they file a 7, all the accounts filed on are removed from the credit report, but that's simply not true. When you file a 7, all of your accounts will indicate something to the order of "Charged Off To Bankruptcy" or "B-K Liq. Reo." which means discharged via chapter 7 or 11. The accounts remain on file for 7 years and the bankruptcy remains for 10 years.

CHAPTER 11

CREDITORS' RIGHTS

Creditors tip the scales over Consumers when it comes to each others rights. But then that's only fair in most cases because the creditors stand to lose more in credit transactions than consumers do. This statement is best supported by: "He who has the gold makes the rules." This chapter would be much too lengthy to describe these rights state by state, so I'll simply generalize.

As a rule, Creditors can assess late charges for bills paid after the due date. Fortunes are made on late payments. The amount they can charge would be found in the original contract you signed with them. Creditors can request you to stop charging on your revolving accounts and if you continue to charge or exceed your credit line limit, they can close the account. Your credit card grantor may also warn other merchants not to accept your card. Some Credit Reporting Bureaus will warn their subscribers if you start showing a pattern of late payments. Banks in which you have a line of credit with may pull money out of your checking or savings account to offset late payments on installment loans or lines of credit with them. However, they must leave a certain amount of money in the account which can vary state to state.

Repossession? Everyone should be aware of the Repo Man by now, after reading Chapter 6. Creditors have the right to repossess anything that was used as collateral on a now defaulted loan. Not only can they repossess merchandise used to secure a loan but, it some cases, they may also sell the security and assess what's called a "deficiency judgment" against you if the proceeds from the sale are less than the pay-off amount on the account; should there by any surplus, you would be entitled to it. If you refuse to turn the property over, they can obtain a Court Order forcing you to turn it over.

In the State of California, the merchant must send you a notice that the repossessed item will be sold. The notice will include instructions as to how you can redeem the property. Usually, for a few days, you'll have the right to make full restitution on the loan and get the item back. Some creditors, not many, will let you have the merchandise back if you make up the back payments and pay for any other costs that may have been incurred in repossessing the merchandise.

Many contracts have what is called an "Acceleration Clause." In the event your contract contains this clause and you get behind even one payment, the creditor then has the right to call the entire balance "due" at once!

Home mortgages are a little more in your favor, though, when they go into default. Each state has separate foreclosure laws. Some lenders in states such as California can foreclose on a piece of property in 111 days from the date of filing a Notice of Default with the County Recorder. Minnesota creditors can take from three months to a year to complete a foreclosure. It all depends on the state's regulations and whether the property is secured by a Contract for Deed or a Mortgage.

Creditors can take you to Court and sue. If you don't show up in Court, you would then lose by default. Beware of some of the more shady creditors who will often times file their suit in a Court way out in the boondocks making it difficult for you to appear. Consult a competent attorney if this ever happens and also complain to the Court where the case was filed. If you are sued and the other side wins the case, you are then placed with a judgment which states the amount you are to pay the other party. You can pay them on the spot, make arrangements for payment or not pay them at all. However, the creditors can have an asset search done on you and place a lien and force the sale of any property (real estate or personal property) which you may own. It's always best to settle out of court whenever possible. This way you avoid a judgment being reported on your credit reports.

Wage garnishment is nearly impossible without the prior approval of the Court; however, with the Court's approval, a creditor can garnish wages. The amount they can garnish solely depends on each particular case.

The IRS and your State Tax Board are creditors of yours also. They don't even make you fill out an application or do a credit check to give you credit. They'll give "anyone" credit. Here's how it works: Should the IRS or your state government ever find that you owe them money on back income taxes, you're given credit, no applications, credit checks or questions asked. They will let you pay the deficiency in monthly payments that fit your budget. You can dispute their claim by filing a petition in Tax Court to have the case reviewed if you feel they are wrong. Now, if you do owe them money and they have to come looking for you, first of all they will usually report a tax lien on your credit reports and secondly, if you refuse to come to terms with them they can levy a tax lien against any real or personal property you may own and force the sale of that property to satisfy the lien. They can also snatch your income tax returns too, even for child support payments that are in the rears.

Your County Tax Collector will give you credit, too. Unpaid property taxes will eventually end up being paid by the sale of your property at auction if you don't pay.

If you ever feel that a creditor may be taking his rights over the line, then look in the white pages of your telephone directory under Consumer Complaint and Protection Coordinators. These Government Offices can be very helpful.

CHAPTER 12

HOMESTEAD PROTECTION
(California Residents Only)

If you are a California homeowner, pay close attention to this chapter.

Because of the unethical actions of some credit grantors, the State of California recognized the need to create a security blanket for homeowners. This need was fulfilled just after the Gold Rush of 1849. When consumers fell behind on their bills, some creditors were suing and placing judgments and forcing the sale of their delinquent customers' homes to receive payment on the debt. People were being thrown from their homes into the street. It was then that the Homestead Law was passed. This law is still alive and well today.

If you live outside of California, your state may have developed a similar law to the California Homestead to protect the homeowner from unscrupulous creditors and their uncanny actions. If you don't have a similar law in your state, then here's an opportunity for you to do something important and of value to your community, city and state.

The California Homestead Law was designed and written by the State to protect the homeowner from most creditors. The State, however, has more than one hat to wear. Tax liens are not included in the protection given by the Homestead Law. Child support back payments and alimony are not protected by the Homestead Law, nor is the mortgage note holder on your home.

Equity protection for people over 65, and the disabled, is $55,000.00, $45,000.00 for Family Declarations of Homestead, and $30,000.00 for single people under the age of 65. A petition for bankruptcy will not affect your homestead. Under the Homestead Law you can file bankruptcy and still keep your home.

The cost to file a declaration of homestead is only $4.00 and can be done with no problem at all. Some companies will send out direct mail advertisements to homeowners and offer to file the Declaration for them. These firms usually charge $30.00 to $40.00. Attorneys will often charge you $50.00 to $100.00 to file a homestead, but you can do it yourself for only $4.00.

It would be foolish for me to attempt to give you all the details on homestead protection in just one chapter of this book. Therefore, I'm going to recommend that you visit your local library and pick up a copy of Homestead Your House by attorneys Warner, Sherman and Ihara. This is a very practical, easy to read book. It will give you step-by-step instructions to file your homestead.

Also in the back of it is a list of numerous other self-help law books that may be of interest to you.

This book can be purchased for approximately $10.00 by writing to:

Nolo Distributing Company
Box 544
Occidental, California 95465

CHAPTER 13

APARTMENT RENTAL ASSOCIATIONS

It seems like no matter which way we turn, someone has our number. Whether it's our social security number, driver's license number, address, phone number or otherwise - somebody has our number.

Renters beware; someone's watching you. Scores of Apartment Rental Associations (ARAs) have been established across the nation over the years, and they have been very busy assisting landlords in screening prospective tenants, shafting renters who've messed up in the past, manager placement and even in representing new legislation locally and on a national basis. After all, real estate is the largest tax paying industry in the country and the landlords can have a lot at stake. Someone has to champion the laws that protect the landlords.

As for the landlord, this system is great but it can be a hassle for the renter sometimes. One of the ARAs in California uses the services of three different sources in screening prospective tenants for landlords (who are members of this association). The first source is an Eviction Service. This firm scans the public records at the County Court House for any eviction papers served on you, whether it was for non-payment of rent, causing problems (parties, fighting, etc.) or for making waste of the property such as anything that would decrease the property's value. A person could have A-1 credit and pay all his bills on time, but he could still owe a previous landlord money without it ever showing up on a credit report.

The next source is the Credit Reporting Bureaus. Here the Association not only sees what their applicants' past credit habits have been, but they can also get a rough idea as to how much the prospective tenant owes and whether or not he may have difficulties in paying rent.

The third source of information the ARAs may often use is the services of a Check Guarantee Company such as Telecredit, CheckMate, Instacheck or Telecheck. The ARAs will use the services of one of these firms to see what sort of responsibility you've demonstrated in the past with your checking account. The Check Guarantee Company will tell the ARA if you ever bounced a check, how many if more than one, and whether they were paid or remain blowing in the wind; they have your number!

As mentioned earlier, these ARAs can be a great blessing to the landlord but, on the other hand, here's another opportunity for a service business to mix your name up with another and supply a derogatory report about you to a creditor like the CRAs often do. I've seen it happen several times.

I don't want to discount the value of the ARA system because I believe in it somewhat providing they don't get sloppy with it. Things can get pretty ugly for the landlord sometimes.

I remember sitting around talking with a group of people after a real estate seminar. Somehow we all in turn volunteered our bad experiences we had had with tenants at one time or another. One of the women there shared her story of how she had rented a home to three single adults who cut a hole in the living room floor and used it as a fireplace. I don't know if they needed it for heat or romantic evenings but that was the worst horror story of them all. Others told how tenants being evicted would dump concrete mix in the toilet or bring their Harley-Davidsons into the house, but the woman with the BBQ tenants had the wildest story of them all.

I was looking at a home in Santa Ana, California one time; the home was being repossessed. The REO manager warned me that he had rented it to a couple who moved in, "along with 18 friends and relatives." I thought to myself, "Come on! Twenty people?" Well, 20 was a little bit too big for me to swallow but I did count 13 bedrooms. It had a 2-1/2 car garage with a bunch of partition walls made of cardboard. This place was the pits! The front lawn was dirt, not a blade of grass on it; I'd imagine there was far too much traffic across the lawn for grass to grow. I only counted eight people while I was there but God only knows how many were at work or running errands. The bank manager could have been right, or at least close. Let's just say there were too many people living there!

Apartment Rental Associations do serve a purpose; they have their place in the business community, too. Let's just hope that they prove to be more efficient Data Processors than the Credit Reporting Bureaus have demonstrated to be in the past.

CHAPTER 14

CHECK GUARANTEE COMPANIES

I remember once standing in line at the check-out stand in a supermarket. There was a heavy-set woman in front of me, unloading two carts of groceries onto the conveyor belt; she must have had a large family. Maybe she was buying for that "family of 20" in Santa Ana I talked about in the last chapter. Anyway, after everything was rung up, the lady goes for her purse and starts writing a check. After signing it, she gave it to the cashier and pulled out her two forms of identification. The cashier turned to a keyboard separate from the cash register and punched in some numbers. There was silence for 10 seconds or so, and then her phone rang. After hanging up the phone she turned to the customer and said "I'm sorry but we are unable to accept your check." The woman customer took a deep breath. I'm thinking, "Oh, come on lady; you must have a few hundred in cash in that big purse of yours; I've only been in line behind you 15 minutes now and this head of lettuce is beginning to wilt." Like Perry Mason, she began presenting her case to the cashier, digging for her deposit slip. They went around and around for a few minutes and then the woman gathered up all of her belongings and stormed out the door grumbling, "I'll never shop here again!"

Everyday, merchants turn away customers paying by check when they cannot get approval on the account from the Check Guarantee Company. Most retail merchants and lending institutions subscribe to the services of one of these Check Guarantee Companies.

First of all, the banks subscribe to this service to avoid opening a new checking account for a person who already has a record of writing bum checks in the past. In most cases upon opening a new account, the bank will make a phone call to one of these firms to see if the new account applicant has any prior record of having an account closed by another institution.

The Check Guarantee Company records the name, address, and driver's license number of any person who has run into difficulties with being responsible in their checking account activities. The bank will supply the Check Guarantee Company with the name, address, and driver's license number to get approval prior to opening a new account. The "path of access" to this information is that of a name, address and driver's license number.

Check Guarantee Companies are then supplied information by the bank on any checks that come back N.S.F. (non-sufficient funds) or that of an account having been closed by them because of misuse of that account. This information is recorded and stored on computer for future use. It usually remains on file for 18 months, whereas derogatory credit is stored on computer with the Credit Reporting Agency for seven years. Does this sound a bit unusual? It does to me. Why only 18 months? The only reason I can make out of this is that the lenders want your *deposits* because they loan them back out for a handsome return on "your" money. If they blackball you for seven years, like they will on credit reports, then they will lose money on "your" money. They want your checking account deposits. They only require your checking history to be on file for 18 months to slap your hands, so to say. They are in essence saying that you've been bad. "We're gonna take away your checking privileges for 18 months, but we'll give you another crack at it after that time because we want your deposits." This is especially so when their cost of money from the Government is higher than the interest they may be paying on savings accounts.

On the bad checks you did write, they don't mind charging you $10.00 apiece. Banks complain about losing money on bad checks but I don't buy it. I've done some work as a contractor in a bank. As a matter of fact, a friend I used to go to school with,Liz, worked at the bank as a check processor. I can remember the machine she used to process checks. It looked like she could process about 300 good checks per hour. As for the bad ones, I'm not sure. It seems that it would be pretty easy though: a check comes back to the bank for payment and the funds are not there to cover it. The machine directs the check to the N.S.F. section. When the N.S.F. section has 50 bad checks in it, the operator takes the checks over to the computer and punches in the account numbers and adds a $10.00 overdraft charge to each account. This takes a good data processor about 25 minutes on her worst day, two checks per minute. She then places the check in an envelope and sends it back to the bank who has the account of the payer on the check, providing it's drawn on another bank. This could take two minutes per check.

We're up to 125 minutes in labor so far on processing 50 bad checks. Let's assume it takes another two minutes per check to mail the person writing the check a notice that their check has been returned due to N.S.F. and that the account has been charged $10.00. Here's another 100 minutes of labor used up. This totals now 225 minutes of labor to process 50 bad checks or three hours and 45 minutes of labor. Let's round it off to four hours. Hopefully, this person processing the checks is earning $8.00 per hour which, at four hours, equal $32.00 in cost to the bank. Add another 25% for taxes and social security which would make the hourly pay around $10.00. Let's include 100 stamps at .22¢. Allow .05¢ for each notice form and envelope = $5.00.

Let's take a look at how this works out to be a "loss" to the bank as they claim.

Labor - taxes, etc.	$ 40.00
Postage	22.00
Notices, envelopes	5.00
Total expenses (approximately)	$ 67.00
Total income - 50 bad checks at $10.00 each	$500.00
Profit to bank on only 50 bad checks	$433.00

How anyone can show profits like this and say with a straight face that they're losing money is way beyond me! I believe that fortunes have been made by banks on N.S.F. charges alone! They have been ripping us off and lying to us at the same time; that's creative!

When the bank records a N.S.F. on your account, that information is usually sent automatically to the Check Guarantee Companies. It's then recorded in their computer. When you write a check for a purchase with a merchant, the cashier will usually punch your account number into her keyboard, which is directly linked to the Check Guarantee Company. Providing there's no record on the computer of you writing bad checks, the Check Guarantee Company will either call the merchant and give verbal approval to accept the check, or if the approval is done automatically by computer, it will provide the merchant with a code being zero. A code one or two would be OK to accept and the Check Guarantee Company may guarantee full payment on the check if it bounced. A code three would mean it's a bad risk; the Check Guarantee Company won't stand behind this one, and a code four means it will most likely bounce! There are many Check Guarantee Companies and each will have its own system, but they operate similarly to the system I just described.

By no means am I saying that it's OK to bounce checks. Sooner or later it will happen to everyone who has a checking account. It could happen for many different reasons. Could be an error on your part in bookkeeping, could be the bank's fault. Maybe your paycheck will bounce, causing all the checks you wrote to come marching home. It can happen to anyone. Just remember that any bad check you write will be recorded and stored for future use to haunt you.

CHAPTER 15

MANNER OF PAYMENT (M.O.P.)

Understanding how the Manner of Payment affects your credit reports is very important. Manner of Payment simply means, the manner in which you pay your bills. Do you pay on time as agreed or are you sometimes 30-60-90 or 120 days late?

Lenders and merchants approving new credit applications will check your credit reports to see how you've paid your bills in the past. They won't overlook the M.O.P. on your other accounts, you can be sure of that. Why? Simply because the creditors understand that we are creatures of habit. Our M.O.P. in the past is usually a reflection of what our M.O.P. will be like in the future. People can and do change their habits but the lenders are skeptical and pessimistic towards people's ability to make such a change. They believe that the "old" you is the "present" and "future" you. They don't really believe you'll ever change. Manner of Payment is important to lenders. They want to know how you're going to pay. They want and expect the money owed them on or before the due date. You and I are pretty much the same; when someone says, "Give me 20 bucks till Friday," you expect it to be paid back on Friday. If it's paid back on Saturday or the following Monday, you won't throw a fit, but you were still "expecting" to be paid back on Friday as agreed. Everyone wants to and expects to be paid back on time as agreed; it keeps things rolling smoothly and it paves the way for future credit even if it's only $20.00 between friends.

Had I made every payment I've ever had to make, on time as agreed - well, you wouldn't be reading this book; it would have never been written. That's not to say it's good to pay late once and awhile; all I'm saying is that I've run into some challenges in paying bills on time and because of it, I found a need to write you, the reader, and warn you not to do it because it will only cause problems.

This chapter is not written to provide you with ways or methods to weasel out on debt; I don't teach that. If you owe a debt you are obligated to pay it and preferably on time as agreed or late if you must, just so long as you satisfy the debt.

Now I must admit to having seen some pretty creative ways to avoid a late payment being reported. For example, one person I know, Mr. Kennedy, related a story to me on how once he was short on cash and couldn't make a credit card payment. He waited for the late notice to arrive. When it came in, he called the bank and asked to speak with the supervisor in the Credit Department. He told the guy that the payment was made on time as agreed but the supervisor insisted that they hadn't received it. Mr. Kennedy then waited for a second late notice and called the bank when he received it, a little angry this time. He chewed out the supervisor and then got off the phone. He called the supervisor the next morning and apologized saying he had just received a manila envelope from the post office stamped "Damaged Mail" and that the check was inside and partially burnt, evidently it had been in a postal fire. He said he would send him the articles received from the post office along with a new check and apologized once again. He bought the time he needed and the late payment was never reported as late.

Now this is definitely a gray area and I don't recognize this as a good practice but it does go to show that some people will go to any extreme to avoid having a late payment reported. Mr. Kennedy does by the way, maintain a "flawless" credit profile even today. He understands the importance of his Manner of Payment.

I will show you in the next chapter how to pay some bills late if and when you must, in a way that it will do the least amount of harm (if any) to your credit reports but not with any methods like the one in the last paragraph. Don't confuse this book with one that teaches you how to weasel out on debt.

I know that someone reading this book will abuse these principles but I really believe that most of you won't. To misuse these principles in a way to get over on someone will only come back to hurt you at a later date. It's not wise to weasel out on debt. On the other hand, it's foolish to ruin your credit when things go wrong with your finances. So why not learn "who to pay late" where it will show up least if you really must pay someone late? A hundred different things can happen in life that would cause you to pay late, or even not at all until your situation turns around. In order to protect your credit reports when the "chips are down," you must learn who to pay late and that's the subject of the next chapter.

CHAPTER 16

WHO TO PAY LATE

Knowing who to pay late, in advance of meeting face-to-face with a financial crises, is very important to the maintenance of clean credit reports. Remember now that these principles are not to be used in getting over on some of your creditors, but only to be used in the event that someone must get paid late.

As mentioned in the last chapter, I said a hundred things could happen that may cause you to pay some or even all your bills late. There are countless reasons one might be late paying their bills; it's almost inevitable and it happens to everyone at sometime or another. For some people, there is plenty of cash to pay bills with, but writing a check and putting it in the mail is always last on their list. Here it's simply a case of developing a new habit. Perhaps this next sentence will help you do just that. Anyone who habitually pays their bills late, whether it's due to a lack of funds to work with or just plain neglect on your part (you've not placed a value on your credit yet), then there is a cancerous growth on your reports, and it's spreading. In other words, it's loading up with black marks. In the eyes of a lender, your credit reports are your soul, and each black mark represents a credit sin. Worst of all, it takes a long time to be "born again," and washed of your sins, so to speak.

In some credit reports like TRW and Trans Union, there is a column provided for recording your Manner of Payment. It will list what your last 12 months of payment activity have been. A "C" on your TRW means you are current. A straight line of "C"s looks great, but a "1" means you were 30 days late, a "2" means 60 days late, a "3" stands for 90 days, "4" means 120 days, "5" means 150 days and "6" means 180 days. (All the codes will be supplied with each individual report.) Here's how it will look on your TRW:

```
                              M.O.P.
                      1 2 3 4 5 6 7 8 9 101112

B of A                  C C C C C C C C C C C C
Current Paid as
Agreed
30 ( ) 60 ( ) 90 ( )

Sears                   C C 3 3 3 3 3 C C C C C
Current was 90
30 ( ) 60 ( ) 90 (5)

Wards                   C 2 2 C 2 C 2 2 C C C C
Current was 60
30 ( ) 60 (5) 90 ( )
```

Some people I've known will argue that they already have plenty of credit so it doesn't matter what their reports reflect because they don't need any more credit. My response to this is that they may need credit in the future, whether they believe it or not. A person could get a job transfer and be forced to sell his home in order to buy a new one. Maybe, there's a balloon payment coming due in a few years on your home mortgage that you forgot about having to pay off or refinance. Maybe you're in the market for a new job. Many large corporations will pull your credit report to help determine whether or not you're a responsible person. Potential employers pull job applicant's credit reports and so do a lot of insurance companies before writing a new policy. Your car could be stolen or wrecked in an accident causing you to apply for a new car loan. Your house could burn down or be demolished by a storm causing you to be forced to buy a new one. Anything can happen, and when it does you'll probably need some credit reflecting a good manner of payment in order to get financed. Maintaining a good credit profile nowadays is nearly as important as maintaining good health is.

When you've received a copy of each credit report from the CRAs in your area, look at each to see how some merchants have supplied information on two or three reports whereas other creditors you have credit with don't report at all.

RULE NUMBER ONE in paying someone late is to pay someone who doesn't report! Who are you making a payment to who is not on your credit report? Is the phone company on any of your reports? Is the gas and electric company? Is the jeweler, the corner hardware store, the oil company (Texaco, Shell, Mobil, etc.)? Is your landlord reporting? Your home mortgage company? Utility companies don't usually report your credit to the CRAs unless it's a collection account. They will, however, shut your utilities off if you don't pay them, but it's much better to receive a late notice from them than from Diners Club or J. C. Penney. Utility companies will usually give you an extension to pay your bill late if you call and make arrangements. They're generally pretty flexible.

Many small merchants you now have credit with may not be reporting. It doesn't pay for them to report. Oil companies don't usually report, nor do mortgage companies. You would think that your house payment would be reported each month, but I've never seen it reported on anyone's reports unless its a second mortgage or home improvement loan by a commercial lender, and even then it's very rare.

Landlords don't report the M.O.P. of your rent, it doesn't pay to do it. As far as I'm concerned, it would be much wiser to pay your rent a few days late versus paying an account late who is reporting.

What's "Late"? Late is when a curious creditor calls and you tell him "It's in the mail." That's late! Late is one day after the due date. Many creditors offer a "grace period." If your car payment with Chase Manhattan is due on the 1st but you're given 15 days grace, then by paying it by the 15th, you're late but there is no late fee and it won't be reported as late. If you wait until the 16th to pay it, then you're "late-late" and there will usually be a late fee, and it will most likely be reported to the CRAs and show up on your reports, not as being one day late but as 30 days late because that's what the billing cycles are: 30 - 60 - 90 - 120 - etc. I realize you might have been only one day late, or one day past the due date, but it still shows up as 30 days late.

Credit card companies usually report your manner of payment every month. People will usually pay a credit card late versus a house payment for fear of losing their home, whereas the worst a credit card company could do is garnish some of your wages. Since this is true, prospective creditors can see in advance if you're about to go under or are already buried in debt and this new $5,000.00 loan you're applying for, that you claim is for education, is actually to pay other bills. They don't want to deal with anyone who is about to go belly-up!

Now if you are short on cash and your credit card payments are current, but you need $5,000.00 to pull your house out of foreclosure, the creditor is more likely to give you a new loan, believing all is fine and dandy with your finances. He doesn't know your home is in foreclosure by reading your credit reports because your mortgage company is not reporting. The only other protection for the creditor would be to call and verify your mortgage payments being current, and they hardly ever do this. Most lenders look at your TRW, or major credit report, call to verify your employment, and then cut you a check. In today's fast times and easy credit, it's surprising that more financial institutions aren't going under. They loan out money very loosely, in many cases, based on clean credit reports and a source of income to verify.

Clean credit reports should carry considerable emphasis here, and knowing who to pay late when you must is one of the keys to success in this crazy world of credit.

With this in mind, in the event you don't even have enough money coming in to pay your accounts which are reporting, much less the ones who don't report, there is still something you can do to save your credit to some degree. If your credit profile contains more than one report, there is still some hope.

Let's presume you live in Southern California like I do, where the three major CRAs are TRW, Trans Union (TU) and CBI. TRW is the largest and most commonly used, Trans Union follows TRW in size and usage, and then CBI. If I were to pay a bill late, even outside of having to pay those creditors who don't report late payments, I would look to my smallest, lesser-used credit report for a merchant who is not on TRW or TU. Do a little study before

paying one who reports late payments. Figure out where it will
hurt you the least. This might sound like a waste of time but
believe me, it's well worth the effort. If my CBI was dirty but my
TRW and TU were clean, I could still get new credit based only on
my TRW and/or TU. Even if my TU was messed up, I could still
get new credit based on my TRW. It's the most commonly used
where I live and many times the only one creditors use.

If I'm in the market for a much-needed new car, and my only
way to buy it is by financing, here's how I would do it. I would
first decide on which type of car I wanted. If I wanted a Cadillac,
I'd call some Cadillac dealers in advance to see who they
subscribe to for credit reports. If they subscribed to TRW and my
TRW was clean, I'd shop that dealership first. Now had they
subscribed to TU or CBI, then I'd hang up and call another car
dealer until I found one I could deal with. Some dealers will pull
more than one report. The only thing to do then is keep calling
around until you find someone you can deal with. Some major
lenders will report to all the major CRAs in their particular area
of trade (this is most common for unsecured accounts), but they
won't always pull a credit report from each to approve a new line
of credit.

Do your homework before paying any bills late if you
absolutely must be late. The effort is worth it in the long run.

A note of caution, if you are current on all your payments but
need a few extra bucks for something or another, don't start
paying the non-reporters late. It's a bad habit to develop.

CHAPTER 17

WOMEN AND CREDIT

This chapter is especially written for women, but you men ought to read it too. Before writing this book, I thought about writing a book designed just for women. I'm always hearing women complain about not having any credit; most of these are divorced or never married. A lot of married women don't even realize they don't have credit, but they'll figure it out if they get divorced or if something happens to their husband - God forbid! The reason behind this is that men are often the ones who have the credit in the marriage. The woman assumes she has credit, providing her husband signs for all the credit. Until he's no longer there to sign for their credit needs, the woman often believes that she has credit, too. Unless it's being recorded on her credit reports (if she even has a credit report), she won't have any credit in her own name. When he's gone, so is his credit, and she finds herself as a middle-aged woman who has no credit. This is a very large problem among women today; I hear about it in the office, restaurants, in elevators - I hear it all the time.

One of the biggest causes for all these women having no credit is because of divorce. Either she didn't have any of her own credit while in the marriage, or the credit she shared with her husband took a turn for the worse as a result of the divorce. Many times, in divorce, a resentful husband or a rebellious wife, or vice versa, will use the credit cards to charge up the world in an attempt to get the better end of the divorce, or to get back at their spouse.

Whatever the case, both reasons contribute to the detriment of credit.

Approximately 60% of our clients who have come in for credit repair are the victims of divorce. Many of these have shared their stories of how their spouse contributed to their having credit problems now. With 50% of all marriages ending in divorce, this creates a lot of credit problems to be cleaned up. There's an answer to reducing all these credit problems, but you must follow what I say to do in this chapter.

It would not be practical for myself right now to set out to lower the divorce rate; therefore, the answer is to lower the credit problems among women. Divorce is here and it's alive and until we value our relationships more, divorce will continue and so will the credit problems. As previously mentioned, over 50% of all marriages end in the actual Court divorce.

Now knowing that 50% of all marriages end in divorce, I feel it's safe to say that 50% of the women reading this book are either divorced now or will be in the future. The numbers never lie. Someone has to support these statistics but it hasn't got to be you. Marriage is a decision and so is divorce a decision. You decide when to marry and you decide when to divorce. As I said, I cannot raise or lower the divorce rate of this country on my own but I can teach a lot of you how to avoid a lot of pitfalls in a marriage that leave women at the age of 30-40-50 with no credit or dirty credit reports.

The key to your credit success, regardless of your marital success, is that you must build your own "sole and separate" credit. You need to build and maintain credit in your name and your name alone. Many of our women clients are startled when we make this recommendation. They sometimes feel as if this would cause a division in their relationship. We do not want to cause division; we are taking a weak link in the chain and making it stronger.

There are a lot of benefits to be gained from doing this. First of all, in the event the marriage doesn't work out, each spouse may part with their own credit. If the wife was always on time in paying her bills, she will have good credit when the marriage is dissolved, whereas if the husband was habitually a poor credit risk, she doesn't have to pay for his neglect or irresponsibility. When one has one's own credit, and divorce is in sight, one spouse cannot take the charge cards and abuse them to get the better end of the divorce or to get back at their spouse like they could if they had joint credit.

Another good reason to have separate credit is in the event a financial tragedy comes your way, leaving you with no alternative but to file a bankruptcy. Providing it's feasible, one of you could file bankruptcy while the other maintains good credit in the marriage. If you're both in the same boat and it's sinking, you're sunk. Having two boats with one going down, there's still one afloat which you can share until you get another boat.

If your husband has all the credit now, have him put you on his accounts as a "sharer" of the account. You want to be sure you only "share" the privileges but not the contractual liability. If he messes up in the future on the account, you don't go down with him on it. It may show up negative on your reports, but you can dispute it saying you only "shared" the account, but not the responsibility of paying it back. If the account remains in good standing, then you can use the account as a reference, saying you share this account with your husband. Make sure it reflects on your credit reports as being positive; if it's negative, get it off of there.

Some men don't have credit, but their wives do. You can apply this same principle. Put your name on your wife's account as a "sharer" of the account.

If neither the wife nor husband has any credit, then both sign on the account as joint in privileges and contractual liability. Do this until you both have enough credit built up to get credit singularly. Then, as your new sole and separate accounts begin to get established, start closing the joint accounts you first shared. The end result is that you both want your own credit to be "sole and separate."

As for who to pay late when it's called for after you both have separate credit, the answer is very simple. If you're the husband, you're saying pay late on her accounts. But if you're the wife, you're probably saying let's pay late on his accounts. You'll have to work this out between the two of you.

If the wife is not working, she can still get credit reported on her reports by being a sharer of the account. If divorce comes along, she might then start working for a source of income to support herself, and she would have some good "shared" credit on

her reports to use as a reference on her applications for new credit
in her own name. This is provided he maintains good credit after
the divorce. If he quits paying his bills right after the divorce, it
will most likely come up negative on her reports, but she can
remove it by saying she didn't share the "contractual liability" on
that account. Providing you didn't sign the application for that
account, there is really no way they can leave negative
information on your report because it would be derogatory. Ask
them to produce an application for credit on that account that
bears your signature. They can't do it providing you didn't sign it
to begin with. How can they hold you liable for something you
didn't authorize? Share the good and dispute the bad. The way to
become a sharer on an account is to have the account holder
contact the lender or merchant in writing and request that this
other person (you) be added to the account. Include the sharer's
name, address and social security number.

In the following chapters, you'll learn how to build credit, if
you don't have any now. This chapter has been mainly on the
need to develop sole and separate credit. In the back of this book
is a reproduction of the Equal Credit Opportunity Act. This will
tell you what your credit rights are as a woman, while applying
for credit. I highly recommend that you read it.

Joint checking accounts can be good or bad. It's easier to
make deposits in and keep records of one account than it is for
two. If your husband is careless and causing problems with your
checking account, then I recommend you set up an account under
your name alone. A clean checking history is very helpful in
building credit. We'll talk more about this later. I'll also show
you how a checking account can be turned into a piece of
revolving credit which is a big plus on your credit reports
providing it's properly maintained.

CHAPTER 18

SELF-EMPLOYED? J.O.B.

The J.O.B. stands for Jumping Over the Bumps of being self-employed while applying for credit. The J.O.B. also spells Job which is the answer to all the problems that stand between you applying for credit versus being approved when you're self-employed.

When I had a job, I could get credit with no problem at all, but when I became self-employed, the tables turned. It was like having a good friend become a total stranger overnight.

There are all kinds of tactics one can use to overcome these high hurdles of getting credit when self-employed but I don't approve of them all. I've seen where people can hire an accountant to create bogus financial statements to substantiate the proper "income to debt ratio" in order to get loan approval but that's not right.

What I do recommend is that you get a job. I'm not saying you should go out and apply for a new job to replace your business or to have a secondary income. I'm saying that you should become an EMPLOYEE of your business instead of saying you're the owner of your own business.

You need to be <u>NORMAL</u> when applying for credit. Banks and merchants are not all that crazy about doing business with self-employed people, especially when the business hasn't much of a track record to base profitability and stability on. Creditors love doing business with the normal everyday man or woman. They don't really want to do business with hot shot real estate investors or "set-the-world-on-fire" entrepreneurs. They will do business with these people, but they would prefer doing business with the average person.

The perfect scenario of a good credit risk is a person who has a 9 to 5 job and has been on that job over five years. Let's call him John Normal Jones. John has lived in the home he's buying for 3 to 5 years. He drives a small to midsize car that is being paid for on time, as agreed, in monthly payments. John is married, his wife works part time outside the home, and they have a few children. John has a savings account, checking account, an Individual Retirement Account, life insurance, some municipal bonds, and a healthy credit profile. John gets up everyday and goes to work, puts in his eight hours, five days a week, collects his paycheck on Friday and deposits it in his checking account and pays his bills before the due date.

John is ultra conservative. He never rocks the boat or makes any waves. He's almost a robot whose actions are automatic. Creditors love John because he is the perfect model of a good credit risk.

However, Don, John's neighbor, is a whole different story. Don is one of these high-risk entrepreneurs the banks are not fond of doing business with. The creditor never knows when to expect payment from Don. He has his own business and is very proud of it. He burns the candle at both ends and sometimes in the middle. Don rocks the boat and makes plenty of waves. He projects the image of being a future mover and shaker. Don is convinced he's going somewhere in life and he understands in advance that there will be bumps to jump over, mountains to move and plenty of risks to take. Don's the high spirited fellow you see in the bank talking to the loan officer. Don looks like he owns the bank. He acts like he owns the bank, and although he may not have any stock in the bank, he very well could be the one who controls the bank.

A really good "Don" can control the bank without having any of his own money in it, simply by being the one who owes the bank the most money. Believe it or not, it's actually better for Don to owe the bank $5,000.000.00 rather than $5,000.00 because the bank will have a vested interest in Don's success. If Don only owes them $5,000.00 and he "needs" another $5,000.00 to cure a problem, the bank may tell him NO because he "needed" the money. As a rule, borrow money when you <u>don't</u> need it. Now if Don needs a million to cure a problem, or to invest in a venture that will pay the five million back he owes them, Don has a much better chance at getting this loan because the bank can't afford to let Don fail on paying back the five million he owes them. Don is a big thinker and a big doer. Don knows how to play the game and it sometimes scares the bank to have someone who's mastered the art of building credit when you (the bank) are the author of credit. Banks are sometimes fearful of Don because there have been other "Dons" who have robbed the bank without a gun.

Don's a high flyer; often times he's found riding out a wicked storm. He can go through life by the seat of his pants. He's the kind of guy who can lose $10,000.00 in a day on a business transaction without blinkin' an eye. Don just keeps on keepin' on. He has a dream, a goal, a vision of a better tomorrow; he follows that dream. Many bizarre events can happen along the way, but nothing can stop a determined Don outside of death itself! Even with death, a "well-seasoned" Don will have his funeral financed!

Is there any question why banks are very cautious in dealing with a "Don?" Being self-employed is the "pits" when applying for credit if you come on as the owner of your own business.

Self-employed people (let's call them entrepreneurs) are usually required to produce their last three years' profit and loss statements, income tax returns, and a balance sheet or "financial statements." Presenting yourself as an entrepreneur to a loan officer can be a real challenge in getting a loan approved. That's why I say, get a J.O.B. Become an employee of your company if you have a hard time getting credit. Don't list yourself as the owner or president; let your wife be the owner and president and you be the vice president of sales, or marketing director, sales manager or janitor, but don't be the owner or president. Become an employee of your company. Make sure that whoever answers your phone is equipped with these four pieces of information about you when your out applying for credit:

#1 - position or title
#2 - monthly/yearly income
#3 - years on the job
#4 - supervisor's name

Have this information handy for lenders, verifying your income and length of employment. Pay yourself a salary and become an actual employee of the company.

If you prefer to remain calling yourself the owner or president of Fly By Night Enterprises, then you should get all your ducks in a row when applying for new credit. The key to jumping over the bumps in applying for new credit is to get a job. If you insist on telling your future creditors that you're the president or owner, then start a file on yourself to give to creditors when you apply for credit. Note: The fatter the file, the more money you can borrow. The loan officer will request a profit and loss statement, tax returns, and balance sheet from the last three years. GIVE IT TO HIM! Throw a bunch of other goodies in with it. Put your credit reports in there, a copy of your high school diploma, a picture of your family, a computer run of your checking account, your college degree or certificate - fill that baby up! He won't read it all - 99 times out of 100, he won't go through all that stuff. To see if he does, put a note in the middle of it all which says: "Dear Mr. Loan Officer: My associates and I are in the process of opening a lending institution just down the street from you. Would you be interested in being interviewed for becoming the Bank President? It pays approximately double the salary you are now getting at Sharky's Thrift and Loan."

Will he call when he sees the note? You can count on it! Twice the amount of pay, and Fridays off to go play golf? You can bet he'll call you if he reads everything in your file and comes across that note, but he'll probably never see it because he'll never fully read it.

Why the big file? Well, that's his "out" if you default on the loan he just made you.

In the event he's ever called into the Board Room on behalf of your bad loan he made, that file is his trump card. He's going to dump that puppy out on the table in front of his superiors and say: "Look at all the information this person submitted; he's the last person I ever thought would default on a loan. Look - here are his financial statements, tax returns, checking and savings account activity sheets, his high school diploma, college degree, and even a picture of his family (standing next to a Rolls Royce you don't own, in front of a nice home you've never been inside of before).

Mr. President, this is the last person I ever thought would default on a loan."

The bigger the file, the fatter the loan. Playing the game. That's how the big shots do it and you can duplicate the process.

If your self employed, either get a job or start building a file like the one I mentioned with all the goodies in it. But don't include a picture of the Rolls Royce and mansion you don't own.

CHAPTER 19

BANKER MENTALITY

Understanding how your personal loan officer thinks is very important to your success in being approved for loans through him.

To start with, we need to analyze where this person comes from, his background and training as a loan officer. As with a new-born baby, so it is for the loan officer in that the first word he learns is "no." He really has to practice at it in the beginning, probably in front of a mirror in the morning before work. He must be persistent in his practice until he masters the art of saying "no." He has to know how to say "no" or he would end up giving the bank away. He gets so good at saying "no" that the word "yes" is erased from his vocabulary and replaced with words like "probably, I suppose, or sure."

The loan officer uses the word "no" to protect his position and the bank's interest. By saying "no" to an unsecured personal loan, he can later bargain for collateral on the loan, or a co-signer to secure the bank's interest better. On a car loan, by saying "no", if the customer persists, the loan officer can ask for a bigger down payment, once again securing the bank's interest in the loan.

People who are weak in the ABCs of banking (attitude, belief, commitment) are easily brushed off with the loan officer's firm but friendly "no." These people are time wasters to the loan officer. Anytime he can talk you out of a loan by just saying "no", he probably just turned down a loan request that in most cases would end up in default.

As far as I'm concerned, the word "no" really means "yes." What he's really saying is, "Yes, I want to give you the loan, but you haven't given me "no" reason to." "No" reason. You need to give him a reason to make you the loan. The best reason you can give him is that it's a sound loan he is making, because you always pay your debts on time as agreed and, besides that, the bank must make loans to stay in business. These are both valid reasons why he would make the loan; but he may be hung up on one particular reason of his own. How do you find out what his reason is?

Well, when he says "no" to your request, ask him why. Why won't he give you the loan?

Now, be careful here. He's just like a lot of us. He has two reasons why he won't make the loan, just like we have two reasons why we won't do something we don't want to do. This is human behavior.

The first reason he gives you is almost always a lie in disguise. He might say that you haven't been on the job long enough, or lived at the same address long enough; these could be good first reasons to deny the loan (always listen for, and pay attention to his second reason). Regardless of whatever his first reason is, always say, "OK. I can see where you're coming from Mr. Loan Officer, but what's the "real reason" why you won't make the loan?" In most instances, he will then tell you the real reason why he won't make the loan. Maybe you're asking for too small a loan or too large a one. Maybe he wants a co-signer or collateral this time around. Also, it's possible that the bank is too short on funds to loan at the time. I know a person who has good credit and plenty of funds available to make good on a debt, and a bank turned down his sound, secure loan request. Here's a case where a good credit risk was turned down, not because of anything wrong with his credit, but simply because the bank had recently made a lot of loans which depleted their reserves of money. The bank made it look like the customer was lacking something or was at fault when, in fact, it was just a matter of the bank being short on available cash for new loans. Banks who run into this problem now and then will never tell a customer they're either short of money or out of money because they're supposed to be a bank, and banks are supposed to have money in them, either for loans or for covering withdrawals.

I was standing in line at a branch office of a very large California bank one time when I overheard the branch manager tell the head teller that they should have ordered more than the usual $25,000.00 the normally get on Fridays.

My first thought, of course, was $25,000.00 on a Friday? That's all the cash they have on hand? How do they expect to cash all the payroll checks of their customers and the cashier checks received on the personal loans that day, and the savings withdrawals, and the people who come in to cash a personal check for $100.00 to cover the weekend? And what about the money needed to fill up the automatic teller machines (ATM's) that are used over the weekend while the bank is closed? What about the business customers who order money for making change on a $20.00 bill in the restaurants, stores and gas stations they own? Twenty-five thousand dollars - that's all you have on hand on a Friday? I immediately realized that this was not a bank where you would want to request a $10,000.00 loan on a Friday, because they probably couldn't even cash the check! I like cash; it's no fun walking around with a silly check . Cash spends better than checks.

Another thing that is drilled into a loan officer's mind are the initials CYA, which stands for Cover Your Ass-ets, or in other words, cover your backside. If for some reason you skipped over the last chapter on "Self-Employed," go back and read it in order to better understand what I'm saying here. The file you want to submit to the loan officer is his way of covering his own personal asset - "being his job." Asking for co-signers, collateral or large down payments are other ways to cover himself. The loan officer is more concerned about his job with the bank than he is with the bank's assets; however, if he makes a bunch of loans that go sour, he's out of a job. His job is first priority, and protecting the bank's interests in a loan is his second priority. They work hand in hand, but his major concern is in keeping his job, bankers love *security*. In order to maintain his status at the bank, he must cover the bank's assets.

Stop being intimidated by the bank and its loan officers. There's really no reason to have any fear. Walking into a bank used to run cold chills up and down my spine. The image they project is "all this money" and, also "we're not leaving town - we're here to stay." Credibility is a combination of trustworthiness and expertise. That's why you see all the glass and marble and brass and oak fixtures and expensive office furniture. These things are used to impress you and me, but I'm not all that impressed. Beneath all these expensive trimmings in buildings made of glass and marble is "dirt." The same kind of dirt that is called the "floor" over at Deuce-Rents-It, your local tool and equipment rental company. In all reality, your bank is really no better than Deuce. Your bank rents money to its customers, Deuce rents tools and equipment to its customers; the motive for both is profit. Stop borrowing money from the bank and start "renting" it from them. The rent on their money is the interest they charge. Rent your money from the bank; it's much easier than it is to borrow.

Renting money is an attitude. When we use the "rent", rather than "borrow", a whole new dimension to credit opens up before our very eyes. The attitude of renting money makes it much easier for you to get the money you want and need because you are no longer trying to borrow money or, should I say, "beg" for a loan. You are now renting it. When you approach it this way, instead of borrowing, you start to shop for price, you don't have to deal with hard-to-deal-with loan officers you never cared for in the first place; you no longer go in on your hands and knees to borrow money. Instead of looking for a bank that will accept and approve your loan proposal, you're now looking to rent money from someone you want to do business with versus finding someone who'll do business with you. The end result is that you get more loans approved at better rates of interest in much larger amounts than if you were to borrow. What's the turning point here? You've created *competition*! Anytime you create competition between banks, your value as a customer goes up.

Banking has never been more competitive than it is today. Where there used to be a gas station on every other busy street corner, there's now either a bank or a convenience store. Some of these convenience stores even have automatic banking centers in them. You don't have to deal with just any bank that will accept you; you can start qualifying banks that you wish to deal with. Competition is where it's at, folks. Create competition between the banks you deal with. Be like Bert Lance, former President Carter's Federal Budget Director. This guy was a "master" in renting money from banks.

Lance's attitude was, "I don't need your dirty, stinkin' money, Mr. Bank President, because I have all these other banks catering to me. I don't need your money."

Many bank presidents have lunch with their competitors. When one bank, not then renting money to Lance, found that his competitors were, then they started prying Lance's fingers open to get a pen in his hand, all the while saying, "How much?", "Sign here." Lance had bankers calling and chasing him with more and more money to rent. This went on for quite some time before the banks renting Lance money found out that he was using this new money to pay off other money he had rented, somewhat like robbing Peter to pay Paul. Well, it must have been fun while it lasted. Lance rented over 20 million dollars from 41 banks, on over 300 different accounts! I have no idea whether or not he paid the 20 million back. But his way of creating competition worked very well in this case of renting money. What was the substance of Lance's key to the vault? OPTIONS. Lance had scores of other banks which would rent him money; why would he need some other bank's money when he had all these other banks to deal with? Who needs your dirty, stinkin' money? That's the Bert Lance attitude on renting money!

Bank loan officers need to know that you have other options available to you. If they think that they're the only game in town, you won't go very far with them. Now, if you let them know that they are really just one of hundreds of banks to deal with (actually thousands), you create the perfect atmosphere for competition and, if they want to play, they have to play by your rules to a certain degree. These principles are best applied once you are already established, but use them even if you are just starting out, or starting over in the world of credit.

My young millionaire friend I talked about earlier, who asked me to find him a house in Bel Air has several lines of credit he can access on his signature alone, the highest single line of credit being a $250,000.

Now if you're an entrepreneur, exercise these practices at your own risk. If you're a normal, everyday person, working from 9 to 5, I recommend that you steer away from these practices. You can get in hock real fast using these methods if you don't have a solid means to put this money into, which will pay the rent on your loan, much less a profit to you.

Renting money is a piece of cake when you know how bankers think. In the next chapter, we'll be talking about choosing the right bank for you. Going one step ahead of myself, when you find the right bank, you'll always want to make an effort to deal directly with the bank president whenever possible. Don't just walk in and ask to see the president because the receptionist will probably ask what it's in regards to, and shuffle you off to a lesser authority such as the personal loan officer. Note: You always want to start at the top in the Chain of Command and work your way down if you must. This way, you can tell the loan officer that Mr. Bank President referred you to him should the president brush you off. You may gain some credibility yourself this way, rather than saying, "Hi, Mr. Loan Officer. My name is John Doe, no one special - just off the street. I'd like five minutes of your time so I can beg for a loan."

No! Call the bank before you go in and say, "This is Irate Slate; what's the bank president's name?" Now, you can go in and ask for him by name and get by his secretary with the least amount of explaining what you want to see him about.

Whenever meeting with the bank president or one of his subordinates, you'll always want to use good mental posture. Act like Bert Lance. Never go in expecting to get loan approval on the same day if you don't have a prior banking relationship established already with that particular bank. Once you have done business with them, the rest is fun. You just say how much you want, and sign the contract. If they are foolish enough to ask what the money is going to be used for, say: "What would you like to hear that it's for?" That's posture, folks. IT DOESN'T MATTER WHAT IT'S FOR JUST AS LONG AS IT GETS RETURNED WHEN YOU'RE THROUGH WITH IT; ON TIME AS AGREED, OF COURSE!

Don't walk into a bank you have never been in before, and expect to get approved on an unsecured signature loan that same day. Instead, go in to meet with the president and pre-qualify him for a possible future banking relationship. Tell him who you are and a little bit about yourself. Explain to him how you're very displeased with the poor service you're presently getting down at Care-Less Bank and Trust. Mention the other banks you do business with, also stating how much more convenient his bank would be, providing he could fulfill your financial expectations.

Make certain you say that you would want to become a "valued customer" if you did decide to bank with him. He's always looking for "new" and "valued customers."

Be sure and mention all of your associates who also bank with Care-Less and how they're dissatisfied with the service they receive for "all that money" they run through their accounts. Ask him if "he would mind" if all your associates moved their accounts over to his bank if you decided to do business with him.

Once again, this is good mental posture on your part. He ought to be reaching into his pocket to give you a key to the vault by now. Qualify him and his bank and his ability to meet your needs and desires. Don't let him qualify you as they often do (this would also be a good time to discuss interest rates). Remember Bert Lance's attitude on renting money: "I don't really need your stinkin' money, Mr. Bank President, but I'd like to have it waiting for me should I ever want it or find a use for it." This is good posture! Remember, the one who asks all the questions is the one who controls the conversation and the outcome. You qualify him - don't let him have all the mental posture by asking you a million questions.

Never commit to opening an account there on the first day. See how he warms up to you. If he's hot, come back in a day or two and put some money in the bank. If he's a weird banker and his response is cold, move onto another bank who wants to do business like you're used to doing business. Be sure and tell him that you despise loan approvals and filling out a bunch of paperwork, but, initially, you'll fill his file with all the necessary information (you know the file) and update it twice a year. By using this posture on even a lukewarm bank president, you'll have what I call a "bank in your pocket" or Hip National Bank. How much is a bank in your hip pocket worth to you. $5,000.00? $10,000.00? $50,000.00? More?

Back in Minneapolis, I had a wonderful banking relationship established. After moving to California, I failed to see the value in maintaining that relationship. I figured that they wouldn't be of much help to me while living in California except for a reference on my experience with them. This bank was a dream. I was only about 22 at the time, but I had made alot of unsecured personal loans there. I had an excellent rapport with the vice president there. My first loan was $1,000.00 and it grew from there.

Based on experience, I'll say that it's vital to maintain your banking relationships when you develop a good one like I just described.

When you develop a good banking relationship like this, maintain it, and keep it active. Don't let it die off or fade away. Rent money, just a small amount, even for three to six months and then pay it off. Do this twice a year to keep it alive.

Invite the person you deal with out to lunch once in awhile. Let "him" pick up the tab when you're through dining. After all, he's the hot shot banker; he's the one with "all that money" over there. Actually, bank loan officers or bank presidents don't make that much money on their job. The ones who are doing well in life are those who have ventures of some sort going on the side. As for "all the money," well, it's not their money. They count other people's money; they personally don't need any help counting theirs because they don't make that much to begin with.

As far as having a job is concerned, being bank president must not be a bad position to hold. There are a lot of benefits that go along with it. Personally, I'd much rather own or control the bank than to be the president of it. To own a bank, you just do a high leverage buy-out like you would with any other business. To start a bank, round up a group of investors and file for a Charter. To control a bank, which is the best position to be in, either be the biggest depositor or the one with the most money rented out. If you rent three to five million from your bank, you'll definitely have some control over that baby when it comes to interest rates, terms, extensions, and additional lines of credit when you want it most. Up until now, you probably thought you had to own the bank in order to control it but that's simply not true.

After having read this chapter, there should be no reason at all for your being intimidated when walking into a bank. Bankers are people, too. Stop looking at them as High Priests in Holy Temples. They only perform a job like anyone else. They're just another profit-oriented company among the business community. Bankers put their pants on like any other man - feet first. They're no different than you or me; they're just people. I will admit that some of the younger loan officers get off on having the power to manipulate your success in borrowing money to some extent, but you don't have to buy that garbage anymore. Now you have "options" available to you, and you no longer borrow money. Remember, you rent it! Remember that banks must rent out their money to stay in business. They don't make a dime on deposits alone; they have to rent out money in order to stay in business.

Renting money is a game. It's a game that involves a winner, far too many times a loser, and a strategy. Make this game be a win/win game. Both you and the bank must win in order to continue your relationship. Since he'll always want to see all the cards in your hand, you might just as well see all the cards in his hand so you can play your cards accordingly. Never let a bank put the monkey on your back - YOU put it on HIS. When developing a new banking relationship, remember that he's on trial, not you. You qualify him and his bank. It's OK to bend a little in the initial stage, but take more and more control of the situation each time you rent from him.

Let him know that you're a player, you play the game of renting money. You know all the rules that govern it and you live by them. Don't ever leave a banker hanging out to dry when you rent from him.

Be somewhat patient when you start building your banking relationships. Bankers are not entrepreneurs and they never will be. They'll remain out in the weeds for as long as there are banks to be bankers at.(This book was not written with the intention of coming down hard on bankers. Its just that bankers and entrepreneurs are like cats and dogs; they always have been and always will be. My being this aggressive is only for the purpose of reducing the number of entrepreneurs who leave the bank empty handed. How aggressive you are personally with this information will be up to you.)

Build more than one good banking relationship. If you're an entrepreneur, build several to start with and always continue to expand your banking relationships. Continue to create more and more "options".

The reason you want to always seek to establish new banking relationships is that even though you get a good rapport going with someone and pay all your loans back on time, you might walk in one day to rent some money and your personal loan officer or bank president may not be there. He could get transferred, fired, or just sick and fed up with that bank's management and quit. Sure, you have good credit with that bank to show the man replacing the guy you knew, but it's not the same. You'll have to educate this bozo on how you're used to doing business, just like you had to do with the first guy. That's why you want to maintain more than one good banking relationship and continue to establish new ones. Another reason to seek new banks to deal with, is because you might pull up one day, all revved up, and ready to rent some money, only to find that the bank is closed, yes, closed, insolvent, bankrupt! This usually takes place on Fridays, though. I'll talk more about this later.

With banks dropping like flies, there's a good chance that the next one could be yours. Where do you stand then if this was the only bank you had established a relationship with?

It doesn't matter how big your bank is and how solid you may think it is. It's a shake-out period for banks. Look at the size of Continental Illinois Bank. How about Seattle First National? Continental was bailed out by the government but, even so, it still became insolvent. What do you suppose happened to all those loan officers? Establish more than one banking relationship.

CHAPTER 20

CHOOSING A BANK THAT'S RIGHT FOR YOU

In choosing a bank that's right for you, keep in mind that the two main objectives are: finding a bank that is aggressively seeking new business, and making sure you can develop a personal banking relationship with them; also, they must be able to meet your credit expectations. Don't just walk into a bank and open up an account. Be fussy about who you bank with. Spotting an aggressive bank to deal with is fairly easy. Just watch for those who are doing a lot of advertising.

Advertising can get pretty expensive. In order to profit from it, they need to pull in new customers for loans and lines of credit. It would be foolish to advertise if they didn't have an abundant supply of money to rent. Another good sign is when you see all these credit applications on top of cigarette machines in hotels, restaurants, and the like. These are the "Credit Card Pushers." They are VERY aggressive in seeking new business. More about these little honeys in a later chapter. Ask friends where they know of aggressive lenders - who's easy and who's not.

Merchants who offer credit terms on their merchandise are a good source for finding aggressive lending institutions, especially car dealers. Any good sales manager knows who's aggressive and who's not. A really good sales manager can put almost anyone in a new car.

My favorite banks are the "Lone Ranger" banks. These banks have only one or two offices, not a thousand branches. They are generally more aggressive, more lenient on qualifications, and much friendlier and more personalized in the service they offer. These little one-office operations are sweet to deal with. They have to be more flexible in their lending because all the big banks create so much competition for the little guy.

With the small, independent bank, you get service with a smile, and often called by name. The tellers remember you enough not to have to see your identification every time you want to cash a check drawn on your own personal account. Small banks don't have a large loan committee that really does no more than shuffle paper. They want to stall you for a day or two, just so they don't look *anxious to give you a loan.* Big banks have forgotten that the customer is always "number one." They want to act like they're doing you a favor when, in fact, you're doing them a favor because without the customer, there can be no bank. Large banks can be very impersonal. Nobody really knows you; in fact, they really don't care to know you. All they want is your money and, occasionally, they'll give you a loan providing you fit into their lending policies.

These large lending institutions have a lot of employee transfers and turnovers. You never know who you'll be turned over to as far as loan officers or personal bankers are concerned. It can change quite often.

I used to do business with a very large bank in Minnesota. It was a mess. Faces changed every time I entered that bank. There was little hope of ever establishing a banking relationship with any one loan officer. I didn't bank there very long. It was from this bank that I chose the smaller one I talked about in the last chapter, where I was granted several unsecured signature loans; what a difference in banking!

Back when I was about ten years old, I had a savings account into which I'd deposit $5.00 or $10.00 a week. My neighbor lady was a teller there. She just retired from that job a couple of years ago. She must have been employed there for at least 20 years. It was a fun bank to deal with - very friendly people. They made you feel of value, not always in words but in their actions. You walked out of there with the feeling that they respected and appreciated you as a customer, even with being a Nickle-Dime depositor like I was. You were more than just "a number" to them; they wanted you as a customer and they were willing to work towards satisfying your needs. I never thought of renting any money from them, but I'm sure my neighbor would have co-signed for a couple of hundred dollars had I thought to ask her.

Deal with smaller banks. Most of these big guys couldn't care less about you on a individual basis unless your already a proven High Roller. Then the banks start calling and chasing you with money to rent.

Maybe as people start swinging over to do business with the smaller banks, perhaps, just maybe, the big banks will catch on and get on the bandwagon of treating people like people should be treated. If you're presently doing business with one of the larger banks in your area, keep your accounts open for a couple of years, but go out and open an account with one or two of the smaller banks in your area. When these new accounts have seasoned for a year or so, close your accounts at the larger banks and do all your business with the smaller ones, providing the big ones are not meeting your expectations.

Don't close your accounts at the big ones until the accounts with the smaller bank have been opened for at least a year. You can even do all your business on the small bank's account, but keep your big ones open because they are good to use as a reference on new credit applications. The people approving your new line of credit will like to see that you've had a checking and savings account open for at least one year.

CHAPTER 21

SIGNATURE LOANS

Here's your passport to success in taking advantage of a good deal or profitable transaction when it passes your way. Signature loans are your *key to the vault*. Signature loans are just that - loans granted on your signature alone. No co-signers or collateral is involved in a real signature loan.

With pen in hand, based on prior credit history and experience with your banker, your signature can draw from $1,000.00 to $250,000.00 or more. It all depends on your ability to pay it back. Even more so than your ability to pay it back, is your "reputation" of paying it back. I've gotten signature loans when my income wouldn't support a way to pay them back, but the ventures I invested this money into did produce enough to pay it back. This is where "income to debt ratios" don't apply.

Signature loans is my way of banking. I like a "no questions asked" banking relationship. I like to go into the bank, tell them to write me up for $5,000.00 or $10,000, sign my name, and I'm on the road again conducting business. I don't like to have to haggle with bankers. Just give me the money and I'll return it as agreed. Who wants to fool around with a stupid loan committee, income and employment verification, and the other nine yards? Just give me the money; my name is well worth the lousy $5,000.00 I'm renting.

Everyone won't be able to handle this approach right off the bat, but with practice you'll get it down to a tee. Once you have this posture and form, don't ever stop using it. If you don't use your abilities, you lose them. You become rusty just like I have done before. It takes a lot of coal shoveling to get the fire burning hot again.

Now, in my opinion, and most loan officers will say I'm crazy, but anyone with a clean credit report and a source of income is worth some amount of money on their signature alone. You bankers reading this book can tell your hair to lie down now, but that's how I feel. If a banker makes you a loan, let's say for $1,000.00 and it's secured by a $1,000.00 Certificate of Deposit, there's really no trust on the banker's part. If you want the C.D. back, you have to make good on the loan. This doesn't leave any room for judging the real *character* of a person. When there is collateral backing a loan, it doesn't give the person renting the money the freedom to default on the loan and express his true inner being, like it would be with an unsecured loan. It's what's on the inside of a person that counts. If on an unsecured basis, the customer doesn't burn you on a loan in the beginning of your relationship, then chances are very much in your favor that he won't put the screws to you over the course of your relationship either. It shows that he respects and appreciates your trust and faith in him. If you, Mr. Banker, distrust your customer, he'll sense it, and anytime you plant seeds of distrust, they will almost always produce a harvest in the form of default on the loan. As we sow, so shall we reap!

As mentioned before, I don't mind using the merchandise I'm going to purchase on credit, such as a home or car as collateral, but it's foolish to ask for collateral or co-signers on signature loans. They just aren't signature loans with any of these added contingencies.

Once you get your first signature loan with a bank, walk in on the day it's due, and pay it off with two cashiers checks or two different stacks of money. The first stack of money will be to cover the principal amount of the loan. As you give him this, be sure and tell him how well you did for yourself in renting that money. "I made a lot of money on that loan, Mr. Loan Officer. Tell him not to spend that money because you might come back to rent it again; hang on to it for me." As you pay back the interest portion on the loan (the rent), make sure you point out how much money the bank made on the loan. Remind him that the bank made a profit based on your performance on the loan. Make him acknowledge that he understands that the bank made money on the loan. Remind him that it's the rent you pay on these loans that keep the bank in business. You have to remind him about this because bankers tend to overlook the fact that it's the rent paid on these loans that keep the bank in business.

Now, let's say your loan was for $3,000.00. As you get up to leave the bank, turn to him and say, "Oh, by the way, I may want to rent $5,000.00 in a couple of weeks. Will you hold onto $5,000.00 for me?" What you are doing is *pre-qualifying* a $5,000.00 loan. You're saying, "Hey, Mr. Loan Officer, are you gonna raise my next signature loan to $5,000.00 or is $3,000.00 the limit?" What can he say? You just paid back the $3,000.00, you paid back the rent, making it perfectly clear that the bank made money on the transaction, and that it's this rent which keeps the doors open and pays his salary. What can he say? If he answers with, "We'll see," sit back down at his desk and say, "You mean you're not sure? What seems to be the problem?" Get a commitment on the next loan from him in advance. He won't answer with the word "yes", but a "sure" or "I suppose" will suffice. Don't leave the bank until he commits to the next loan. With each new loan, raise the amount $2,000.00 or so until you're getting signature loans of $10,000.00 at which time you'll start raising future loans in $5,000.00 increments.

When shopping for aggressive banks, ask the person you're dealing with if they are a "commissioned" loan officer. They are the most aggressive loan officers of all, because they get paid a commission on all the loans they write. These people will be more eager to make you a loan.

Another rule of thumb in renting money is to always ask to rent more money than you want. Here's why. Let's say you want $10,000.00 to purchase a home that needs repairs which will return you a nice profit upon resale. If you need $10,000.00 to successfully complete the transaction, ask for $15,000.00. Providing you receive the entire $15,000.00, you then have $5,000.00 to put in reserve or play with on another project. Now if the loan officer says he can only give you $12,000.00, say, "That will be just fine; that's what I really had in mind anyway." Now if he says the $15,000.00 is a little too much, but that he will loan you $10,000.00, say, "Fantastic! I was just going to recommend that; you stole the words right out of my mouth."

Had you originally asked for $10,000.00 and he made a counter offer of $8,000.00, you would come up $2,000.00 short of your needs, it's always easier to "come down" than it is to "go up".. Always ask for more than you need. We don't always get what we want, but in most cases, we seem to always get what we need.

CHAPTER 22

APPLYING FOR CREDIT

Here are the actual steps you'll want to take in putting your best foot forward when applying for credit. For those of you who are already well established, keep reading. I'm sure you'll find some more bases to cover when filling out your next credit application.

The first step in applying for credit is to make sure your credit reports are in their proper form. There's no sense in applying if there is still derogatory information on your reports. Be sure everything is up to date and accurate.

Next, a checking and savings account are vital in applying for credit. At least one of each is necessary but two would be even better. Savings accounts should have some money in them - at least $100.00. You'll also want to make deposits and withdrawals from time to time just to keep them active. Otherwise the accounts get turned over to your State Government after a period of time and become a part of the "$25 Billion" kitty that they aren't real concerned with in finding the rightful owners of.

Checking accounts must remain active but, most importantly, they must be free of any bounced checks. Creditors are looking for stability and responsibility here. They want to see how you handle your checking privileges. If you have a history of writing bad checks, chances are very good that you won't handle your charge card payments with tender loving care either.

There are several different types of credit you may apply for. Let's take a look at a few of them, and then continue with going over the proper steps to take in applying for credit.

The most common types of consumer credit are:
- Installment Loans
- Signature Loans
- Revolving Charge Accounts
- Closed End Charge Accounts
- Open End Revolving Accounts
- Lines of Credit
- Letters of Credit
- Overdraft Protection
- Consolidation Loans
- Mortgage Loans
- Home Improvement Loans
- Hard Money Loans
- Home Equity Credit Lines
- SBA Loans
- Auto Loans

Installment Loans, in brief, are described as a loan in which the total principal and interest are divided into equal monthly payments in spreads of 12 months, 24 months, 36 months, etc.

Signature Loans should only require one signature. They are not based on collateral or co-signers. They are based upon your character of having successfully rented money and paid it back on time. These loans can be a 30 day note, up to a one year note. You may be required to pay the interest each month and then the principal amount when it finally comes due. The more sophisticated entrepreneur will generally ask that the principal and interest be paid at the end of the term, and then when it comes "due", he'll "roll it over" for another 6 months or so.

Revolving Charge means a balance on an account can be paid in full or in monthly payments. Providing you're not over your credit limit, additional charges can be made on this account and added to your next month's billings. The most common charge cards are Sears, Wards and J. C. Penney.

Closed End Charge Accounts are American Express, Diners Club, Carte Blanche, etc. These are charge accounts which must be paid in full each month. Often, these are referred to as Travel and Entertainment cards (T & E cards).

Open End Revolving Accounts are your Visa and Mastercard accounts. These are the best of all. The credit limits on these are based on your ability to make the payments on them. The interest rates are generally high, but I know of some low interest cards I'll share with you later. These accounts can also be paid in monthly payments or in full. Fully 75% of the banks issuing these cards still have a float or grace period. These are the hardest cards to obtain at first in building credit.

A Line of Credit is most commonly used by businesses where they are granted a line of credit. These can be reserve lines of credit for meeting taxes and payroll or overhead expenses. They are designed to help see the business man through the lean periods.

Letters of Credit are most common among the business community; often they are used in the import/export business. This is simply a letter on the bank's stationery stating that they will guarantee the specified amount as payment to the business person to which the letter is addressed; this is a service to you as the bank's customer.

Overdraft Protection is a form of credit which essentially allows you to bounce a certain dollar amount of checks on your account with the bank picking up the tab and billing you in monthly payments - with interest, of course.

Well, you should know what **Consolidation Loans** are after having read Chapter 8. These are more easily obtained when your financial position in life is stable rather than when your ship is already on the rocks.

A Mortgage Loan is also known as a Contract for Deed or Note secured by Deed of Trust. These have sharp variances about them but they all pertain to the financing of real estate. Mortgage loans come in hundreds of different makes and styles to choose from. A friend of mine, who is vice president of a large lending institution in Seattle, once told me that he stopped counting all the different home loans on the market when he reached the "100" mark.

The interest rates will vary with different market conditions and costs of money to the lender. The most popular mortgage is the one which is amortized over 30 years at which time it's paid in full.

Fifteen year mortgages have been coming on the scene lately and offer some very attractive advantages. For another $100.00 per month or so, depending on the amount of the mortgage, you can pay off this loan in 15 years instead of 30 years and save "a bunch" of money.

Mortgage loans come with either fixed or variable rates, depending on which one you choose. Variable rates start out real low but can cause severe problems when payments are raised in the future. I believe this is a big part of the reason that the rate of foreclosures is at an all time high. Variable rate loans are designed to help the "unqualified", qualify. Fixed rate mortgages are harder to qualify for but they are easier to maintain when you know exactly what your payment is each month. Each has their own advantages and disadvantages.

Home Improvement Loans are just that - they are designed for home improvement. These loans are based on the equity in the home and the homeowner's ability to make the payment on this new loan. The interest rates on these are generally higher than the first mortgage rates are. They also range in terms of one to fifteen years.

Check with your local government for low interest rehabilitation loans. They may be able to provide just what you need and can afford. They may even have a Block Grant Program if you live in a target area. Also, there are special low interest rate loans designed for the elderly and the handicapped. Contact your local HUD office.

Hard Money Loans or Hard Money Lenders, also known as equity-only lenders or finance companies, are outfits which will often times make a loan when banks won't. Some equity lenders don't even require an income or good credit history. The loan approval is based on the equity in your home. These people are similar to loan sharks in that they have high interest rates and outrageous loan fees. Finance companies will often make hard money loans, they will also do car loans and personal loans; the rates of interest can be a little steep.

Home Equity Credit Lines With the new tax reform laws going into effect, interest and finance charges on credit cards will no longer be tax deductible. So, what's been coming on the scene lately is the Home Equity Credit line because of its' special tax benefits. Basically what you have here is a revolving credit line secured by the equity in your home, which allows you to write off interest on your taxes again. See your banker for more details.

SBA (Small Business Administration) Loans are available from the government but I've never received one. I hear about them all the time but I've never even met a person who has received one. I would imagine they exist - I see ads in the paper by brokers who advertise to get you one, but, personally, I've never seen it happen. I guess there's some status or prestige in saying: "I'm in the process of getting a SBA Loan". Good Luck!

I am much more familiar with **Auto Loans**; I've had several myself. They run between 12 and 60 months. The interest rates can be high or low, depending on the lender, and they usually require a 20% down payment and good credit in order to get approved. Also, based on experience, I know that if you fall behind a couple of payments, you'll get a visit from the Repo Man in Chapter 6.

Now that we have covered some of the more common types of credit, let's get back to applying for them properly.

All of these types of credit, in most instances, will be approved initially based on scoring enough points on the standard scoring system lenders use. Many facets of your personal life come into play here; they are as follows:

- Residence, Own or Rent, Buying
- Length of Time at Residence
- Employment, Years There
- Professional, Skilled, Laborer
- Annual Income
- Marital Status
- Education Level
- Age
- Dependents
- Credit References

Look to the next page, at a sample point system and see how you add up. Remember now that this is only a "sample" point system. Each lender will assign their own numerals to each category.

SAMPLE POINT SYSTEM

Residence

Own	3
Buying	2
Renting	0

Income (Annual)

$12,000 - $15,000	1
$15,000 - $25,000	2
$25,000 - $35,000	3
Over $35,000	4

Length of Residence

0 - 2 Years	0
3 - 5 Years	1
6 or More Years	2

Marital Status

Married	2
Single	1

Length of Employment

Less than 2 Years	0
2 - 3 Years	1
3 - 5 Years	2
Over 5 Years	3

Age

18 - 25	0
26 - 65	1
Over 65	0

Type of Employment

Professional	2
Skilled	1
Laborer	0

Dependents

One	3
Two - Three	2
Four - Five	1
Over Five	0

Education - Years Completed

Under 12	0
12 Years	1
2 - 3 Years College	2
4 - 6 Years College	3
Over 6 Years College	4

Credit References

Checking	3
Savings	2
Credit Card	3
Bank Loan	2
None	0

Naturally, the idea is to score as many points as possible without being dishonest. Some people will lie on their applications, stretching, their assets or holding back from listing all their liabilities. Although I cannot stop you from doing it, I highly recommend you don't.

Let's run through the sample point system. Look for areas in which you can improve upon to score more points in the future.

Residence. Notice how you get more points if you own your home outright than if you are buying. To rent your home, you don't receive any points at all. The reason behind this is that you're not building any equity and you don't have any roots planted. You can pack up and leave in the middle of the night before the lender has a chance to place a repo order on your new car or furniture. On credit card applications, they don't call to verify whether you own your home or not. It would cost a fortune to do an ownership of title check on each application. Banks or finance companies, on the other hand, may call to verify ownership, as well as the condition of the loan.

Length of Residence. If you move around a lot, it would be a good idea to get a P.O. Box. I'm not talking about the kind at the Post Office, but one with a "suite number" with an address. You can get one of these at a check cashing center. If the mailing address for the check cashing center is 321 Main Street and your post box is #10, your mailing address would be 321 Main Street, Suite 10 (or Unit 10). This looks a lot better than using a P.O. Box number. This system also protects your privacy to some extent. Bill collectors can't just drop in on you at home.

Education Level. This is just to give the creditor an idea of how sharp you are. They associate continued education with success. Personally, I think they have it backwards. To me it seems that the less normal education a person has, the better they will do in life, providing they have some "Success Education" under their belt. There is a big difference between the two.

Annual Income. The more money you earn, the more points you earn. With some credit card companies, I have found that often they won't even call to verify income. This sounds crazy but it's true.

Marital Status. You get more points being married than with being single. The reason is that they feel you're more responsible when you're married.

Age. Being 18 to 25 years old doesn't earn you any points. They don't feel you're responsible yet. These are the years most people are likely to neglect their credit privileges. Not that you can't get credit in these years of life, but most people are not established before the age of 25. The productive years for most people are between 26 and 65, but most people over 65 suffer a drastically reduced income, leaving very little to pay bills with after having paid their living expenses. A lot of health problems set in after people retire which also adds to their being a bad risk.

Dependents. Having one dependent is good because it supposedly adds to responsibility, but any more than one becomes a financial burden in the creditor's eyes. The more mouths you have to feed, the more clothes you must buy. More than one dependent is an added expense which cuts into the money you pay bills with.

Credit References. It's important that you have had some past credit experience to share with your future creditors. Here's where the importance of having a checking and savings account come into play. You need at least one of each just to score points. You get added points for having a charge card or credit card to list as a reference. The same holds true for a bank loan or a car that's being financed. Some credit applications will also give points based on your zip code. Insurance companies will also do this in determining the cost of your car insurance policy.

Length of Employment. This is important. Do you change jobs every six months like I used to do? Lenders are looking for stability here. The longer you've been on the same job, the more points you will get.

These are the main characteristics that creditors are looking at. With being honest, look for ways you can increase your number of points on this scoring system. Creditors all use a standard point system similar to this. Each may have a different set of numbers assigned to each category but this is a sample of the scoring system they use. Using the numbers as listed, to pass this test you would need a minimum of 20 points. Check your score and see how well you did. Look for ways to increase your number of points in the years to come.

On credit card applications, once you've passed the point system, they then pull your credit reports. If your score is marginal or borderline, clean credit reports will put you over in many cases.

Before applying for any credit, get a copy of all your credit reports and make sure they are accurate and up to date. If you don't have a credit report with anyone of the major CRAs in your area, start one. Write to them and ask that a file be started on you. Supply them with all the necessary information. Make sure the person who will be verifying your employment and income has all the necessary information.

If you want to add unrecorded credit information to your credit profile, I'll show you how later. In the meantime, don't go out and apply for a bunch of credit if you are getting denied. Check your reports because something is wrong. You don't want to pile up a bunch of Inquiries on your reports. An inquiry is listed on your report every time a creditor pulls your file to do a credit check on you. These remain on your file for one to two years. Don't keep applying for credit if you keep getting denied. The very reason for your denials may be because a lot of inquiries are showing in your profile. An inquiry which is not followed by a new account opened by the creditor making the inquiry, tells other creditors that you were probably denied credit for one reason or another. Several inquires without new accounts being opened, and reflecting on your file, will tell a prospective creditor that everyone is denying you credit. Why should he grant you credit if no one else has? Why should he take a chance on you if no one else will?

I'll show you how to avoid a lot of inquiries later on.

CHAPTER 23

CREDIT CARDS

I believe you'll find this chapter to be most helpful in obtaining credit cards. I'll be talking to both the normal everyday person and the entrepreneur. Watch for and recognize the difference between the two. I don't want you normally more conservative people to go out and obtain 100 Visa and Mastercards, only to be used in creating consumer debt.

In the beginning stages of building credit, the oil company cards are easiest to obtain. They usually start you off with a minimum limit of $300.00. They'll check your reports before granting you credit, but, in most cases, they won't report your manner of payment. Some of the major oil companies who issue credit cards are Texaco, Mobil, Shell, Exxon, Unocal, etc. These are the easiest cards to obtain when first establishing credit or reestablishing credit. If you ever filed bankruptcy or let a bill go unpaid with them, chances are that you're still on file with them, only to block you from getting over on them a second time. Many of these companies will maintain an indefinite file on any person who already defaulted on an account. Since they don't usually report to the credit bureau, this indefinite list of deadbeats is their main source of protection from getting screwed a second time by the same person.

Department store charge cards are the next easiest to obtain. Who's the easiest of the department store cards to get? To the best of my knowledge, it would have to be J. C. Penney. The reason here is that J. C. Penney's customers are overall in a lower income bracket than Wards or Sears. Wards would be the next easiest to obtain in regards to major department store cards, then Sears. Sears is a good department store card to have if you desire their new Discover card. Sears has entered into banking to capture their share of the billions of dollars to be made in these times of high finance. They just completed a promotion asking some of their 60,000,000 Sears card holders to apply for the Discover card.

Before applying for credit with a department store, it's often wise to call their credit department and ask what CRA they use for getting their credit reports. For the longest time, I didn't have any credit information on two major reports of mine and was constantly denied credit because of it. Each department store may pull different reports on you. Call in advance to see who they get their reports from, particularly if one or more of your reports are lean on credit information of past success. You'll avoid any unnecessary inquiries on your reports this way.

After you have a couple of department store cards, you're then ready to apply for a Travel and Entertainment card. Probably the easiest of these T & E cards to obtain is the Diners Club card. The reason behind this is that Diners Club is owned by Citibank who just happens to be one of the most aggressive credit card pushers in the industry. Another good thing about the Diners Club is that people who maintain a good account with them will probably receive a promo application for a Citibank Visa or Mastercard. American Express is very aggressive also but harder to obtain than Diners Club in my opinion.

American Express does the highest dollar volume in sales than any of them. In 1984, American Express did over 38 billion in sales. Citicorp, with all their different credit cards, had 14 billion dollars in sales. Next was Sears at 13 billion, Wards at 7 billion, Bank of America at 6 billion, J. C. Penney at 5 billion, AT&T at 5 billion, Shell Oil at 3.7 billion, First Chicago Bank at 3.3 billion and Amoco Oil did 3.2 billion dollars in sales. These cards are listed as the highest in dollar volume.

Now, as for which cards are used most in transactions, American Express leads the pack again with 461 million transactions in 1984. Next was Sears with 365 million transactions, Citicorp with 360 million, Shell Oil with 197 million, Amoco Oil with 186 million, Texaco with 179 million,

J.C. Penney with 165 million, and Exxon with 162 million transactions.

Once you have a T & E card, it's easy to get a Visa or Mastercard. Visa, the name given it by the founders of the card, found that the word itself is the "most common word" used in all the countries of the world. It's accepted by over three million merchants in over 135 countries. It is, by far, the most popular credit card of all. Mastercard, previously called Mastercharge, was developed by a group of large California banks. Over 150 million Americans have Visa and Mastercard among the seven credit cards the average person carries in his or her wallet. There are over 725 million credit cards in circulation in America. This is what I call "Plastic Pursuit;"

Of these 725 million credit cards, there are four Premium cards that you should know about. A step up from the American Express Green Card is the American Express Gold Card. The annual fee for this card is $65.00 and offers cash advance features and credit lines to $5,000.00; about three million Americans have at least one of these in their wallets. But that's not all. A step up from the Gold Card is the American Express Platinum Card. This one carries a whoppin' $250.00 annual fee and has no credit limit.

Mastercard has a Gold Card also; the annual fee is $55.00 with a credit line of $5,000.00. Two million Americans have at least one of these. Visa's Premium Card is called the Premier Visa. With annual fees ranging from $30.00 to $50.00, and credit lines of $5,000.00, there is no reason to wonder why two and a half million Americans have at least one of these cards among the many others.

Interest rates on these cards run between 18% and 21%, with the average interest rate being 19.4%. That's highway robbery when compared to the 10.5% Visa and Mastercards coming out of the State of Arkansas. Them Good Ol' Boys are regulated on the rates they can charge, and in some cases, they will accept applications nationally. The lowest rate on a Visa that I know of is 10%. One of these banks is in the State of Virginia and the other is in California. Look in the Appendix for a list of low interest rate credit card issuers.

Before getting your first Visa or Mastercard, you really can't be too selective on interest rates, but, when you have one to list as a reference, then you can shop around more. There are a lot of card issuers out there who offer rates of 14% to 16% which are much better than the average rate of 19.4% but some of these have limited market areas.

Why the big push on credit cards?

Money is the answer, the entire motive is for profit, and the name of the game is Plastic Pursuit. The three biggest players in the game are Citicorp, Sears and American Express. The strategy here is to cash in on the huge profits realized between the cost of money to the bank and the rate of interest charged for credit card purchases. Banks love to buy money at 5 or 6 percent and loan it out at 19% or 20%. These are big spreads, leaving the bank with a "pitch black" bottom line. Citicorp, the nation's largest banking company, is, in my opinion, the most aggressive credit card pusher of them all. They have the "shorty application," unlike some bank card issuers who want to know your life story. A couple of years ago, my roommate got a pre-approved credit card with a $1,000.00 line of credit - when he was unemployed. That's aggressive!

I read a newspaper article a couple of months ago which told of an 11-year-old boy being sent an application by one of these pushers and a 14-year-old girl was sent a pre-approved credit card with a credit line. The article went on to say that there was proof of pre-approved credit line applications being sent to prison inmates, unemployed teenagers, and household pets. I don't know if this would be considered as being aggressive or careless but it does go to show that the Plastic Pushers are on the prowl.

American Express has targeted the Ivy League students with the Green Card, saying, "Don't leave college without it." They plan to offer nearly all the traditional services of a bank through its Shearson Lehman Brokerage offices to its customers. Sears' new Discover card doesn't have a membership fee; this is unlike most other credit cards. It also offers a host of other benefits to be taken advantage of by Discover card holders. Sears has done very well in all the other services they offer, so there is no reason to doubt the success of the Discover card.

Another big reason for the push in credit card lending versus traditional lending practices is because of the Federal Regulations that restrict interstate banking. There's a gap in the law that allows limited consumer banking services on a nationwide basis. The pushers are taking advantage of this loophole to establish multimillion dollar banking networks without the actual bank. What used to be land, concrete, glass and marble has now been replaced with plastic, about 2 inches by 3 inches and a thumbnail thick. With all the other financial services being offered along with being a card holder with one of these giants, it's almost possible to carry your bank in your wallet. That's some progress we've made over the years; these people are sharp cookies.

With all this loose credit available, I think we'll see some major problems follow in the near future. Mail boxes now being stuffed with applications for credit and pre-approved applications may one day be replaced with hate mail from the pushers saying, "pay up or else!"

It's not just the banks and other financial institutions making the big push but a lot of retailers have entered into the game of Plastic Pursuit as well. Retailers feel that if a one-time customer can be approved for a charge card, then chances are very likely that they'll come back for more since they have the plastic to purchase with. With the charge card customers, they can also maintain a mailing list of active customers to solicit with sale information, whereas with the cash paying customer, it's hard to get and maintain a current address to send notices of special sales to.

Be careful with all this easy credit. You can get into financial trouble terribly easy. If you're a "set the world on fire" entrepreneur, take on this easy credit at your own risk. I've personally run into problems with this and it's not hard to do. It's much easier to get into debt than it is to get out of debt! I think we'll see a record rate of bankruptcies in the future as a result from all this easy-to-obtain credit. Credit can be great if it's properly used, but, in many cases, it's not. American people use credit cards today to pay for things they didn't really want, didn't need, and couldn't afford to start with, only to be paid for in the future. Surprisingly enough, delinquency on these accounts are only 3% but I think that the rate will double by the mid 1990s.

Entrepreneurs can often find a way to cover their credit card debt but even the wisest entrepreneur runs into problems now and then that are beyond his control.

For you normal everyday people, let me suggest that it would be wise to get an oil company card and a couple of department store cards. Then get a Visa and a Mastercard. Once you have this Visa and Mastercard, apply for a low interest Visa and Mastercard, cut up your other high interest Visa and Mastercard and any other credit cards you have and close the accounts. The only cards you really need are one or two low interest rate credit cards. You don't need department store cards once you have Visa or Mastercard. You only need a few department store cards to get a Visa and Mastercard.

Now, for all of you "forever enterprising" entrepreneurs, let's get some Visa and Mastercards so we can take advantage of their Cash Advance features and get on with building our empires. I must, however, disclaim having any responsibility for the results of your transactions. Since I don't share in the profits of your business ventures, I surely won't take on any of the risks involved in this kind of activity either.

I'm sure most of you are familiar with what cash advance features are. A Visa with a $5,000.00 credit line usually has a $3,000.00 cash advance in which you can draw on the card at most any bank that issues Visa cards. The major credit cards which have cash advance features are Visa, Mastercard and the American Express Gold Card. If a Visa is drawn on Bank of America, you don't have to go to B of A to exercise your cash advance. If you have 20 Visa's and Mastercards with a $3,000.00 cash advance on each, all of which were issued by different banks, you can walk into any bank that issues these cards and get a cash advance on each, all at the same time. In other words, by showing the bank teller 20 cards with $3,000.00 cash advance on each, you can walk out of that bank in less than 30 minutes with $60,000.00 in cash and cashiers checks. This is my way of banking. No questions asked is my way of doing business. Do you think you could get a $60,000.00 business loan from your banker in less than 30 minutes with no questions asked? Of course, they charge a small cash advance fee on each card used, but that's the price you pay for the convenience of "no questions asked banking."

On the American Express Gold Card, you get checks that can be written for cash as their form of a cash advance feature.

The highest credit card limit I know of is $100,000.00 which is issued by a California bank. The highest credit card limit I ever heard of was over $2,000,000.00. What do you suppose the cash advance limits are on these credit cards? A good way to access your total line on a credit card is to open a checking account with the issuing bank and have your Visa or Mastercard linked to it for overdraft protection. That way you can use Visa and Mastercard (via overdraft protection) to cover purchases that could not normally be purchased with a credit card, simply by writing a check.

The most Visa Cards, Mastercards and American Express Gold Cards ever obtained by an individual that I know of is just over the "200" mark. The most I ever heard of was over 400 credit cards. How much money do you suppose could be raised on cash advance features just on 200 credit cards? I'd say at least $250,000. Now, how many cards do you want? How much money do you need available to you through cash advances? Now do you understand what I mean by Plastic Pursuit?

Yes, you can obtain 100 Visa and Mastercards if you want, but do you really need all those cards? What would one do with all those credit cards? Well, if you could buy a foreclosure piece of property from your bank's R.E.O. Department for $50,000.00 which was appraised at $80,000.00 to $100,000.00, would you use your cash advance features on 20 of your cards to raise the cash to purchase the property? If you said "yes" to that question, then you'd be doing what thousands of others have done before you.

Don't buy non-productive merchandise at retail prices that will just end up lying around the house or end up in the trash. Use these credit cards as a tool to make short term purchases at or below wholesale prices to be sold for a profit. (See the chapters on Hidden Bank Treasures, and Making Money with Credit.) If you start using these credit cards to buy the luxuries of life like boats, motorcycles, TVs and stereos, you'll probably end up in trouble financially. Don't use those credit cards to increase your lifestyle; use the cards to make cash profits which, in turn, can be used to increase your standard of living. Far too many people use these tools, made for building their empires, as a means of taking a short cut in life and, in essence, buying their empires. I'm using the word empires here for dreams. Whatever your dreams are, they are the substance of your empire; that's what empires are made of.

I've known some people who have five or six of these credit cards but are afraid to use them. Inactivity is not good, either. Your credit reports reflect your highest limit ever achieved on any card. If you have five Visa Cards with a $5,000.00 credit line, but only used one or two of them for up to $1,000.00, then other credit card issuers will see that you're not even using the credit lines you do have, so why should they solicit your business for taking one of their cards which you won't use either? To have credit lines and not use them in a productive, profitable manner is poor stewardship.

"To whom much has been given, much is expected."

The Scriptures support such a statement, having just read the Parable of the Talents. A talent was a measure, could have been gold or silver. The King went away for a while on vacation in Palm Springs. Before leaving, he gave three of his servants each 1,000 talents to care for. When the King returned after some period of time, he called them into his chambers and asked what they had done with the talents they were given to care for. The first servant said, "Master, I have taken the 1,000 talents you have given me to care for, invested it while you were gone, and now I have 5,000 talents." The King said, "Well done; you shall keep the 5,000 talents and be given 5,000 more." The second servant turned his 1,000 talents into 3,000; the King said that he had done a good job and that he would be given 3,000 more. The third servant said, "Master, I took the talents you gave me and buried them so that I would have them when you returned." The King turned to his guards and said, "Stone this man to death, for he has been an evil servant."

This was done in paraphrase à la David B. Triemert, but the principle remains the same. To have credit lines and not use them is poor stewardship. To have credit lines and use them to purchase merchandise or services that won't return a profit or save you money is foolish. I've met alot of people who live only to "get all they can", "can all they get" and then "sit on the can". That's not the purpose of money or credit. Both are to be used in creating Profit!

Now, the people who issue Visa and Mastercard are probably shaking their heads "no" to what I just wrote. They want you to be indebted to them, but only to the amount you can afford to pay. They don't want their credit line to be only "one" of the 50 credit cards you have. They'll say that this practice of obtaining a lot of credit cards to produce a profit is simply not right. On the other hand, however, they'll spend millions and millions of dollars on advertising, saying, "Don't leave home without it!" They don't mind sucking every last available dime out of your paycheck, but they don't want you using these credit cards for questionable business ventures or practices. It's just a matter of opinion to me.

When you first receive a credit card and if you actually want more cards, draw at least the total cash advance amount available, and then use it to pay the card off. This way it will reflect as having been used and paid back on time as agreed. A card with no activity on it will eventually stop other card pushers from giving you their cards.

Float periods on credit cards are important. About 75% of all card issuers still offer a float period. Each will vary in length of time but the average is a 25-day float. This means that if you get a new credit card in the mail and, let's say, you charge $500.00 on it, when the statement comes for that billing, paying off the entire $500.00 within the float period or before the due date will preclude your being charged any interest on the $500.00. Now, if you only paid the minimum monthly payment, interest will be added from there on. Some card issuers will attach interest to your charges the day they are made and others will start adding interest at the beginning of the next billing period.

To bump your limit on a credit card, you simply pay three or four times the amount of your minimum monthly payment. If your credit line is $2,000.00 for instance, and your balance on the account is $1,000.00, your minimum payment let's say would be about $50.00. If you pay three times the minimum or $150.00, and you continue to do so for three or four months in a row, your limit will be raised automatically by computer in many cases. Not all banks will do this, but many will. Their computer is programmed to recognize accounts which have been paying more than the minimum amount. If it finds you have the ability to pay more than the minimum payment, then, with many banks, your limit will be raised accordingly. And why not? Why wouldn't they raise your limit if you've demonstrated the ability to pay more than required?

They are in the money rental business and they want to rent as much money as possible to anyone who can pay it back. Looking at it in this sense, if you can afford to pay three times the minimum payment on the $1,000.00 balance, won't they want to raise your limit to $3,000.00 knowing you can still afford to pay the minimum payment of $150.00 on that amount? Sure they will, but I must say that every bank doesn't subscribe to this practice. However, many banks do. This is what I call the "Silent Bump."

If you request them to bump your limit by phone or mail, they usually send you a long, ridiculous application form to increase your limit. On this form, they want to know it all. It's worse than the original application you filled out. Furthermore, they scrutinize every detail you give them. Again, instead of a hassle, I like "no questions asked banking." That's why I love to use the "Silent Bump" as a way to increase my credit card limits versus having to ask for it.

Another more common way to bump your limit, is to go over your limit and send in the amount over the limit plus your minimum payment but this isn't really a good practice. First of all, the card issuer may close your account, and it could appear as "account closed at grantor's request" on your credit reports. This is not good. Also, by charging over the limit, it will show on your reports as such and it may discourage other card pushers from soliciting your business with them. Some people I know have been successful with this method but I don't practice it. You could if you wanted to but I don't recommend it.

Here's how it's done. Let's say you have a $2,000.00 limit on a Visa and your balance is $1,950.00. If you make a charge on that card to make a $100.00 purchase, the merchant will usually call in to the card issuer and get authorization, a "guarantee number" from the bank that they'll pay the merchant on that purchase. Now, if the merchant calls in for authorization and your bank (who issued the card) is a little flexible, they will OK the purchase. Now if the bank says, "No way, $2,000.00 is the limit and it's already at $1,950.00, we won't honor your request;" then the merchant must deny your purchase in order to cover his assets (C.H.A).

A way around this is to make some purchases with the credit card that are under the Floor Limit. The floor limit on Visa is

$50.00. The floor limit on Mastercard is $75.00. If you go out for dinner ten times over a 30-day period, each time spending $20.00 (equaling $200.00) you are now $150.00 over your credit limit. Don't do this unless you can afford to send the amount over the limit plus your minimum monthly payment when your billing statement comes in. Any amount under the floor limit is guaranteed by the issuing bank. Because of this, merchants don't have to call in for authorization on charges under $50.00. Some banks will raise your limit when you go over it but I believe the majority of credit card issuers won't. It's risky business doing this and you just might end up losing your credit card. There are much better alternatives to expanding your credit lines than this last method I have just explained.

Recently I was sent a Visa and Mastercard by a large California bank. The credit limit was set at $1000.00 on each. After receiving the cards I wrote a letter to the bank thanking them for the accounts. I also added that I was somewhat embarrassed about the credit limit, being my other credit cards all have a $5000.00 limit. I went on to say that I am a big spender ect. They ended up raising each account from $1000.00 to $2,500.00. That's a total increase of $3000.00 just for writing a letter. I do this same thing on every credit card I receive regardless of the initial limit they start me at.

Earlier I mentioned that I'd show you a way to avoid a lot of inquiries on your credit reports and still get as many credit cards as you desire. If you apply for say ten cards, you'll end up with ten inquiries on your credit reports. This is not good. Lenders don't like to see a lot of inquiries on your reports, especially if none of the inquiries gave you a card or opened an account for you. Some card issuers have a standing policy to automatically deny a credit application for having over five inquiries that didn't follow up with at least one open account. The best way to avoid a lot of inquiries is to get your name in what is called the Interconnect System. Many of the smaller banks want to be a credit card issuer but, because of limited facilities for credit card processing and such, it's sometimes difficult for the smaller banks to cash in on the credit card boom. What's been developed is the interconnect system. This is where a large bank will process credit card applications and issue the credit cards for the little banks.

For example, let's say that Mini Savings and Loan wants to get in on the Plastic Pursuit. Mini, however, hasn't the facilities or staff to process card applications, or issue cards. Mini then contacts Maxi Bank to hire their services for card processing. Maxi has several others like Mini which they serve. Mini has a credit application drawn up with their name on it. They place these applications in their business community to solicit business on their new credit card. Now you come across Mini's credit card application while shopping one day. You fill in out and drop it in the mail to Mini Savings and Loan. Mini then forwards the application to Maxi Bank for processing. Maxi Bank pulls your credit reports and processes your application. Assuming you're approved on the application, Mini is notified and requested to assign you a credit line. Maxi then sends you a credit card, Visa or Mastercard, with the name of Mini Savings and Loan on it. You make your payments directly to Mini; Maxi Bank is out of the picture now and your account is with Mini Savings and Loan.

Even though Maxi Bank is out of the picture, your credit information is still in their computer. Maxi Bank can then sell your name to all the other institutions like Mini Savings and Loan or even to the other big aggressive banks so that they can solicit your business as well. This is where pre-approved applications come to you in the mail.

Now the way to avoid inquiries is to ask Maxi Bank (once you know who Maxi Bank is) who else they process cards for. Then go to those other small banks they give you the names of and apply for one of their cards. Let's say you apply at Tiny Savings Bank. Tiny will forward the application to Maxi Bank. Being Maxi Bank still has your credit information on file, and providing it's somewhat current, Maxi Bank will use that information versus pulling new credit reports on you. This way you avoid another inquiry on your report.

Pre-approved credit cards are the best of all. These show up as a promotion on your credit reports versus an inquiry. Pre-approved cards are a result of one bank who now has you as a customer, and sells your name to another bank or series of banks so they can have you as a customer, too. Another source that sells your name is the CRA. And why shouldn't they? It just so happens that they can program their computer to print a list of names and addresses of people with clean and healthy credit files.

This list is then sold to lending institutions and merchants who want to send you a credit card. They even have what's called a "hit list" of names, addresses and social security numbers that are believed to be credit card frauds. This is part of the protection they can offer their mailing list buyers.

The lender who buys the mailing list will then do one of two things. First, he might send you a normal application to apply for his credit card. If you fill it out, he will pull your credit reports (an inquiry) and decide whether or not to issue you a card. If you're approved, you'll get a card in the mail but if you're denied he will send you a letter stating the reason why. If you have bad credit or insufficient credit information on your reports or if it's not been on the report long enough, he'll say his denial was based on information received from TRW, TU, CBI, etc. If it's for another reason you are denied credit, it will be listed as so. Some other common reasons for denial are collection accounts, judgments, unpaid tax liens, insufficient income, not on the job long enough, unable to verify income, excessive inquiries, etc. If you feel that their reason for denying your application for credit is weak, get on the phone and call them up. Blow a little smoke at them, not a lot, but just enough to let them know you feel you deserve the card. They might bend a little and give it to you.

Anytime I was rejected on a credit card application I always sent them letters until it was approved. And then once they did approve me, I bitched about the credit line they gave me. Its fairly easy bumping your credit line up once you have been initially approved for the accounts. Just don't accept "no" for an answer.

Secondly, a lender buying the mailing list might send you a letter which says: "You've been noticed as a good credit risk in your community. We at New York Credit Pushers Bank understand your credit needs and will make ourselves available to meet your needs. This is the reason we are sending you this letter stating you've been pre-approved for a $5,000.00 credit line. Just sign this agreement and your new credit card is on its way."

Credit card pushers hire writers to draft those silly letters to make it sound sweeter than I just did, but you get the idea. "Just sign on the dotted line and get $5,000.00 credit on your new Visa."

That's aggressive, folks. One of my more recent callers who was seeking credit advice, stated that he just applied for a Visa a few weeks ago and was approved. He then went on to say that he filed a Chapter 7 bankruptcy on about 30 creditors just three years ago. How this slipped by I have no idea.

Each lender will be a little bit different. The majority of credit cards are issued by only 25 banks and savings and loans. There are some 3,000 credit card issuers out there, though. My list of pushers can be found in the Appendix. At the time of this writing, these pushers have proven to be very aggressive. Some will change their policies with the weather; however, out of all the lenders I know of who have been aggressive in the past, this list of lenders has proven to be the most consistent. It's also wise to apply for *out of state* credit cards because many times the inquiries won't show up on your reports back home.

Whenever applying for cards, if you want to get a bunch of them, follow these other steps. On most applications they provide a "box" which you will want to fill in. It allows you to give your spouse or friend a credit card on the same account. Always put someone's name in there, here's why. After you've been approved for the card, the person whose name is in the box will get one too. Now what happens many times after the account has had some time to season, the lender who issued the card will send a letter to the sharer of the account asking if he or she would like their "own" credit card with their "own" credit line. If you were to put your wife's maiden name in there, she would probably end up getting an account in her name as well. That's what I call a two-for-one credit card special. Many lenders will do this but I cannot say that everyone of them will.

If you're after alot of cards, find a friend who wants to get some too. Have your friend apply to five banks, and you apply to five different banks, putting your wife's maiden name in the magic box on the application. Chart your applications. Make a list of who each of you applied to, were you approved or denied; if approved, how much was the credit line? Who was the fastest to respond? Etc. Find out who was easy and who was hard. Try five more banks 30 days later and once again, chart the response. Now you and your friend each have ten banks in which the other can apply to the easiest and most aggressive, skipping over any stubborn credit card issuers so to avoid any unnecessary inquiries. You women can get cards in your name while your husband is getting cards in his name. It's just a matter of how aggressive the two of you are.

When filling out credit card applications, be sure to fill in all the blanks, but never list anything in the "other income" section unless you need your other income to qualify for even the minimum credit line.   To list other income is only asking for trouble. If it's possible or feasible, it's better to inflate your normal income to include any additional income you actually have than it is to list it separately. The reason behind this is that the person scoring these applications is making about $5.00 an hour and like the rest of us, they too are lazy by nature. If they see another income, they probably won't even bother to verify it, and if they did verify it with the source, providing it could be verified, they probably wouldn't believe it anyway. Never list an "other income" unless you must have it to qualify for even the smallest credit line with them, which usually requires $12,000.00 a year income.

If you're just getting started in building credit or if you're starting over, remember that the "hardest" Visa or Mastercard to obtain is your "first one." The reason here is that no one really wants to be the first one to give you a card; after you have the first one, then the others would like you to have theirs too.

There are some short cuts to getting your first Visa or Mastercard. Even with some bad credit showing on your reports, there are still some lenders who will give most anyone a credit card, providing you put a deposit in a savings account with the issuing bank. My favorite institution to deal with on a secured Visa or Mastercard, is Home Trust Savings in Vermillion, South Dakota. They only require a $380.00 savings deposit and in turn they will issue a card with a $380.00 credit limit. You can increase your credit limit up to $2,500.00 simply by adding the additional increased amount to your savings. Providing you pay your payments on time as agreed over a 12-month period, Home Trust will then refund your deposit with interest, and you maintain the credit card now on an unsecured basis like any other Visa or Mastercard.

They may require that you apply for this credit card through Service One Corporation, located in Chatsworth, California, but I would call or write Home Trust directly . When you have this

Visa or Mastercard from Home Trust, you can then use it to obtain a charge card from many of the participating retail merchants across the country who have what is called an "Instant Credit" program. With these firms, just show them your Visa and they will give you one of their charge cards after your account has been verified. The whole process generally takes fifteen minutes or so.

Key Federal Savings and Loan in Perry Hill, Maryland has a similar Secured Visa Card Program. They charge $18.00 to process the application and require a savings deposit of $500.00 My clients haven't had much luck with them though.

Your local savings and loan may have a similar program. It would be wise to call around and see what programs the lenders in your community have to offer on the Secured Visa Program.

Home Trust and Key Federal are more geared towards helping people obtain a credit card when there is some past credit problem on the report, or no credit at all, than any other lender would be. Again, you can find the address and telephone number for Home Trust and Key Federal in the back of this book.

Another source for these secured credit card grantors can be found in papers like the National Inquirer, Star and Globe. These outfits guarantee to get you a credit card and usually charge a fee of around $30.00 to $35.00. I would guess that they too must get their credit cards from Home or Key. There are not as many institutions offering secured cards as there once was because a great deal of people have abused their privileges.

Be careful of these offers in the paper because I've found that many of them will charge you a referral fee, only to turn your name over to an Exclusive Firm who will charge you an application fee on top of that and then forward your application to the issuing bank itself for approval.

CHAPTER 24

CHECKING ACCOUNTS

Here's another form of "no questions asked banking," somewhat similar to a Visa card, providing you want it. This form of credit which can be added to the checking accounts of qualified individuals is called Overdraft Checking Protection. Before we go into depth on this, though, let's just cover the general information about checking accounts themselves.

To begin with, checking accounts can be a real pain if you don't have a good record keeping system. I still round off all my figures to the next highest dollar. A check for $11.29 is the same as a $12.00 debit to me. The biggest obstacle I've found is simply taking the time to record each check as I write it. I don't bounce checks but still I find myself fighting with names, dates and dollar amounts. It can become a hassle tracing checks when I have a dispute with the billing department on one of my credit accounts.

Checking accounts should be kept as clean as a whistle. Don't bounce any checks on the account. If you find yourself bouncing a check every now and then, I suggest that you go open up another account and never bounce even one check on it. You need at least one clean checking account to use as a reference on your credit applications. Prospective creditors may verify the account you list. They'll be looking for your demonstration of "responsibility and stability." They'll ask your bank whether or not you bounce checks (responsibility) and how long the account has been opened (stability).

One thing you'll want to do when your monthly statement and canceled checks come back, is to make sure that the bank has all of their figures correct. Looking at your statement alone won't do it. Next to your account number on the bottom of your canceled check, in the far right hand corner, is the actual amount the bank debited your account. Make sure that amount matches the amount you wrote in the box. Usually they're pretty accurate about this but it's a good idea to double check their figures.

Some banks offer a "safe check keeping" service where they will store all your checks for you. I like to get my checks sent back to me each month. I don't want my account number and signature left out in the world any longer than it has to be in order to be processed. It could take days, perhaps weeks, for them to retrieve a check if I ever were to need it to show proof of payment on an account. Plus they'll charge a fee to retrieve the check. They already have a photocopy of the front and back sides of every check I ever wrote; they don't need the checks themselves. They maintain these check photos on microfiche in case the IRS wants to monitor or audit your check writing activities. This government of ours is in on everything we do.

By the year 2000, the IRS should be able to tell you exactly what 95% of your income was spent on. We are moving into the Electronic Age. They want to keep tabs on every dime we earn and spend. They want to do away with cash altogether. All these electronic banking systems that some of you people think are so neat, are going to be used to monitor your life in the future. It won't be so cool when the government can punch your name into a computer and recall more information on you than you can remember yourself. Think about it. The federal government already has 3.2 billion files on us - that's equal to 18 files on each.

Get back to carrying cash while there's still cash to carry. I see some of you people writing a check for a lousy hot dog. You have the checkout stands in the grocery stores all tied up. I seen a guy use his Mastercard to purchase a magazine and a quart of beer! Next time you find yourself becoming impatient while standing in line at the checkout stand, start looking around and see what people are using to pay for their purchases with. What are you paying with? Start carrying some cash with you. Some of you can hardly even remember what cash looks like. If it weren't for the game shows on TV, you probably wouldn't remember what color the ink was.

If you're afraid of getting mugged, that's all the more reason to carry cash. Those little bandits aren't gonna stand around waiting for you to cut them a check for $50.00. They want and need cash; that's why you're being mugged. I have an old family friend who lives in New York. He carries a $20.00 bill in his pocket. He calls it his "mugger money." It's a lot cheaper to give away $20.00 than it is to be resistant and wind up in the hospital, if not the morgue, he said.

Now, let's get back to the checking accounts themselves. Here are a few special situations that may occur with having a checking account. First of all, you know about bouncing checks. The average fee on a NSF check is $10.00 but you'll see that raised to $15.00 before you know it. I'm sure the bankers will whine some more about losing money when you bounce a check on their bank, before they raise the NSF charge to $15.00, but you'll see it happen shortly. They used to raise this fee in one dollar increments. But now they raise it in $5.00 increments. After $15.00 comes $20.00 and then $25.00, and so on down the line. When a check bounces, they charge you the set NSF fee. If you deposit before the check hits your bank a second time, you save yourself another NSF charge. If they do run it through twice and it bounces twice, then you pay twice. The merchant you wrote the check to can also charge you a fee if the check is returned a second time unpaid. If it bounces twice, the merchant can send it in for collection with your bank. Your bank sits on the check until you deposit some money again. The laws on bouncing checks are getting pretty stiff. You had better stop bouncing them if it's presently a habit of yours.

"Stop Payment" on a check is done at your branch office. It usually costs about $6.00 or $7.00 to do it. They'll raise that fee to $10.00 before we know it, too. Providing they haven't paid a check of yours before you contact them, you can demand that they stop payment on that check. Many times it's hard to convince a merchant that the blender you purchased from him was defective before you used it. Some will be reluctant to exchange the merchandise or make a refund. Providing your bank didn't pay the check yet, you can give yourself the refund by stopping payment on the check. You can later discuss whether the merchandise was defective before you bought it or not. This puts you in a position to negotiate a deal, to settle the matter.

Lost or stolen checks should be reported to your bank immediately. This way they will do a signature check before paying on your checks and avoid any forgeries.

Never write a check out to cash and carry it with you or leave it lying around. Anyone can cash it and you won't have any recourse on being reimbursed for it.

Whenever you open a new checking account, take control of the situation. Bank personnel who open new accounts are trained to start your check numbers at #101. Don't let them start you with such a low number. Many merchants won't even accept a check under #500. Request that you be started at #1001 or #1501. This will help in cashing checks. Anytime I see a check come into our office that's #156 or so, I get this preconceived idea that it may end up bouncing. If you ever want to accept a check that you're not sure of, just call the bank and ask to verify funds. They'll tell you if the money is on account or not.

If you've been closed out on a checking account within the last 18 months, you may have a problem getting a new account opened. The New Accounts person at the bank will usually call Telecredit or CheckMate, or one of those companies to see if you've been closed out on another account. Well, if Telecredit or one of those firms has a line on you, here's how you get a new account opened. First, call the banks in your area and see if they subscribe to Telecredit or someone else. If Telecredit has your name on file for having had an account closed but the institution you call says they subscribe to CheckMate or Instacheck or Crosscheck, then go there and open your new checking account. Should one of these have your name and dominate the check service market in your area, then watch for a new bank that's soon to open in your neighborhood. Look for the landscaping phase of the project to begin. The bank should be opening right around then. Walk in and apply for an account with them before they get hooked up to the Check Guarantee Service. Many times a new bank can be open several months before they are actually set up with this service.

Another way to do it is to open a savings account at a bank you want to do business with. Make a lot of deposits and withdrawals as a means of getting to know the person in the new accounts department. After a couple of months, go in and open a checking account. If you built a good relationship with that person in New Accounts, it would be very unlikely that she'd call in to the check service to see if you ever had an account closed by another institution.

Another way to get around this check service, if you've been closed out before, is to have a friend go in and open an account. Have him put you on later as a sharer on the account. Once you have this one, you can get however many more you may need.

Note: If you live in California or one of the surrounding Western States, there's a very large interstate bank which does not subscribe to any check guarantee companies. With this bank, anyone with proper identification can open an account, regardless of previous check writing experience.

I stress the importance of having a checking account for two simple reasons. First, you need it as a reference and for scoring points on your credit applications. Secondly, these checking accounts can later be turned into an unsecured line of credit, or a "no questions asked" loan.

Overdraft Protection is the name of this line of credit. It will show up on your credit reports as a revolving account which is a strong piece of credit to have as a reference for future credit. Credit lines on these can vary with each person. I believe that the minimum amount is $300.00. The maximum? The sky's the limit - there really are no bounds. It just depends on your ability to pay it back. As it is with Visa and Mastercard, once again there's no limit as to how many checking accounts you can have that carry an overdraft protection credit line.

I remember when I first learned of overdraft protection. I thought, "Hey! This is great! Someone has finally designed a program for people who habitually bounce checks; how thoughtful of them." Well, to my surprise, I found out that this program was designed for people who DON'T bounce checks. People who bounce checks show themselves as being irresponsible, and lenders don't want anything to do with irresponsible check writers. Of course, it's to cover any overdrafts that may occur on your checking account. But it was not designed for habitual check bouncers.

As with your Visa or Mastercard, this, too, is a revolving account which means you can pay your billing in full or in convenient monthly payments. If you want to establish alot of unsecured credit, this is a good way to achieve your goal. A friend of mine has a $25,000.00 line of overdraft protection on one of his accounts.

Some institutions offer an overdraft protection service which draws funds out of your savings account. To me, this is not a genuine form of overdraft protection. All this is is a funds transfer service. I'm still not satisfied. I want a sole and separate unsecured line of credit as overdraft protection - no substitutions! Any bank will transfer funds from one account to the next, but how many will give you a sole and separate, unsecured, "no questions asked" line of overdraft protection? Deal with those who will deal with you. All the others can go fly a kite.

CHAPTER 25

FINANCE COMPANIES

Finance companies should always be considered as a last resort as a source for renting money. First of all, they have very high interest rates, and it's not a "super plus" on your credit reports even if you pay on time as agreed, because it tells other, more conservative lenders like banks, S & Ls, and credit unions that you had to lower yourself to the point of dealing with a high risk, high interest rate finance company.

If you're new to the world of credit, or making a fresh start with credit, then it may be necessary to deal with one of these outfits to get started with credit. Having a couple of satisfied accounts with a finance company on your credit profile is better than no credit history at all, but it's best to find a bank or S & L to deal with.

Two of the bigger names in the finance company business are Dial Finance and Household Finance. Both are very aggressive and their interest rates reflect it. Dial does a lot of direct mail advertising. They are the ones who send you a fake check for $5,000.00 with your name on it. They say something to the effect that "this check could be yours by simply filling out the enclosed application and returning it at your earliest convenience."

One thing nice about these aggressive lenders is that, once you do business and complete a loan with them, they usually send you an invitation (pre-approved) to borrow again. I like that idea. I wish banks would practice that more but they have to take a much more conservative approach. After all, they are bankers and bankers don't chase people (supposedly) to put a new loan in the hands of just anyone.   Well, that's the banker's train of thought, but look at them push the credit cards.

Finance companies are good to have in your hip pocket for emergency cash. They make personal loans just like anyone else in the business but at higher rates. Some firms advertise Loans by Mail, or "Borrow $25,000.00 Overnight On Your Signature." Watch out for these ads. They may bait the hook and then reel you in. It's called "Bait and Switch" or "strings attached." What they will do is grab your attention on an ad similar to this and then try to get you to use your home as collateral. What they are doing in essence, is bringing you in on a signature loan which actually ends up being a second or third mortgage on your home. Watch out for these guys; they can be pretty creative.

Don't use finance companies unless it is the only source you can find to rent some money from. Many merchants who say "We Finance," don't actually finance in-house. What they usually have is an agreement with a finance company to carry the paper (contract) on merchandise they sell on credit terms.   The merchant usually has a good rapport going with the finance company agent. Many times he can boost the agent over the fence to finance a marginal loan request.

One of my associates and I were out looking at cars one time. We found a Cadillac Seville we liked, and filled out a credit application.   The sales manager called in the information and told us to call him in an hour. It was approved - didn't take long at all. Finance companies are the most aggressive of them all.

Car dealerships who advertise, "We Carry Our Own Contracts" are just as aggressive as the finance companies. They buy their cars wholesale at bank REO auctions and impound lot auctions.

Let's say they buy a car for $800.00 and sell it two weeks later for $1,500.00. They'll advertise something on the order of "No Credit Needed" or "Bad Credit OK." They'll always try and recapture their investment in the form of a down payment by the customer. On this example, they would ask for $800.00 down and, perhaps, $100.00 to $150.00 per month. If the customer pays as agreed, fine. But if they don't get paid as agreed, they are "quick" to repo the car and keep the down payment. As long as they get their investment back as the down payment, the rest is gravy.

These guys can be some pretty slippery dudes. Watch what you get yourself into.

Finance companies of any sort are a great source for special situations, but avoid dealing with them whenever possible. A bank loan successfully paid in full will look much better than a similar account with a finance company.

CHAPTER 26

CREDIT UNIONS

Credit Unions are my very favorite to do business with. They are often the best source in town for establishing valuable banking relationships. They seem to treat you like family - it's a family affair.

I was a member of a railroad credit union back East. My older brother was an employee of the railroad. I received some of the best banking service from that credit union than I've ever received elsewhere. They seem to have a genuine interest in helping you with your financial needs and desires. I can't speak for each and every credit union, but this particular one I'm talking about was the closest thing to old fashioned banking I've ever come across.

I get a kick out of these TV commercials where some old gold prospector comes out of the hills and into town with his find. He gets approached by several bankers who try to reel him into their banks. He ends up going to the one at the end of town, and here's this old fashioned, honest looking, about-to-retire banker who weighs the precious metal and says, "That's what it's worth, and that's what I'll pay you for it." What they are trying to do with all these advertising dollars, is to project an image of something they are not. They'd like to be old fashioned but all these computers and electronic banking aids have polluted their real purpose in business. Instead of being on a first name basis with a bank or S&L, you're just another number to them. They've moved out of

the *people business* and into a computer state of mind. They don't
even think for themselves anymore; it's all done by computer.

One large bank has recently come out with an advertisement
that is way off base. They speak very highly of service but
judging by their branch offices I've been in, they haven't got the
faintest idea what service is.

Yesterday, I stood in line for 15 to 20 minutes at a bank,
waiting to reach the counter to cash a check from one of my
clients. They had 15 teller windows, only three or four were open,
and there were 20 to 30 customers standing in line scratching
their heads. On busy days, it's even worse. I won't even go near
one of their branch offices on the 1st or 15th day of the month
when most people get paid and do their banking.

I can't believe it. They spend millions upon millions of dollars
on advertising. Everyone knows that the message they try to
relay to the general public is usually a crock. Why don't these
banks take some of those advertising dollars and use it to put
some tellers behind the counter so they can live up to providing
the service they speak of ? Why don't they use that money to pay
some people as tellers to serve their customers properly. They
spend their money in all the wrong places, on all the wrong things
such as expensive TV and radio advertising.

Who do you think is the one who's really paying for all this
advertising? Well, if you spend more than five minutes in line
waiting to be served, then you're paying for that expensive
advertising with the "rotten to the core" service you receive. If
every teller window is open and there's a ten minute wait, then
it's understandable. But if there are 15 teller windows and only
three or four tellers working, and there's a line of people forming
a Z-line in the bank lobby all the way to the front door, then you
had better deal with someone who really does want to serve you.
If these banks continue to operate this way, it will eventually
become faster to get a heart transplant, than to get a check
cashed! I've always believed in word of mouth advertising. Sure,
a business would want to advertise heavily when it's just opened,
but some of these banks have been around longer than dirt, and
still they spend millions of dollars on advertising that could be
much better spent in other areas of their business. They
continually search for a new "Band Aid" when they're really in

dire need of a "tourniquet." They need to start serving people again.

In California it's very rare that a bank has a drive-up teller. There's thousands of housewives who would rather use a drive-up teller than have to drag their children into the bank only to stand in line with them for 20 minutes. A lot of banks used to have drive-up facilities but they've closed them, probably to save a few bucks on the cost of maintaining the equipment. They don't serve people like their advertisements claim they do.

In California, banking hours are from 10 am to 3 pm. On Fridays though, they stay open until 6 pm. There's only one bank that I know of out here who is open on Saturdays and they tend to be one of my favorites to deal with because they are still *service oriented* to some degree. They even have drive up tellers.

It's a wonder how anyone can operate a business on only 5 hours a day, and still remain in business; how do they do it? I'll tell you how they do it. They set their business hours according to their own desires without giving any consideration to what you and I as *customers* might want or need. From here,the rest is quite simple. They jam us into the lobby like sardines and make us wait in line for 20 minutes to let us give them our money. With our money in hand, they pay us a whoppin' 5% interest and turn around only to charge us 18% interest on a personal loan or credit card.

The more I think about their mode of operation and procedures, the more attractive the thought of owning a bank becomes. I wonder if one could stay in business being open only 3 hours a day?

Find a credit union to deal with. I'm still convinced that they, for the most part, still want to fill a respectable and valuable service, and they will go out of their way to achieve such a task. Most will at least stay open until 5 pm.

Credit unions have Visa cards, too, at much better rates than the banks. They have good rates on everything. Often times, their rates are under market on all the different credit lines they offer.

CHAPTER 27

LOAN BROKERS

Here's a source which can be very helpful to anyone wishing to obtain a real estate or business loan of some sort. Loan brokers can provide a very meaningful service to you. Any loan broker who plans on staying in business must know who the aggressive lenders in town are and what types of loans they make. Loan brokers act as a fact gathering, information exchange service between borrowers and lenders.

Lenders love doing business with loan brokers. First of all, loan brokers save the lenders from having to do a lot of work. Loan Brokers will have the borrower complete all the necessary paperwork in the loan package prior to submitting it for approval to the lender. Suppose the lender approves the loan, then they pay the loan broker a small percentage of the loan as a loan fee, also known as *points*. A point is a percentile. Two points is two percent and so on. Loan fees or points to the broker will usually range from two to ten points. The lender usually pays the broker but, in all reality, you are the one paying the points through the lender.

One thing you really want to be aware of is the broker who asks for a loan fee or application fee up front, before the loan package is even submitted or approved. There's big business in selling loan applications to applicants who pay from $25.00 to $250.00 as an up-front application fee. When you pay an up-front fee, who knows if your loan package was ever sent out for approval? It may have gone into the trash without ever being sent out or called into any lenders.

Don't pay any up-front application fees. That would be like paying a realtor a commission to sell your home before it's even listed for sale in the multiple listing book. You need to be aware of these rip-off artists who do nothing more than cash your check. Never pay a pre-application fee. If the broker really feels he can find a lender to make the loan you request, then by no means should he ask for an up-front fee. He'll get paid for his service after he's done his homework and gets your loan approved.

Loan brokers are a dime a dozen. Don't just let the fact that there is no up-front fee steer you in that firm's direction. Qualify the brokers as you call around searching for the right one. Ask them who's aggressive in making your type of loan. Ask them how busy they've been. If they've been sitting around staring at the walls while the loan brokerage industry is booming, then either they're not aggressive and hard working, or they're not established yet. They may have just opened their business last week for all you know. It doesn't require very much at all to get in this business and call yourself a loan broker.

Some loans, such as real estate mortgages, will require a broker to be licensed by the State to broker such loans. Be cautious in whom you do business with. Even if they don't charge an up-front fee, you still don't want them pulling your credit reports unless they are established and aggressive. You don't need any unnecessary inquiries added to your credit reports. Don't be afraid to use a loan broker, but don't pay up-front fees or deal with any thumb suckers in the industry.

A good loan broker can be worth his weight in gold. He knows what the lenders expect in a loan package and which lender is best for each type of loan. Lenders would much rather deal with a loan broker than the borrower himself because a good loan broker knows the business well, and also, he speaks the *language*.

Be cautious but not afraid of dealing with loan brokers. They can often get a loan approved that would otherwise be rejected were the borrower to attempt it himself.

CHAPTER 28

HOW TO BUILD CREDIT

Here, we're going to get into some more meat and potatoes of building credit.

To begin, what are your credit reports reflecting? Are they clean of any derogatory remarks? Is everything accurate and up to date? Would you lend you money based on your reports?

Your credit reports are the *heart* of credit. Clean reports will help insure your obtaining future credit and dirty reports will insure your being denied over and over again.

Don't begin building any new credit until your credit reports reflect a clean bill of health. Remember, the way to remove derogatory information is to keep squeaking until someone oils ya.

Don't let these CRAs blow you off with their stupid "form letters" which are designed to simply get the workload off their backs, telling the consumer to go stick it. Some CRAs are masters at this practice of dodging consumer disputes but we don't buy it in our credit consulting office. Maybe when this book is published, I will go to work on revising the Fair Credit Reporting Act laws. The main emphasis would be in getting the CRAs to perform and live up to their grave responsibilities to the consumer as a Credit Reporting Agency. My greatest accomplishment would be to force these giants to investigate and remove any derogatory credit information <u>within a reasonable period of time</u>!

What are your credit reports reflecting on you? Do you have a savings account opened? How about a checking account that's never had a check bounced on it? Can your employment and income be verified? Did you figure out your income to debt ratio? Do you have any money left over to debt service additional credit accounts? Don't let these things go undone; they are very important steps to take in building credit.

Now, once all this is in order to the best of your ability, it's time to start building credit - credit that will be *paid on time as agreed* and reported on your credit profile. The following chapter will cover adding unrecorded credit to your profile, but first we'll cover the steps of building credit.

Only to begin, you may need a co-signer. This is where a second party - could be anyone you know - signs on the dotted line, stating that he or she will pay off the new credit account if you don't. They become contractually liable on the debt and, by law, are legally required to make good on the debt if you, the primary applicant, default on the account. The person you would want to co-sign your first credit transaction should have good credit, or a least a substantial income - enough to cover his expenses plus this debt. A high income alone may not be acceptable. More times than not, the co-signer's credit rating will play the biggest part of it. A co-signer with good credit will prevent a lot of red flags from being raised, more so than a co-signer with just a large income.

Asking people you know such as friends, relatives, and associates to co-sign is a lot of fun. It's fun providing you don't mind finding out who really believes in you and who doesn't. It's crazy but I've asked some people to co-sign a loan when I was getting started with credit, and I was amazed at how bent out of shape they got. It's like they went into withdrawals; some get all panicky, fear sets in and dominates their decision-making process. They just plain get flustered. It's great fun. I still ask people to co-sign loans with me. Some people literally flip out when you ask them to put their name on the line with yours. Try it, it's fun.

I'm constantly expanding my circle of friends and business associates. With each new person who comes into my life, I usually put them through my own acid test. Either I'll ask them to co-sign a loan, or rent me some money. Many people will fall to the wayside; they just don't have it in them. Yes, in most cases they either have the cash or the credit to fulfill my request but they just don't have the guts. They don't "BELIEVE." What's credit? Isn't it belief?

Most of you reading this book will encounter the same results I have when it comes to finding a person who wholeheartedly believes in you. If you don't come to the same conclusion, you're very fortunate.

As I've said, the larger part of my credit experience has been with individuals whom I've known. If you think you're already a master at finding co-signers, see how many people you can find who will "invest in a business venture" of yours, where the only way they get their money back is if the venture is successful. Investors are even harder to find than co-signers. Either way, it's fun to find out who believes in you versus those who say they do but really don't. Put some people to the acid test and see what their level of belief in you really is. Certainly there must be someone who believes in you who will help you get started with credit by co-signing a loan.

Who do you know who has good credit? How about your mom or dad, brother, sister, friend, relative, co-worker, boss, acquaintance, associate, or neighbor? Surely you must have at least one person in your life who believes in you who can be of help in co-signing your first piece of credit. If you're a total hermit and have absolutely no one to co-sign, there's still hope, providing you have some money in your savings account.

Prior to asking anyone to co-sign anything, go back and read "What's Credit" and "Banker Mentality" before getting with them about helping you out. Remember, renting money is only an *attitude*. Whoever it is you have in mind as a co-signer, here's one way they can be of help to you. First see if they will co-sign a credit application with you. This would be your best bet. I'm not talking about a department store card or an oil card; I'm suggesting they help you obtain your first unsecured Visa or Mastercard. Just a $1,000.00 line of credit will be fine. If your co-signer is nervous about this idea, tell him you will cut up the credit card and close the account once you can obtain a credit card on your own to replace it, or let him use the card and make the payments - just as long as it's getting reported on your reports. Then you can get one on your own.

Another way to get credit card activity in your profile is to have him add you to his account as a sharer of the account. This can be achieved by writing the merchant or lender who the account is with. You don't want a joint account; you just want to share in the credit information reported.

The reason I stress getting a co-signer for a Visa or Mastercard over a department store card is because of the power it adds to your report. A Visa or Mastercard which reflects a good rating on your credit report will be the strongest piece of credit you can maintain because, after all, it's the hardest to obtain at first.

A car loan which has been paid back on time as agreed is a good piece of credit history, but any credit granted on an unsecured basis is always better. Find someone who has good credit and ask them to let you share some of their accounts until you can get some on your own.

The other way I mentioned, about getting a secured Visa from Home Savings is a good way to build credit, too. What you are doing with this type of credit is "buying" a credit rating. A secured Visa or Mastercard is a great tool to use as a stepping stone to your first unsecured Visa or department store cards (as mentioned in talking about the instant credit programs among retailers).

Another source I've used to build a credit rating is the passbook savings loan. This method can be turned into the "round robin" banking procedure. First of all, the passbook savings loan is one anybody can obtain. You need to have at least $1,000.00 in your savings account to do this. Banks will normally lend you up to 80% of the amount you have in your savings or certificate of deposit or what have you of "like kind." "Like kind" in this example is any asset which is liquid and can be held as security and can be turned into cash without a discount which would cause the lender to lose money if you defaulted on the loan.

Let's say you have $1,500.00 in the bank. You ask the loan officer for $1,000.00 over 12 months, secured by your savings. Now, the principal amount ($1,000.00) and the rent over a one year period of time might be 12% ($120.00) or a total payback of $1,120.00. Your $1500.00 savings account would have an $1120.00 freeze on it until the loan was paid for but it would still collect the normal 5-1/4% interest. Your monthly payments on

the loan would be just under $100.00. You would now have
$1,000.00 cash against your savings to use for payments on this
loan. Let's say you put the $1,000.00 into another savings
account where it, too, collected interest. That would decrease the
cost of this loan even more. Now, let's assume you make monthly
payments on this new loan, on time as agreed, for six months.
Then you go in and say that you want to pay the loan off. When
all the smoke settles, here's what you end up with.

First, the $1,500.00 you once had in the account, which
secured the loan, is now down to about $1,450.00 and it's no
longer frozen; you can have access to it anytime you choose.
Second, you have a credit experience recorded on your credit
reports of having rented $1,000.00 which was paid back six
months earlier than anticipated. Third, you now have the
grounds to go into the same bank a few weeks later and say, "Mr.
Banker, I'd like to rent $1,000.00 again." He'll say, "Fine, but
we'll need to secure it with your savings again." (Here's where
Chapters 1, 19, and 21 come in.)

When he mentions security or collateral, stand up as if you're
about to leave and say, "No, this time I would like to do it on my
signature alone. We secured the last one, and I paid it back on
time; we don't need to secure this next loan." If you develop the
same attitude I have and spoke about in these three chapters,
you'll walk out of that bank with your first signature loan! Don't
leave that bank until you do. You're not asking him for
$50,000.00. You're only asking to rent a lousy thousand bucks. If
he gives you a hard time, twist his arm. Remind him that he
needs to rent money or else they'll go out of business. Say, "Hey,
six months ago, we discussed this matter and you said you would
like to have me as a "new and valued customer." You said you
would be able to meet my desires concerning credit. I don't need
that lousy thousand bucks. I'll go pull it out of one of my savings
accounts. I do have other banking relationships outside of this
one. I don't have to do business with you. You're not the only
game in town; I have other sources I can rent money from when I
want it. I don't need your stinkin' money." (Make him aware of
all your options; remember Bert Lance's attitude on renting
money.)

Now hit him with, "Are you going to rent me the $1,000.00 I
request, on my signature, or shall I go do business with one of my

other sources?" Now - SHUT UP! Don't say a word, because whoever speaks next loses. If you say another word, he'll probably say no. If he speaks first, then he loses the battle and you get your loan. Don't be afraid to lose, and you'll find yourself a winner almost every time. If he does speak first and says no, then you still didn't lose because you never had anything going with this guy to lose in the first place. Make him well aware of the fact that your signature is worth well over a lousy thousand bucks!

Renting money is an attitude. You'll be able to rent all kinds of money when your attitude towards you and it are of the proper mind. If you have a problem with developing this attitude, then start looking in the mirror every morning when you get up, and say, "Your signature is worth thousands, baby; you're the best money renter there's ever been; you aren't a Small Fry or McNugget, you're the BIG MAC when it comes to renting money, your The Value Pak." Develop this attitude and the banks you deal with will be yours. Now, important step here. Pay the guy his money back as agreed to in the contract. Don't leave him hanging out to dry. After you do a thousand or two, raise it to $5,000.00, then to $10,000.00, and so on. Find out what his limit is.

Now, the "round robin" procedure is really nothing more than a duplication of how you got your first passbook savings loan which was later turned into a signature loan the second time around. The only difference is that you do the same process with two or three banks at the same time instead of just one. It will require a little more money to do it with more than one bank but let's run through the process real quick.

With $2,000.00 in bank #1, rent 80% or ($1,600.00) and use that to open a savings account at bank #2. With $1,600.00 in bank #2, rent $1,280.00 and use the proceeds to open a savings account at bank #3. With $1,280.00 in bank #3, rent $1,000.00 and put that in a savings account to make the payments on these three loans for about three months. Then go into bank #3 and pay if off, using any money you have left over plus the money frozen in #3. Now, use the proceeds to make a payment to banks #1 and #2. When the next payment comes due on #1 and #2, go in and pay off bank #2. Use the proceeds remaining from #2 to pay the payments on #1 as they come due. When the proceeds from bank #2 are gone, go in and pay off bank #1 with the money in its account.

Now go back to bank #3 and get a $1,000.00 signature loan, hit #2 for $1,500.00 on your signature, and #3 for $2,000.00. Pay these off and keep repeating the process. Ask for more each time you rent from them.

The rent you pay to do this procedure is the "cost" of buying your credit rating and signature loan sources. You could easily spend $500.00 on rent doing this. You'll have to be the one who says "enough." Credit cards are easier but this is an added line of "no questions asked" banking when it's fully developed.

This method is rather high tech compared to some of the softer, less aggressive methods. There are some slow boats to China in building credit (I'll cover a few) but they take just as much effort as with using the major league approach; may each of you cut your own path in building credit.

Local merchants who provide a product or service will often have some kind of credit terms you can take advantage of to establish some credit experience with. I'm talking mainly about the smaller, independent "one store" operations. These are the ones who don't require "everything you own" plus your "first born" as collateral to secure the account. I remember when I was a building contractor. I set up credit accounts without even knowing it really. I was just conducting business is all. If I needed 20 gallons of paint to shoot a house with - but didn't have the money for materials, somehow I always seemed to get whatever I needed to get the job done. With all my contractor accounts, never once did I sign a contract or sales agreement between the supplier and myself. My objective was not to build credit; it was to get materials to do a job with, to create a profit, so I could pay my living expenses and have some cash in my pocket. I bought a couple of work trucks with the same idea in mind, not to build credit with, but to make a living with. I never looked at it as building credit. Many times I set up credit terms to purchase something I needed when really, the person selling what I wanted, didn't offer any credit terms. I even had an account with a restaurant years ago who displayed a sign next to the cash register which read, "In God we trust, all others must pay cash." I've made hundreds of credit transactions in one form or another. If all of them, over the last ten years, were listed on my credit report, it would take a good banker two hours to pull my file up on the computer, and a week to read it!

Building credit is no big deal. You've just been looking at it from the wrong point of view. Credit is a tool; it's like a wrench set. There are different wrenches for different purposes; shapes and sizes vary and there's a special wrench for every need.

Do you want to build credit? Then start turning some of your cash paying purchases into credit term purchases. Are you going to lay out $400.00 on a new set of radial tires for your car? If so, are you going to pay the service station in cash, or are you going to say, "Hey, look. I need to build some credit; I need to eventually get a credit card because I can't even cash a check without one. Tell you what we can do. I'll give you $200.00 down on four new tires and $50.00 a month for five months; you're making an extra $50.00 by helping me build some credit. Have we got a deal?" If he says no, then argue the point that the tires only cost $200.00, and if you never paid him another dime, he really wouldn't be losing much, but if you do pay him as agreed, not only is he getting full retail on the sale, but he's making $50.00 on top of that and, one step further and most important, he'll have you as a customer for as long as he's in business. If he still shakes his head from side to side, get out of there because he's not your man; go find one that is. Do business with people who want to do business! There is one more thing this merchant who sold you the tires must agree to, and that's to report your credit experience to the CRA when the balance has been paid in full.

What are you presently paying for by cash or check that could be converted into some form of credit account? Start looking around; there are at least a hundred sources right in your own community that you can use to establish credit.

You younger people reading this book should be made aware of the fact that you can start building credit before your eighteenth birthday by having your mom or dad co-sign for you. A lot of department stores have developed a program which assists students in building credit so they will have it when they need it most. Well, that's the pitch they use anyway. Of course, they want your money to increase their sales volume, but, so what? You're getting some credit established.

What are you about to pay cash for? I had a caller the other day who wanted to know how to build credit. I asked several questions about his past experience, and his response was like a lot of others I hear. He said he'd always paid cash. He had just laid out 2,000 in dead presidents for a new motorcycle. I said that the next time he does a transaction like that, put the purchase money in a savings account and borrow against the savings to complete the purchase; then make payments on the loan as if paying yourself back. Do that a couple of times and you won't have to call me about wanting to build credit.

What will your next major purchase be? How will you pay for it?

One more way to build credit is to find a small aggressive bank that wants to serve you and ask them to loan you $1,000.00 with which in turn you will put the entire $1,000.00 in your savings account which they can put a freeze on as a means to collateralize the loan. Now make the payment on that loan "on time as agreed" and then you have credit. This method works - you just have to find a small bank that wants to be of service to you.

CHAPTER 29

ADDING CREDIT TO YOUR FILES

Whenever you negotiate credit terms with a merchant who does not report to the CRAs, make certain that he'll agree to either send a letter to this effect to each CRA, or that they'll give the credit information to the CRAs when they call or write to verify it.

Any good credit experience that is not reflected on your credit reports isn't doing much good when you're starting to build credit. In the beginning, you'll want as much positive credit information on your reports as possible. After you've obtained all the credit you desire, then it's no longer important to have your non-reporting accounts report to the CRA

TRW is really picky about what information they'll add to your report. If a merchant does not subscribe to TRW for credit reporting services, TRW won't report your credit experience with that merchant but they are required by the FTC to update and keep current their files as per their subscribers. Trans Union and CBI, on the other hand, will record your unreported credit information for a small fee upon verification. I just recently requested that six of my unreported credit experiences be reported to TU and CBI. These were all large unsecured loans that I received and paid back over the last three years. I had them added to my report because these are strong pieces of credit I had obtained. It cost me about $12.00 to have them added to each report. If you just have one entry added, it's about $8.00 per report. It gets cheaper as the number of entries to be added increases.

Following are some sample letters you can use to have unrecorded credit information added to your report. Write your requests in a similar manner.

SAMPLE - CONSUMER LETTER

Credit Bureau, Inc.   (Date)
2223 Wellington Avenue
Santa Ana, CA 92701

Dear Sir:

In review of my credit report you hold on me, I've noticed that some of my credit experiences over the years have not been reported to you. I would like them added to my report to reflect my true and complete credit history. I request that you verify the information with the source(s) given below and have them added to my file. Please tell me if there is a fee for this, which I'm willing to pay.
The credit references I want listed on my report are as follows:

Diamond Jewelers, Inc.
1234 Golden Avenue
Your Town, U.S.A.
Acct. # 615893
Opened 1/11/84
Closed 1/11/86
Amount $2,400.00 @ $100.00 per month
Paid on time as agreed
No present account with them

United Finance Company (your best friend)
213 Gimmycash Drive
Any Town, U.S.A.
Acct. # (make your own) 6-8 digits
Opened 5/85

Closed 5/86
Amount $1,000.00 unsecured
Paid as agreed - no present account

United Finance Company could be anyone who has loaned you money. If your friend, Sonny Smith, loaned you $500.00, then you would list it as Smith Finance. Add all your credit experiences when you're first getting started in the world of credit.

SAMPLE - MERCHANT LETTER

Trans Union Credit   (Date)
1400 North Harbor Boulevard
Fullerton, CA 92635

Re: Peter Pest
*   Address*
*   Social Security Number*
*   Acct. # 711777*

Dear Sir:

At the request of our customer, we are writing to state that a loan in the amount of $10,000.00 was made to Mr. Pest on July 1, 1982 and paid in full, on time as agreed, in 48-monthly installations. Mr. Pest does not have any open accounts with us at this time. Mr. Pest has requested that we supply you with this information so that it will be added to his report. He is willing to pay a fee for this service, whatever it may be.

Once again, this has been done at Mr. Pest's request.

Thank you.

Sincerely,

Donald Dontbugme
Accounts Supervisor
Grump Thrift and Loan

It would be wise to call your local credit bureau (CRA) and ask about the cost and procedure of adding unrecorded credit information to your files. Most merchants will be willing to supply the CRA with your credit activity, but they are not required by law to do so.

CHAPTER 30

CREATIVE CREDIT TECHNIQUES

In this chapter, I want to cover just a few methods I've used in obtaining credit for special situations.

We have already covered passbook savings loans, the round robin method, the interconnect system, and several others that can be used in the world of credit, and the "how to's" of building credit. We also covered the attitude behind the "how to" when we covered What's Credit in Chapter 1; Banker Mentality in Chapter 19, and so on. These chapters are based on developing the right mental posture - the proper attitude towards credit. When your attitude towards credit is in the right form, you'll obtain any credit lines you truly desire. Here are a few methods I've used in special situations.

First of all, in applying for a real estate mortgage, if your credit reports are dirty, or if you don't earn enough income, or if it cannot be verified, there are several solutions to this problem. If your credit reports are full of black marks which would prevent you from obtaining a real estate loan, one way of getting around this is to watch for homes that have an FHA or VA assumable loan on them. For these types of mortgages, there is no qualifying; you just pay a $50.00 application fee and anyone can assume these types of loans. This method of purchasing a home allows even the person with the worst credit to buy a home. All they need is the down payment.

Another way to get around having to have good credit to purchase a home is to find one that you can buy on the terms of "subject to" rather than "assume" when it comes to purchasing a home with an existing mortgage on it. For example: You find a home that you want to purchase; the asking price is $75,000.00 with $5,000.00 down, and assume present financing. The owner is firm on his price; he's more concerned with getting his asking price than with how you take over the existing financing. You say, "OK, I'll give you the $75,000.00 you're asking for on the house, and I'll give you the $5,000.00 down payment you request, but you'll have to do one thing for me, Mr. Owner." What's that? "Well, it may prevent me from buying your home if I have to go in and qualify for assuming your loan because I have a few little black marks on my credit from a recent divorce (or what have you). But if I can buy this home "subject to" the terms and conditions of your loan, then we have a deal and can start the closing process." He'll usually say yes to this if you're honest and sincere about your offer to him. When the deal closes, his name is still on the loan but the title goes in your name and you make payments to the seller and then the seller cuts a check to the lender. Rather than doing a "formal assumption" of the loan, you bought the home "subject to" the mortgage's terms and conditions.

Now there are some things that can go wrong with this approach. One would be that some mortgages contain a "due on sale" clause; if the lender finds out the home was sold, he can demand that the entire loan be paid. Most prudent lenders won't call it "due" but they may ask that you sign a new mortgage with them. If you're paying your payments on time, they'll generally let you slide, especially when there's only a little equity behind their loan. It would be foolish to call that loan "due" if you're making the payments on time; the last thing they want is to have that house back. For further information on this matter, consult a competent real estate broker.

Another way to qualify for a loan if you presently have bad credit or insufficient income, is to bring in what's called a "straw buyer", aka a co-signer. Let's say you've only been on the job for six months, or you're self-employed and cannot provide proof of income. You want to buy a home; maybe you can't afford the monthly payments. Maybe you can afford the monthly payments but you can't seem to raise the down payment. Here's where a "mouse" meets an "elephant." You're the mouse, you can't raise the down payment but you know a person (an elephant) who has the money just sitting in the bank but that person does not have time to search for real estate investments, and furthermore, he doesn't want the headaches of being a landlord. Here's your proposal: "OK, Mr. Businessman, or Mr. Doctor, or Mr. Anyone with money; I have this home over on Main Street that I want to buy as an investment, and also as a home for me and my family to live in. I can afford the monthly payments but I don't have the down payment. They want $10,000.00 down, but I just don't have it. Why don't you make the down payment, and I'll make the monthly payments. I'll also do all the maintenance and upkeep at my expense; we can split the cost of any major repairs over $500.00 which may occur. We'll keep the house for five years at which time we'll sell it and split the profit." This is "profit participation;" it was also known as "equity share" until the IRS began to scrutinize this term and procedure. Being the elephant will be half owner, he'll also share in half of the tax benefits.

Folks, these types of transactions are created and take place everyday of the year. It's nothing new; it's just a form of being creative with credit. I can't go into every little detail on these methods in this book; I'm just throwing out ideas to spark your imagination. You'll have to do some research on the nuts and bolts of these methods if you're interested in utilizing them.

Let's say there is a nice home you'ld like to buy; you can raise the down payment but the monthly payments are a little bit more than you can handle. Let's say the payments on this new home are $800.00 monthly, but you're presently leasing an apartment for $600.00 a month and that's about all you can afford. Tell the elephant that you will make the down payment on the home, live in it, do the maintenance and upkeep if he'll put $200.00 towards the house payment each month. At the end of five years, you'll sell it and split the profits.

Once again, why would anyone want to shell out $200.00 a month for house payments, or $10,000.00 for a down payment on a home he's not even gonna live in? Well, two reasons: Number one is for future profit (that home is going to increase in value in five years) and, number two, tax benefits that are available with owning investment property. Once again, these transactions are going on all around you every day of the year.

The big Hyatt and Hilton Hotels? Hyatt doesn't buy those buildings outright; a group of investors pool their money to build those fancy buildings and then Hyatt or Hilton is the tenant who leases or lease-purchases the building from the investors. Hyatt then cuts that big building up into little sleeping quarters and rents them out to you and I on a daily basis. Here you probably thought that Hyatt paid to have those buildings built. No, it's "profit participation." It's being done every day on anything from single family homes to shopping malls and office buildings. Why can't you be creative and structure a deal like one of these?

In business, it's Leverage Buy Outs (LBOs). A couple of years ago, in one of the major business newspapers, I saw an article about three men who teamed up and bought an 1100 room Holiday Inn with "no cash down." LBOs are taking place everyday across the nation, too. Basically what happens is that you purchase a business, using the business' assets and cash flow as a means to finance the deal. This takes some specialized knowledge, but if you can ride a bicycle, you can learn to do LBOs with practice, too. Be creative with credit.

I developed a saying I want to share with you in closing this chapter.

If there's a will, there's a loan; you just have to be creative and find it. If you can't find it, create it!

Any time you create a void or a vacuum, it must be filled with something, somehow. If you take a bucket of water out of the ocean, the ocean fills the hole up with water again. The same holds true for creating a loan when you cant find one. Providing you have the need and the will to do it - you'll get it somehow. Create a void, commit to that void and watch it fill itself.

If *broke countries* can borrow millions and billions of dollars, then why can't you obtain the financing you need?

CHAPTER 31

PREPARING A FINANCIAL STATEMENT

Financial statements are a two-part system. First, there's the Income and Expense statement, and then there's the Balance Sheet. The balance sheet will reveal what your true worth is (financially). If you sold everything you own today (assets) and used that money to pay off every debt you have (liabilities), how much would you end up with? That figure is what's called your "net worth." That's how much you're really worth in dollars and cents.

The income and expense statement is what's used to list all the sources of income you may have coming in. On the other side of the sheet you would list all of your expenses. This is how a budget is developed. The income and expense statement can be used to target areas where expenses can be reduced. By listing all your income on one side of the paper and all your expenses on the other, after deducting your expenses from your income, the figure you arrive at is called "cash flow." Positive cash flow means you end up with money after the expenses are subtracted from the income, and negative cash flow means you're in trouble. It means that your expenses are greater than your income.

Income/expense statements can be drawn up monthly, quarterly, bi-annually or annually. It's a good idea to do one on yourself or your business at least every six months so that you can monitor your progress and where you're going financially.

You will probably be listing two different types of expenses on your statement. They are "fixed expenses" and "variable expenses." Fixed expenses are payments you know of in advance and the exact amount like rent, mortgage or car payments, etc. Variable expenses are items such as food, gas, telephone, babysitter, etc. To arrive at your variable expenses, just average out what those items have cost you per month over the last six or twelve months.

Look to the next page at a sample income and expense statement.

INCOME AND EXPENSE STATEMENT

FROM _____ TO _____

INCOME		EXPENSES	
Gross Salary	$ _____	Mortgage Payment	$_____
Minus Deductions	_____	Rent	_____
Net Take Home	_____	Other Property	_____
Other Income	_____	Utilities	_____
Minus Deductions	_____	Food/Household Goods	_____
Net Other Income	_____	Transportation	_____
Gifts (Cash)	_____	House Maintenance	_____
Commissions	_____	Auto Maintenance	_____
Bonus/Tips	_____	Insurance	_____
Alimony/Child Support	_____	Installment Contracts	_____
Business Income	_____	Credit Card Payments	_____
Professional Income	_____	Property Taxes	_____
Rental Property Income	_____	Income Taxes	_____
Net Profit from Sale	_____	Other Taxes	_____
of Merchandise	_____	Self-Improvement	_____
Refunds/Rebates		Personal Care Items	_____
incl. Income Tax	_____	Entertainment	_____
Income from Trusts	_____	Lease Payments	_____
Life Insurance Benefits	_____	Alimony/Child Support	_____
Disability	_____	Savings Program	_____
Social Security	_____	Charity Contributions	_____
Royalties	_____	Dues/Memberships	_____
Unemployment	_____	Medical Expenses	_____
Veterans Benefits	_____	Child Care	_____
Pensions	_____	Other	_____
IRAs/Keoghs	_____		
Other	_____	Total Expenses	$ _____
		Total Income	$ _____
Total Income	$ _____	for Savings,	
		Investments, Debt	
Cash Flow Available	$ _____	Service, Etc.	$ _____

BALANCE SHEET

ASSETS (Present Market Value)		LIABILITIES (Total Amount You Owe)	
Cash on Hand	$ _____	Real Estate Mortgages $_____	
Savings	_____	Taxes	_____
Checking	_____	Notes Payable	_____
Real Estate	_____	Accounts Owed	_____
Time Deposits	_____	Contracts Owed	_____
Vested Pension	_____	Other Debts	_____
Automobiles	_____		
Other Vehicles	_____		
Accounts Receivable	_____	Total Liabilities $ _____	
Notes Receivable	_____	(Subtract Liabilities	
Life Insurance		from Assets to	
(Cash Value)	_____	Determine Net Worth)	
Stocks/Bonds/Securities	_____		
IRAs/Keoghs	_____		
Rebates/Refunds	_____		
Other Assets	_____		
Tools and Equipment	_____		
Antiques/Art/Jewelry	_____		
Household Furnishings	_____		
Patents/Trusts	_____		
Other Interests	_____		
Other Assets	_____		
Total Assets	$ _____		
Less Total Liabilities	_____		
Net Worth	$ _____		

You can get a standard copy of the balance sheet and income and expense statement from any bank. It's wise to fill out both as completely as you can, just so you know where you are financially. Also, save them over the years so you can chart your progress with what your financial goals in life have been versus what you actually achieved. The numbers never lie. People lie with numbers sometimes, but the numbers always tell the true financial position you're in. These two sheets that make up your financial statements are a "direct reflection" of your financial position in life.

CHAPTER 32

WHEN A BANK GOES BELLY UP

It's been strictly "Rock-N-Roll" among the key figures participating in the banking industry. The Great Quake has struck - the shake-out period is underway as the winners and losers emerge. At one time, the fastest growing banks in the nation were in Texas; now, they are the hardest hit of them all. Oklahoma has their share of problems in banking also. The Southwest has suffered the worst losses of all. Due to the sluggish oil economy, millions upon millions of loan dollars are being written off as bad loans. Banking in the states where a lot of agriculture loans have been made are the next hardest hit. Barriers to interstate banking have been whittled away, causing massive competition throughout the industry. Most of the bank failures to come will be small banks but we'll see some of the major banks being restructured.

As of this writing, there are over 1,400 banks on the federal watch list (hot-sheet). These banks are being monitored because of excessive red ink in their loan portfolios. Of these 1,400 on the hot-sheet, fully 160 of them will be considered insolvent and taken over by the Federal Depositors Insurance Corporation (FDIC). Some 200 banks are predicted to fail in 1987 and only God knows how many will fail beyond 1987 and when it will cease.

It's very interesting and somewhat dramatic how the FDIC pulls the curtain on a failed bank. No one outside the FDIC really knows who is next or when it will happen. It's a "hush-hush" situation. Of the larger banks that are to be bailed out and sold to another banking firm, the top officials of the bidding firms are the only other ones who know who's next. These firms could be the failing banks' rival, standing ready to take their position in the bidding for acquisition. The FDIC liquidator stands by with sweaty palms, waiting to get his hands on the asset list to be liquidated in an effort to repay uninsured depositors and creditors. Manpower could be 50 to 100 federal auditors who are moved into a nearby hotel, close to the failed bank. They're known to hotel employees and car rental agencies as art collectors or photographers or whatever sounds good. Game plans are developed, who's gonna do what, and in what order it will be done? The clock strikes five bells on a Friday afternoon and the command is given to start their engines. They want the timing to be just right. A swarm of federal auditors, along with a couple of armed guards, arrive at the bank. The auditors go in, the guards lock the doors. Transactions in progress among bank customers are quickly consummated. Bank employees are stunned, they haven't any idea what is going on, but the branch manager or president is probably well aware of what's happening.

The FDIC announces that this bank has been declared insolvent. All of the employees are asked to gather their personal belongings and leave; they are no longer employees of this bank. Each employee must be checked over: handbags, brief cases, etc. are examined before leaving the building. The Feds don't want any money, or important documents, going out the door which are assets of the bank. With the bank employees gone, and the curtains drawn, the race gets underway. Auditors figure out the bank's complete financial picture, while investigators search for the main cause of the failure, always keeping an eye out for any unlawful banking practices. Bidding procedures get underway - who will be the new owner on Monday morning when it's re-opened under a new name? Who'll be awarded the bid? How much will it sell for? The Feds ought to have it down to an art form by now. With an estimated 160 banks doomed to fail in 1986, that nearly equals one every other day of the year.

In 1980, there were 200 federal liquidators, and less than six years later the number of "liquidators at large" has topped 3,000. This increase in bank liquidators reflects the increase of bank failures. I'm sure it will be a few more years anyway before the shake-out is over. And there you have a general idea of what happens when a bank goes belly up. It is very similar to a giant drug bust, lots of drama and emotion.

CHAPTER 33

HIDDEN BANK TREASURES

Call any bank in town and ask for the REO Department and most will say they don't have an REO Department. Well, they just might lie about other things, too. The point I'm making here is that every bank has an REO Department somewhere within their corporate structure. But no one wants to admit it because it represents *failure*.

REO stands for Real Estate Owned. It's the Foreclosure Department in a lending institution, and they also handle the goods the repo man brings in from collecting collateral on defaulted loans. Every lending institution has got to have a REO Department to liquidate the collateral that comes back to them.

When I first called around to banks seeking to speak with the REO Department, I was brushed off with, "We don't have an REO Department." In other words, they were saying, "We don't make any bad loans; all of our customers make good on all of the loans we give them." They act very innocent, but it's just a cover-up. They don't want the public to know they make loans that go bad.

The biggest fear a lending institution can have is of the general public catching wind that the bank has got alot of bad loans which could cause severe financial problems. They don't want any rumors started about the bank being on the verge of failing. A rumor like that could spread like wild fire and cause a *run on the bank (or run on deposits)*. That's where its depositors rush in and withdraw their money, or try to anyway. Banks are scared to death of such a thing happening. It would be similar to the restaurant owners' fear of serving some contaminated food which caused food poisoning.

How do you get into the REO Department? First, let's cover the "why you would want to" get into the REO Department. With real estate foreclosures being at their all time high, banks are loaded with properties that have come back to them because of loans going bad. They may have been the first, second or third mortgage holder on the property when the owner stopped making the payments on the loan. This forced the bank to start the foreclosure proceedings and sell the property at what's called a Trustee's Auction on the Court House steps. Now the only people who attend these auctions usually are the trustee (auctioneer) who represents the bank and, occasionally, a few passer-bys (bag ladies and street corner bums) will stop and check out what's going on. What happens usually is that the bank is the only bidder on the property and they take possession as its new *legal owner*.

Now, the property belongs to the bank legally and sits vacant for several months; in some cases it could sit vacant for years. The bank is forced to "write down" or depreciate the home over a five year period of time. On their books, it becomes a depreciating asset. The FDIC only allows the bank to have a very small percentage of bad loans on their books or it's "lights out" for the bank. The bank is stuck with the property. They don't want to advertise "Bank Repo" contact Belly-Up Bank. This would bring public attention and awareness that the bank has some financial problems.

Some banks will turn the property over to a realtor in hopes of selling the property. Many banks will sit on the property, telling people who call looking for the REO Department that they don't have any foreclosed property. A lot of banks, who sit on property, will be the ones who will sink with it on their books. Some institutions pride is so strong that they'll go under, versus admitting they have some collateral from bad loans they made and move it off their books.

I cannot go into a foreclosure seminar in this book. Once again, these are only the basics, but with gathering more specialized knowledge on the subject, you can use credit as a tool in this method of buying distressed property at prices that leave room for a profit to you upon resale. I've bought property from REO Departments before. They have some super deals in them.

The key to your success in the foreclosure business is getting into the REO Department and establishing a rapport between you and the REO manager. Once you have one foot in the door, the rest is easy. You now have access to the bank's hidden treasure.

I won't go into a lot of "how to" because I don't want you going off half-cocked. You need some specialized knowledge in this field and it can be obtained by going to various real estate seminars and/or there's several good books on the subject which can be purchased at most any bookstore. Which seminars should you attend? It's hard to really say. My teacher in California is a very sharp real estate attorney and seminar instructor named Ione Young Gray. I like to learn from the best. Although her seminars are pretty much limited to California, there are people teaching many of these systems and principles in your area. You have to take caution though because not all real estate instructors will have your best interests at heart; they will be more into giving the seminar to profit themselves rather than helping the students in the seminar. A seminar offering a backup support system will be of great importance.

All I'm saying is there's a pot of gold in these REO Departments that you can make withdrawals from and help the bank at the same time. Not only will you find homes that can be bought at or below wholesale prices, but also you'll find cars, boats, planes, business machinery, office furniture and equipment. They have to move these items off their books; help them do it - and reach your goals at the same time.

There are several ways to get into the REO Department. First, you can visit the bank and ask for it outright; you may get the name of someone to see, or they may brush you off. The next way to get in there is to call the bank and ask to speak with the person who manages a particular piece of property the bank owns. Get a name, call back and ask for that person by name. You are now in the REO Department.

Once you're in, you'll want to present yourself the exact opposite of if you were applying for a loan. You want to be low-keyed, soft spoken and reserved. Tell the loan officer that you're looking to buy a home for you and your family. Say, "I know you people occasionally get a home back because of foreclosure, and I know you're not in the real estate business; I felt that you may just be able to give me more home for my money than I could find otherwise in the marketplace. I'm looking for a two or three bedroom house. I can do repairs; my price range is in the area of $_____. How many homes do you have that might fit into what I'm looking for?" If he says none, ask what he does have. Do you know of any that will be coming back on your books in the near future? Can you refer me to anyone who might have a home like the one I'm looking for?

Soft soap this guy. Don't be aggressive. Play it cool. The REO Department has more tension in it than any other department. The reason is that this department is the "loser" in the bank. REO managers are the first ones to catch hell when the FDIC says for them to <u>clean up their act</u> "or else."

Build a friendship. It can really go a long way. He can turn you on to deals that are not available on the street. This is the only guy in the bank whose arm you don't want to twist. Be nice to him and respect his position in the bank. He holds the toughest job of them all. He's under pressure and he doesn't need you putting any more pressure on him. When he gives you a couple of addresses, suggest how much easier it would be if he were to just give you a copy of his REO list.

Fortunes are being made today by people who are in the REO Department negotiating deals. If you have a lot of credit lines, see what his price is. What would the cash price be? With paying cash, you would expect at least a 30%- 40%discount of the market value. He can also arrange special financing on this home that the bank wouldn't make otherwise. Get your foot in the door of the REO Department and you, too, will see the hidden treasures in these banks.

Don't contact banks only. Contact the Thrift and Loans (Finance Companies), the Savings and Loans and the Mortgage Companies. Large corporations have REO Departments also. These are not repossessed properties but it could be old buildings they used to use in business but are now vacant. Also, when large corporations transfer employees who are homeowners, often times they will buy the home from an employee so that they can move and buy one in the next town.

REO Departments have hidden treasures in them. You'll just have to do your homework and negotiate your first deal.

CHAPTER 34

MAKING MONEY WITH CREDIT

Here's the main reason one would desire to obtain many Visa and Mastercards and American Express Gold cards. What I'll be discussing is "forced sales," most of which are conducted by the government, on the city, county, state and federal levels.

Please keep in mind that I can not cover every little detail involved in these sales. Caution should be taken and research should be done prior to attending these sales and you should attend some of these sales while leaving your cash at home. I don't want you to get overwhelmed with all the excitement generated at these sales; you might purchase something you may later regret.

Let's cover the federal government's forced sales, first. The **Internal Revenue Service** has two types of sales. The first kind is the **Tax Lien Sale**, levied against real estate of individuals and businesses who have not paid their federal income tax. These sales generally have a substantial amount of equity in them. The owners of the property have been given many warnings and notices. The IRS will make arrangements for a payment plan. If the IRS sells this property, you can be sure that the owner was either a tax evader or didn't want the property. When you buy these properties, you're buying it subject to any other liens or mortgages against the property. A lot of research should be undertaken. To get on the IRS bidders' list, simply call the district field office in your area and request to be put on it.

The IRS personal property tax sale is the other form of a tax lien sale. Here's a great source for buying cars, boats, airplanes and any other thing a person might have. Unlike the real estate tax lien sales where the owner of the property has 120 days to redeem the property (paying you 20% per annum on any money you laid out, plus your expenses), all personal tax lien sales are final. Your local Court House or Post Office will usually have these sales posted prior to the sale. Also, watch the legal newspapers for such auctions. Attend a couple of them and see how many people show up at the auction. Don't bring any money the first time or two. Just go to observe the process and profit potential of such forced sales. If it looks like your cup of tea, pursue it further.

U.S. Marshals' Sales are really great. I remember the first time I went to the Marshall's office in Los Angeles. I was reading all the different cases that had merchandise to be auctioned. This information can be viewed by the public. Most of these sales are the result of a "controlled substance" bust. I remember one sale which had over $500,000.00 worth of jewelry which was seized in a drug bust. It sold in lots at about .20¢ on the dollar. They also seize alot of Mercedes and airplanes that are sold at auction. View your local U.S. Marshall's records, usually found in the Federal Court's building. There are some great deals to be had at these sales. A lot of cash is seized too but they don't auction it off. I was hoping they would.

U.S. Customs' Sales are similar to the Marshals' sales except they tend to have a lot more yachts. These sales have everything else you could imagine, too. Some areas of the country are better than others. The Southern states along the Gulf seem best, but don't overlook your own state. Prices paid at these sales can be very high or very low, depending on how many people show up on the date of the sale. I clipped an article of a sale I was unable to attend where a yacht valued at $458,000.00 sold for $22,000.00. Can you see what I mean by making money with the cash advance features on your credit cards? Contact your local U.S. Customs' office in your area.

FBI Sales - this one in particular was a joke. A man at the auction paid $4,000.00 cash for $200,000.00 worth of Persian rugs; quite a profit there. What was really wild about the whole deal was when his employees started to unroll all the rugs; they found that each rug contained a long plastic tube filled with cocaine. The FBI wouldn't admit to "selling" the drugs though.

The Department of Alcohol, Tobacco and Firearms doesn't have any sales. They claim that everything they seize gets destroyed (or so they say).

General Services Administration (GSA) sales can be very profitable. The GSA holds public auctions for several different departments of government. Sometimes they will sell merchandise for the Post Office or the State Highway Department or the Forest Ranger Offices and even the U.S. Customs' office. The GSA offices nearest you can be found in the white pages of your phone directory under U.S. Government Offices. Have your name added to their mailing list so you are notified of when the sales are scheduled and what items will be auctioned off. Some GSA offices have the last few sales sheets on file for your viewing. By looking at these, you can get a general idea of the merchandise sold at these auctions and how much it sells for.

The **FDIC** Sales have some great bargains, especially in Oklahoma and Texas where bank failures are the highest. Anything a bank would loan money against can be found at these auctions. It can range from something as small as 600 pairs of cowboy boots to a dozen Rolls Royces. I highly recommend these sales. An associate of mine teamed up with a friend and bought 15 cars at half of their market value. They really made a haul on that one. For as long as there are banks, there will be FDIC sales. The list of FDIC offices can be found at the end of the Fair Credit Billing Section in the Appendix.

Among **Housing and Urban Development** (HUD) and **Veterans Administration** (VA) are some great bargains to be had. HUD and VA, both, guarantee home loans. They give the lender a guarantee that he will not suffer any loss by financing homes approved by HUD or VA. When a homeowner defaults on the loan, the bank or savings and loan who made the loan will try to sell the home and, if they fail, the government will reimburse the lender for the loan. HUD or the VA must then dispose of the property if the lender can't, and most times at reduced prices and interest rates. They only require a minimal down payment; some can still be bought with "no money down". Other properties are sold for "all cash." These are usually the "yuk" houses, sometimes in need of major repairs. Your local realtor can easily sign up to become an authorized HUD or VA broker if he isn't already. Don't be afraid to use him. HUD also sells multiple unit dwellings at auction.

I would contact my local HUD office if I were you, and ask to be put on their mailing list of HUD properties going up for auction. Call the VA and ask to be put on the Home Disposal Program mailing list. Millions have been made already by people purchasing these repos; I recommend that you look further into it if you seek to make money with credit.

Your **State Highway Department** might have some deals waiting for you also. With them, you can often buy homes that are to be moved. A good friend of mine has done very well in moving homes onto new lots and selling them for profit.

The County Sheriff's Sales are an excellent source for making money with your cash advances. The sheriff's function concerning these sales is that he's the one who an unsecured creditor sends out to enforce their judgment when they win a lawsuit against you. He doesn't just attach a lien - he seizes your property, both real estate and personal property. He'll seize both individual and business property. He sells the merchandise at auction and uses the proceeds to settle the creditors' claims. Caution should be taken here, too. On real estate that's been seized, and is up for auction, what looks like a great deal may really not be. Do your homework first.

Bankruptcy Auctions are a very good source for buying merchandise at distressed prices, too. You would want to contact your county "Chapter Seven Bankruptcy Trustees" and let them know that you're interested in attending their bankruptcy sales. Businesses which go bankrupt have a lot of assets that are auctioned off for pennies on the dollar. I highly recommend that you look into these types of sales. Fortunes have been made.

Trustee Sales can be most profitable but they also carry the highest risk factor. Let's say a bank has a $70,000.00 first mortgage on a $100,000.00 house. The homeowner has stopped paying on the loan. The bank starts the foreclosure process and eventually the home is sold at a trustee's auction and the bank is the only bidder in most cases. Now, if you wanted to bid on the house, let's say you bid $70,100.00. Normally the bank will not overbid you; they don't want the house, they want their loan settled plus legal fees and such. If you were the successful bidder, you would be required to pay the trustee the entire bid amount in "cash" or cashiers checks. Now you own the property, but there could be additional liens on the home as well and they would be a part of the package, too. You just may end up paying more money for the house than it's worth.

The best and safest way to buy foreclosure property is from the lender after he has finalized the foreclosure process. Or, you could buy the loan and his position in the foreclosure, then hold the trustee auction yourself. There is great potential in buying property at trustee sales, but the risks involved are equally as great.

Property Tax Lien Sales are very common and very profitable and, in my opinion, the safest of all forced sales, but you still would want to be cautious. If a homeowner or property owner doesn't pay his property tax, the County Tax Collector can place a lien on the property. If the owner doesn't pay off the lien, the County in which the property is located, can elect to sell the property at auction to get the tax lien paid. Each state is different in their policies regarding tax liens.

There are basically two different ways a property can be sold. In some states (deed states), the successful bidder gets title to the property upon completion of sale; there is no redemption period. The other states (certificate states) will sell a certificate in the amount of the tax lien to satisfy the lien. Now the person who owned the property will have between six months and four years to redeem the property. If he does choose to redeem the property, he must buy the certificate back from you at the price you paid for it plus interest. The interest rate in Florida is 18% and Michigan certificates will yield 50%. Not a bad return on your investment. I've seen properties sell for 50% of their true value in deed states. I know that these same bargains can be found in certificate states as well.

Go down and see your county tax collector and ask them for a list of delinquent tax lien properties that are going to be sold or certificates which will be sold, depending on whether you live in a deed state or certificate state.

This is one of the best methods to use in making money with credit. Do your homework, though; you'll need to know what you're doing to minimize any known risks. If you want to find out how many counties are in your state, just open up to the back pages of a road atlas where all the states are broken down into each city and county and their populations. The counties of each state are in "bold" print. Count how many counties are in your state; then imagine how much opportunity there is available to you in these tax lien sales. Some states, like Minnesota, have as many as 85 counties in them. Whatever the number of counties in your state, there is more opportunity than one could possibly pursue. Don't go to land auctions which are held by private businesses. Go to the county tax collector sales, the same place these land auctioneers get their properties to sell.

Now let me just say that these ideas may sound like the "hackers" way of making money. Well, you be the judge. These owners have been given plenty of time to satisfy their situation, but, for various reasons, they haven't and that's why the property was seized and is being sold at auction.

If you were to buy the entire stock of property at any of these auctions, the person doing the auctions won't go right out and get some more to sell just because his supply is low. The forced sales are the result of someone else's neglect. If they lose their property, be it real estate or personal property, they can whine and complain but it's still their fault. How can I say this? Simply because I've suffered losses due to my own irresponsibility and/or just stupidity.

Research these sales - you, too, can make a fortune at them providing you dig into them and apply action in a conservative manner. As I stated before, these methods work and they are being used everyday by someone to make money, but since you take all the rewards for your successes, you must take any risk involved, too.

CHAPTER 35

CREATING BALANCE

Success in any endeavor requires an even balance among all the different substances which the achievement is made up of. As for becoming or remaining successful in the world of credit, one must search for that "perfect center" which gives even balance and continued success.

You don't have to go into the depths of "technical analyst" to know where your perfect center is. You know when your getting in over your head.

To create your perfect balance, fill out a balance sheet and income and expense statement. Understand what your financial position in life is. Next set "your own" personal credit limit according to what you want to and can afford to pay for on credit terms. It would be wise to pay yourself first from each paycheck. Ten percent of your gross income should go into a savings account only to be used for emergency cash and investments.

Don't get caught up in all the trappings of life with all these advertisements seen on T.V. You'll find that once you bought a product, the thrill or benefit you thought would enhance your lifestyle in one form or another actually was somewhat deceiving and short lived.

I see far too many people using credit to purchase a lifestyle they cannot afford. Some people use credit as a "Placebo" (an I shall please). Well, it will pull them out of their depressing state, at the longest, until the time the bill comes in for that purchase.

Another big mistake I see people make is letting someone charge a purchase on their charge card , saying they'll pay it back. Many times it doesn't get paid back and you the account holder start getting late notices in the mail and even worse, the manner of payment is being recorded on your credit reports.

It's okay to help out a friend but a more sound method would be to say: Go ahead and use my card and then pay "me" back the money plus any finance charges. Now, before giving them the approval to use your card, decide whether or not you can pay for this additional charge if the other person fails to. If you would find it a bit out of reach, then don't give them your charge card to begin with.

One of my friends has some $10,000 out on cards in which two well meaning friends of his failed to pay back. He's responsible and so will you be if you let someone use your cards and they don't pay it back.

It's okay to share your credit info on their reports with them but be careful of letting them make purchases on accounts for which you are contractually liable.

For those of you who are having financial difficulties right now, whether your neck deep in debt or just always a day late and a dollar short; your long term "balance" will only come from raising your self-image. Most of us were programmed with a lot of negative thoughts about money. We affirmed our financial position with the words and phrases such as "I'm broke," "I can't afford it," I'm always late on my car payment," "I don't earn enough money on my job," "I'll always be poor," "I couldn't get a loan if 'God' were to co-sign," etc.

Our mind is the most magnificent computer ever known to mankind. It's made up of a conscious and subconscious mind. At birth our memory banks are blank. With each year that passes, it gets programmed by the society we grow up in.

All the data that we are exposed to each day passes through our conscious mind and stored for future use in our subconscious mind. We hear people use the negative phrases as listed earlier. Our conscious mind picks up every word and sends it into that abundant warehouse called the subconscious. Not only do we hear people use all these negative phrases, but we begin to use them too. They start out as flimsy cobwebs at first but grow into steel cables to shackle our lives as the years go by.

Like any series of thoughts that are put into our mind through consistent repetition, the subconscious mind performs the task just as it was designed to do which is to move us towards our currently dominant thoughts. When we say we are broke through a series of repetitions, the subconscious mind sets out to achieve the goal. Our subconscious mind is a very sophisticated target seeking, goal achieving device. It gets for you (with time allowing) whatever you set before it as a current thought or goal.

If you worry about your bills, the goal is what? More bills! If you worry about lack, debt, insolvency, bill collectors, etc., the subconscious mind moves toward these things and (with time allowing) scores a perfect hit every time.

Some of you are not buying these principles I'm sharing with you because they are much to simple to be true. Well, "worry," (the word, means to "choke"), is a goal in itself. If you worry about something and continue to worry about it and back up your thoughts with equal strength emotions, that which you fear gets even worse and you spend "even more" time worrying about it until it makes you physically sick! At which point, it drives you to the edge; here's where you say "enough" - there's "got to be" a solution. Now your goal changes from a state of worry and frustration to a new mindset of creative problem solving and (with time allowing) scores a direct hit almost every time and then the once massive problem is now behind you.

What's all this have to do with creating balance in the world of credit? I'm glad you asked. Most everything in our lives originates in the mind first.

Our mind operates not on words but on "word pictures." Mental pictures we create. When I say car, you see a car. When I say a red car, you see a red car. When I say "far," you don't see "far;" you relate it to something which resembles distance. When I say "Visa," some of you smile and some of you frown. Some of you see pleasure and some see disaster. All I said was Visa, but you each individually assigned your own mental pictures to the word Visa.

Our mind operates on "word pictures." Whenever we worry about something, we must first create the appropriate mental pictures in our mind to give substance to our fear. As we continue to fear a certain event or outcome, we create more negative mental pictures to compliment the ones we are presently using. *Worry is "negative" goal setting.*

When we fear loosing our job or going into debt, we create pictures in our imaginations to color in our fear. When we fear being in debt we create a mini series in our mind which is vivid and complete in detail. The more we worry about this certain fear, the clearer it becomes.

The subconscious operates off this continuous loop cassette and sets out to achieve, to bring this motion picture into real life, with time allowing. And then, you wonder why your "always" broke!

My conclusion, based on the experience of scores and scores of the world's top achievers and even my own personal experience is this: I have found that through the process of "self-imaging" we can create any type of mini series on the continuous loop cassette between our two ears which our achievement mechanism operates off of (subconscious mind) and enjoy prosperity using the same process we've used to create debt, fear, worry, and frustration. We can create pictures of being debt free or solvent. We can create pictures of having excess cash on hand and in the bank. We can create pictures of paying off the credit cards each month to avoid paying any interest or finance charges. We can create these pictures in our mind of our own free will and with continuous repetition and time allowing, we can create a perfect balance in the world of credit and in our other finances as well.

Although we cannot erase the last cassette in which we used to create the mess we were in (it gets put in storage), we can start a new cassette, a new video, a new mini series in which we can create pictures in our minds, and bring this new motion picture to life!

This practice of self-imaging was formally referred to as the "art of visualization." Neil Armstrong used this visualization process in his practice sessions here on earth to be later used in real life to set foot on the moon. In his imagination, Neil Armstrong completed 300 successful mini series using the art of visualization before he actually set foot on the moon. When he actually did set foot on the moon, he told the people back on earth that "it's just like drill," I feel as if I've done this 300 times before.

Tom Watson, Lee Trevino, and Jack Nicklaus all use "self-imaging" as a tool in their profession. The current dominant thought is "The ball is in the hole." They practice a shot in their imagination before ever stepping up to the ball. These people are "masters" of self-imaging. If they miss a shot, they immediately replay the shot in their imagination as a perfect shot. You to can master this art of Positive Self Imaging if you practice it everyday.

Tennis greats will take some 300 hours of video which views them playing and edit 298 hours leaving them with a two-hour video of *perfect* tennis. They then view this two-hour video of themselves playing a perfect game of tennis over and over and over again until it's embedded in the subconscious mind and the end result in real life on the court is a perfect or near-perfect game of tennis.

Airline pilots use self-imaging or visualization whenever they run up against bad weather. Pilots are trained to do "mental 180's." This is a half turn, they go back, in their imagination as to when they flew in nice calm weather. They imagine flying in perfect conditions as they cut through this storm and land as planned with little or no problem.

Walt Disney used self-imaging. He walked through the once orange groves in Anaheim, California with an amusement park in "rough draft" on a paper napkin, preplaying in his imagination what has since become Disneyland.

Every top entertainer, athlete, business professional, scientist, inventor, and all the other dynamoes in our present day or even as far back as the creation of man, all top achievers have used self-imaging or the art of visualization to create mini series which later become real life events.

I cannot go into every detail about self-imaging or all the success stories I know of in just one chapter. But, what I can do is recommend that you buy a copy of Norman Vincent Peale's book, Positive Imaging, which is available in paperback, published by Fawcett-Crest.

Creating perfect balance in the world of credit must be done in the "mind first," before you can ever experience it in real life. No other means will give lasting results until it happens in your mind first. What you *see* in life is what you will *be* in life.

All of the answers to life are deep within you. Don't search for an external source for solving life's toughest problems - look within yourself because God is within and he has all the answers.

It's your nature to have *perfect balance* in every area of your life. You were created to live your life to its fullest expression. There are no limits but the ones you place on yourself. Your peace, joy, harmony and balance in every area of your life should be searched for by consulting your inner self, and then trust in that inner voice and do what it says.

You can have anything you deeply desire and are willing to work towards. It's all yours, you just have to stake your claim. And then go for it! Be of good courage and **DO IT!**

Thank you.

APPENDIX

Corporate Headquarters: 505 City Parkway West, Suite 110
Orange, California 92668

ALASKA	NEW HAMPSHIRE
ARIZONA	NEW JERSEY
CALIFORNIA	NEW MEXICO
COLORADO	NEW YORK
CONNECTICUT	NORTH CAROLINA
DELAWARE	OHIO
FLORIDA	OREGON
GEORGIA	PENNSYLVANIA
HAWAII	RHODE ISLAND
IDAHO	SOUTH CAROLINA
ILLINOIS	TEXAS
INDIANA	UTAH
MAINE	VERMONT
MARYLAND	VIRGINIA
MASSACHUSETTS	WASHINGTON
MICHIGAN	WEST VIRGINIA
MISSOURI	WISCONSIN
MONTANA	WYOMING
NEVADA	

NOTE: TRW is also known as Credit Data Southwest in some states.

TRW also holds credit information on over 3,500 public companies.

Corporate Headquarters: 444 North Michigan Avenue
Chicago, Illinois 60611

ALABAMA	MISSOURI
ALASKA	MONTANA
ARIZONA	NEBRASKA
ARKANSAS	NEVADA
CALIFORNIA	NEW JERSEY
COLORADO	NEW MEXICO
CONNECTICUT	NEW YORK
DELAWARE	NORTH DAKOTA
FLORIDA	OHIO
IDAHO	OREGON
ILLINOIS	PENNSYLVANIA
INDIANA	RHODE ISLAND
IOWA	SOUTH DAKOTA
KANSAS	TENNESSEE
KENTUCKY	UTAH
MAINE	VIRGINIA
MARYLAND	WASHINGTON
MASSACHUSETTS	WEST VIRGINIA
MICHIGAN	WISCONSIN
MISSISSIPPI	WYOMING

Corporate Headquarters: 1600 Peachtree Street, N.W.
                            Atlanta, Georgia 30309

ALABAMA	SOUTH CAROLINA
ALASKA	TENNESSEE
ARKANSAS	UTAH
CALIFORNIA	VIRGINIA
CONNECTICUT	WASHINGTON, D.C.
DELAWARE	WEST VIRGINIA
FLORIDA	WYOMING
GEORGIA	
IDAHO	PUERTO RICO
KENTUCKY	
LOUISIANA	CANADA
MARYLAND	ALBERTA
MASSACHUSETTS	BRITISH COLUMBIA
MISSISSIPPI	MANITOBA
MONTANA	NEW BRUNSWICK
NEVADA	NEWFOUNDLAND
NEW JERSEY	NOVA SCOTIA
NEW YORK	ONTARIO
NORTH CAROLINA	PRINCE EDWARD ISLAND
OHIO	QUEBEC
OREGON	SASKATCHEWAN
PENNSYLVANIA	

Corporate Headquarters: 12606 Greenville Avenue
Dallas, Texas 75243

ARIZONA	MISSISSIPPI
ARKANSAS	NEBRASKA
COLORADO	NEW HAMPSHIRE
CONNECTICUT	NEW MEXICO
HAWAII	NEW YORK
ILLINOIS	OKLAHOMA
IOWA	RHODE ISLAND
KANSAS	TENNESSEE
LOUISIANA	TEXAS
MAINE	UTAH
MASSACHUSETTS	VERMONT
MICHIGAN	WYOMING
MINNESOTA	

ASSOCIATED CREDIT SERVICES, INC. STATE FILE COVERAGE

(Formerly Pinger System)

Corporate Headquarters: 652 E. North Belt, Suite 400
Houston, Texas 77060

ALABAMA	NEBRASKA
ARKANSAS	NEW MEXICO
GEORGIA	NORTH CAROLINA
ILLINOIS	NORTH DAKOTA
INDIANA	OHIO
IOWA	OKLAHOMA
KANSAS	SOUTH CAROLINA
KENTUCKY	SOUTH DAKOTA
LOUISIANA	TENNESSEE
MICHIGAN	TEXAS
MINNESOTA	VIRGINIA
MISSISSIPPI	WEST VIRGINIA
MISSOURI	WISCONSIN
MONTANA	

ALABAMA

Credit Bureau, Inc. Anniston
1316 Noble St.
Anniston, 36202
(205) 237-5484

Credit Bureau, Inc. Dothan
Colonial Square Executive Park
715 S. Foster St.
Dothan, 36302
(205) 794-3102

Credit Bureau of
  Huntsville, Alabama
807 Franklin St., S.E.
P. O. Drawer E
Huntsville, 35804
(205) 533-9310

Credit Bureau of Mobile
118 N. Royal St., #202
P. O. Box 2167
Mobile, 36652
(205) 433-5554

Credit Bureau of Montgomery
  (CBI Affiliate)
  (Central Alabama Area)
435 S. McDonough St.
P. O. Drawer 830
Montgomery, 36112
(205) 834-2710

Merchants Credit Association
2119 1st Ave., North
P. O. Box 10286
Birmingham, 35202
(205) 252-7121

Trans Union Credit
  Information Co.
Mobile Division
605 Bel Air Blvd.
Mobile, 36606
(205) 471-5387

ALASKA

Credit Bureau of Alaska
3400 Spenard Rd., Suite 6
P. O. Box 4-C
Anchorage, 99509
(907) 279-5689

Interior Credit Bureau, Inc.
910 College Rd.
P. O. Box 1619
Fairbanks, 99707
(907) 452-2157

Juneau Credit Service Co.
197 S. Franklin, #202
Juneau, 99801
(907) 586-1300

ARIZONA

Credit Bureau Services of Arizona
  (Chilton)
100 W. Washington, #1330
Phoenix, 85003
(602) 252-0757, 258-5328

Credit Bureau Services of Arizona
  (Chilton)
5151 E. Broadway, Suite 420
Tucson, 85711
(602) 745-8105

Credit Data of Arizona, Inc.
  (TRW System)
705 N. First St.
P. O. Box 2070
Phoenix, 85001
(602) 252-6951

ARKANSAS

Credit Bureau of Fort Smith, Inc.
513 Garnson Ave.
P. O. Box 1707
Fort Smith, 72902
(501) 782-8861

Credit Bureau Services
  (Chilton)
Plaza West Building, Suite 260
McKinley & Lee Streets
P. O. Box 1002
Little Rock, 72203
(501) 661-1000

Credit Bureau Services
  (Chilton)
1500 Linden
P. O. Box 8228
Pine Bluff, 71601
(501) 535-1130, 535-1133

CALIFORNIA

Credit Bureau, Inc.
Credit Reporting Center San Jose
  (serves San Francisco market
  and much of California)
6389 San Ignacio Ave.
P. O. Box 23016
San Jose, 95119
(408) 224-2803

Credit Bureau, Inc.
Santa Rosa Credit
  Reporting Center
50 Old Courthouse Square,
Suite 301
Santa Rosa, 95404
(707) 546-0551

Credit Bureau Inc.
2223 Wellington Ave. #301
Santa Ana, 92701
(714) 834-1685

Retailers Credit Association
  or RCA
Credit Bureau of Sacramento
1801 J St.
P. O. Box 1318
Sacramento, 95806
(916) 444-6811

Trans Union Credit
  Information Co.
Southern California Division
(including L.A.)
1400 N. Harbor Blvd.
P. O. Box 3110
Fullerton, 92635
(714) 738-3800

Trans Union Credit
  Information Co.
Southern California Division
(including San Diego)
770 B St., #40
P. O. Box 12069
San Diego, 92112
(619) 232-6461

TRW Credit Data
1065 E. Hillsdale Blvd., Suite 400
Foster City, 94404
(415) 571-1000

TRW Credit Data
1300 E. Shaw Ave., Suite 147
Fresno, 93710
(209) 226-5271
24-hr. recording: (209) 225-1998

CALIFORNIA (continued)

TRW Credit Data
(Los Angeles area)
505 City Parkway West, #110
Orange, 92668
(714) 937-2000
24-hr. recordings: (714) 991-5100
(213) 254-6871

TRW Credit Data
966 Fulton Ave.
Sacramento, 95825
(916) 481-9232
24-hr. recording: (916) 481-3115

TRW Credit Data
2423 Camino Del Rio South
Suite 103
San Diego, 92108
(619) 291-4525
24-hr. recording: (619) 296-0148

COLORADO

Credit Bureau of Colorado Springs
(Chilton affiliate)
418 S. Weber
P. O. Box 26
Colorado Springs, 80901
(303) 473-0960

Credit Bureau Services
(Chilton)
(serves Denver and Boulder)
Suite 311-A
2323 S. Troy St.
Aurora, 80014
(303) 695-0844

Pueblo Credit & Collection Bureau
425 W. 8th St.
Pueblo, 81003
(303) 542-7554, 7550

TRW Credit Data
2260 S. Xanadu Way
Aurora, 80014
(303) 695-4787
(303) 695-8999

CONNECTICUT

Credit Bureau, Inc.
Bridgeport Credit Reporting
Center
144 Golden Hill St.
P. O. Box 484
Bridgeport, 06601
(203) 366-7951

Credit Bureau, Inc.
New London Credit Reporting
Center
61 Bank St.
New London, 06320
(203) 443-8941

Credit Bureau of Connecticut, Inc.
71 Elm St.
P. O. Box 1801
New Haven, 06507
(203) 772-3420

Credit Bureau Services
(Chilton)
25 Pratt St.
P. O. Box 3398, Central Station
Hartford, 06103
(203) 527-2601

TRW Credit Data
211 State St., Rm. 418
Bridgeport, 06604
(203) 384-0791
24-hr. recording: (203) 579-7857

DELAWARE

Credit Bureau of Del-Mar-Va, Inc.
106 W. Circle Ave.
P. O. Box 244
Salisbury, MD 21801
(301) 742-9551

DISTRICT OF COLUMBIA

Credit Bureau, Inc.
1345 University Blvd.
Langley Park, MD 20783
(301) 891-3000

TRW Credit Data
5565 Sterrett Pl.
Clark Bldg., Suite 527
Columbia, MD 21044
(301) 953-2360
24-hr. recording: (301) 596-4811

FLORIDA

Credit Bureau, Inc.
Miami Credit Reporting Center
14701 N.W. 7th Ave.
P. O. Box 680010
Miami, 33168
(305) 685-8507

Credit Bureau, Inc.
Orlando Credit Reporting Center
2250 Lee Rd.
Winter Park, 32789
(305) 647-1400

Credit Bureau of Greater
St. Petersburg, Inc.
6666 22nd Ave., N.
St. Petersburg, 33710
(813) 381-9686

Credit Bureau of Greater Tampa
(Trans Union affiliate)
134 S. Tampa St.
P. O. Box 3307
Tampa, 33601
(813) 273-7841

Credit Bureau of Jacksonville
240 E. Duval St.
P. O. Box 52179
Jacksonville, 32201
(904) 353-4801

TRW Credit Data
1525 N.W. 167th St., Suite 320
Miami, 33169
(305) 624-8471
24-hr. recording in English and
Spanish: (305) 625-7858

GEORGIA

Credit Bureau, Inc.
Atlanta Credit Reporting Center
3 Executive Park Dr.
P. O. Box 95007
Atlanta, 30347
(404) 329-1725

Credit Bureau of Columbus
(CBI Contract Bureau)
703 20th St.
P. O. Box 1598
Columbus, 31994
(404) 327-0201

Credit Bureau of Macon
(CBI affiliate)
484 Mulberry St., Suite 270
P. O. Drawer 4185
Macon, 31212
(912) 743-3771

GEORGIA (Continued)

TRW Credit Data
6201 Powers Ferry Rd., Suite 200
Atlanta, 30339
(404) 953-9265
24-hr. recording: (404) 953-3743

HAWAII

Credit Bureau Services
   (Chilton)
1164 Bishop St., Suite 500
Honolulu 96813
(808) 536-3741, 536-7372

IDAHO

Credit Bureau, Inc.
Boise Credit Reporting Center
6100 Emerald Dr.
Boise, 83704
(208) 376-2122

ILLINOIS

Credit Bureau of Decatur, Inc.
260 E. Wood St.
P. O. Box 1279
Decatur, 62525
(217) 424-1200

Credit Bureau of Greater Peoria
330 S.W. Adams, Suite I
Peoria, 61602
(309) 671-0500

Credit Bureau of Rockford, Inc.
3920 E. State St.
Rockford, 61108
(815) 229-1550

Credit Bureau of Springfield, Inc.
825 E. Carpenter
P.O. Box 202
Springfield, 62705
(217) 544-4661

Trans Union Credit
   Information Co.
Chicago Division
444 N. Michigan Ave.
P. O. Box 11036
Chicago, 60611
(312) 645-6028

TRW Credit Data
1699 Wall St.
Mt. Prospect, 60056
(312) 981-9400
24-hr. recording: (312) 981-0295

INDIANA

Credit Bureau, Inc.
New Castle Credit
   Reporting Center
1426 Broad St.
New Castle, 47362
(317) 529-3230

Credit Bureau, Inc.
Muncie Credit Reporting Center
1535 N. Walnut St.
Muncie, 47303
(317) 289-1816

Credit Bureau of Evansville, Inc.
103 N.W. 2nd St.
P.O. Box 3677
Evansville, 47708
(812) 424-2461

Credit Bureau of Ft. Wayne, Inc.
315 Washington Blvd.
Ft. Wayne, 46802
(219) 422-2240

INDIANA (Continued)

Credit Bureau of South Bend-
Mishawaka
312 W. Colfax
P.O. Box 1757
South Bend, 46634
(219) 236-5620

Merchant Association of Indiana
42 N. Pennsylvania
Indianapolis, 46204
(317) 633-1555

IOWA

Chilton Corporation
Suite H-5
600 5th Ave.
Des Moines, 50309
(515) 288-9130

Credit Bureau of
  Cedar Rapids, Inc.
200 SGA Bldg.
P.O. Box 4291
Cedar Rapids, 52407
(319) 365-0401

Credit Bureau of
  Greater Des Moines
505 5th Ave., Suite 600
P. O. Box 1817
Des Moines, 50309
(515) 247-8900

KANSAS

Affiliated Credit Bureaus, Inc.
212 S. Market St.
Wichita, 67202
(316) 263-9161

Affiliated Credit Bureaus, Inc.
  (Independent, serviced by Pinger)
201 Kaufman Bldg.
Wichita, 67202
(316) 263-9161

Credit Bureau of Topeka, Inc.
915 Kansas Ave.
P.O. Box 2607
Topeka, 66601
(913) 357-4411

KENTUCKY

Lexington Credit Bureau
  (Independent, serviced by
  Trans Union)
135 W. Main St.
P.O. Box 934
Lexington, 40588
(606) 233-3300

Trans Union Credit
  Information Co.
Louisville Division
455 River City Mall, #1233
Louisville, 40202
(502) 584-0121

LOUISIANA

Credit Bureau of Baton Rouge, Inc.
4950 Government
P.O. Box 1427
Baton Rouge, 70821
(504) 926-9640

Credit Bureau of
  Greater Shreveport
620 Crockett
P.O. Box 1107
Shreveport, 71163
(318) 222-3276

LOUISIANA (Continued)

Credit Bureau Services
(Chilton)
First National Bank Tower, #500
666 Jefferson
Lafayette, 70501
(318) 237-1749

Credit Bureau Services
(Chilton)
110 Veterans Blvd. Annex
#200-A
Metairie, 70005
(504) 838-8030

Credit Bureau Services
(Chilton)
1811 Tower Dr.
Monroe, 71201
(318) 387-1153

Credit Bureau Services
(Chilton)
1539 Jackson Ave.
P.O. Box 24060
New Orleans, 70184
(504) 838-8030

MAINE

Credit Bureau of
Greater Portland, Inc.
(Chilton Contract Bureau)
66 Pearl St.
P. O. Box 32 DS
Portland, 04112
(207) 772-3771

MARYLAND

Credit Bureau of Baltimore, Inc.
(CBI affiliate)
300 Cathedral St.
P.O. Box 926
Baltimore, 21203
(301) 332-4635, 4600

Credit Bureau of Del-Mar-Va
106 W. Circle Ave.
P. O. Box 244
Salisbury, 21801
(301) 742-9551

TRW Credit Data
5565 Sterrett Place
Clark Bldg., #527
Columbia, 21044
(301) 992-3000
24-hr. recording: (301) 992-3055

MASSACHUSETTS

Credit Bureau, Inc. of Western
Massachusetts
145 State St.
Springfield, 01103
(413) 736-4511, 4517

Credit Bureau Services
(Chilton)
6 St. James Ave.
P.O. Box 73
Boston, 02116
(617) 423-6400, 423-7417

TRW Credit Data
16 Lakeside Office Park
Wakefield, 01880
(617) 246-2800
24-hr. recording: (617) 245-5150

MASSACHUSETTS (Continued)

Worchester Credit Bureau, Inc.
  (Chilton affiliate)
1115 Mechanics Tower
Worcester, 01608
(617) 756-1561, 1567

MICHIGAN

Credit Bureau of Greater Lansing
  (Chilton affiliate)
520 S. Washington
P.O. Box 40297
Lansing, 48901
(517) 487-6561

Credit Bureau of
  Metro Grand Rapids
  (Independent, serviced by
  Trans Union)
1155 Front Ave., N.W.
Grand Rapids, 49504
(616) 456-6544

Retailers' Credit Bureau, Inc.
3201 S. Dort Hwy.
Flint, 48507
(313) 742-4000

TRW Credit Data
P.O. Box 321
24450 Evergreen Rd.
Southfield, 48037
(313) 352-6450
24-hr. recording: (313) 357-5320

MINNESOTA

Credit Bureau of
  Duluth-Superior, Inc.
  (Pinger affiliate)
21 E. Superior St.
Duluth, 55802
(218) 722-2861

Credit Bureau of Minneapolis
700 Plymouth Bldg.
Minneapolis, 55502
(612) 370-9292

Credit Bureau Services
  (Chilton)
300 Midwest Bldg.
St. Paul, 55101
(612) 298-6600, 6606, 6555

MISSISSIPPI

Credit Bureau, Inc.
Gulfport/Biloxi Credit Reporting
Center
Security Savings & Loan Bldg.
2301 14th St., 5th Fl.
Gulfport, 39501
(601) 863-7171

Credit Bureau, Inc.
Natchez Credit Reporting Center
106 S. Wall St.
Natchez, 39120
(601) 442-2841

Credit Bureau, Inc.
Tupelo Credit Reporting Center
1145 W. Main St.
Tupelo, 38801
(601) 842-2424

MISSISSIPPI (Continued)

Credit Bureau, Inc.
Jackson Credit Reporting Center
200 E. Pascaquola
Jackson, 39205
(601) 969-5570

Trans Union Credit
  Information Co.
Jackson Division
514 S. President
P.O. Box 221
Jackson, 39205
(601) 969-3430

MISSOURI

Credit Bureau of
  Greater Kansas City, Inc.
906 Grand Ave.
P.O. Box 476
Kansas City, 64106
(816) 221-5600

Credit Bureau of Springfield
950 St. Louis St.
P.O. Box 1325
Springfield, 65805
(417) 862-3711

Trans Union Credit
  Information Co.
St. Louis Division
406 Olive St., Suite 600
St. Louis, 63102
(314) 241-4333

MONTANA

Credit Bureau of Billings
209 Stapleton Bldg.
P.O. Box 1019
Billings, 59103
(406) 259-3828

NEBRASKA

Credit Bureau Services of Omaha
  (Chilton)
Collection Consultants, Inc.
4822 Dodge St.
P.O. Box 31159
Omaha, 68132
(402) 554-9600

NEVADA

Credit Bureau of
  Southern Nevada, Inc.
  (Trans Union Contract Bureau)
1055 E. Tropicana
P.O. Box 19060
Las Vegas, 89132
(702) 736-2951, 2949, 2940

TRW Credit Data
1105 S. 8th St.
Las Vegas, 89104
(702) 382-7031

TRW Credit Data
495 Apple St., #110
Reno, 89502
(702) 329-3106
24-hr. recording: (702) 825-0252

NEW HAMPSHIRE

Credit Bureau Services of
New Hampshire
(Independent, serviced by Chilton)
168 Manchester
P.O. Box 127
Manchester, 03105
(603) 624-2629

TRW Credit Data
16 Lakeside Office Park
Wakefield, MA 01880
(603) 627-7583
24-hr. recording: (603) 627-7433

NEW JERSEY

Credit Bureau Associates
  (Independent, serviced by TRW)
817 Carpenter
P.O. Box 203
Camden, 08101
(609) 541-4292

Credit Bureau, Inc.
Tinton Falls Credit
  Reporting Center
  (Serves New Jersey)
766 Shrewsbury Avenue
Tinton Falls, 07724
(201) 842-7500
(800) 392-6807 toll-free in
  New Jersey

TRW Credit Data
5 Century Dr.
Parsippany, 07054
(201) 285-4840
24-hr. recording: (201) 285-4900

NEW MEXICO

Credit Bureau of Albuquerque, Inc.
300 San Mateo, N.E., Suite 500
Albuquerque, 87108
(505) 265-1261

NEW YORK

Credit Bureau, Inc.
Albany Credit Reporting Center
3 Corporate Plaza
Washington Ave. Ext.
Albany, 12203
(518) 869-6699, 2057

Credit Bureau, Inc.
Long Island/New York City
Reporting Center
2234 Jackson Ave., 2nd Fl.
Seaford, L.I., 11783
(516) 785-5300

Credit Bureau Reports
  (Serves all of western New York)
1040 Payne Ave.
North Tonawanda, 14120
(716) 692-4421

Trans Union Credit
  Information Co.
New York Division
95-25 Queens Blvd.
Rego Park, 11374
(212) 459-1800

TRW Credit Data
69 Delaware Ave., Suite 800
Buffalo, 14202
(716) 849-1266
24-hr recording: (716) 849-1288

NEW YORK (Continued)

TRW Credit Data
5 Century Dr.
Parsippany, 07054
(212) 267-0981
24-hr. recording: (212) 233-8569

TRW Credit Data
2450 Ridge Rd. West
Rochester, 14696
(716) 225-3054
24-hr. recording: (716) 225-0585

TRW Credit Data
299 S. Warren St., 4th Fl.
Syracuse 13202
(315) 474-1044
24-hr. recording: (315) 474-1048

NORTH CAROLINA

Credit Bureau, Inc.
Raleigh Credit Reporting Center
5000 Falls of Neuse Rd.
P.O. Drawer 26868
Raleigh, 27611
(919) 876-1460

Credit Bureau of Charlotte, Inc.
 (CBI System affiliate)
1515 Mockingbird, #512
P.O. Box 34488
Charlotte, 28234
(704) 525-9943

Credit Bureau of Greensboro
 (CBI System affiliate)
210 W. Friendly
P.O. Drawer A
Greensboro, 27401
(919) 373-1200

Credit Bureau of Winston-Salem
514 First Union National Bank
Bldg.
P.O. Box 3136
Winston-Salem, 27102
(919) 725-7292

NORTH DAKOTA

Credit Bureau of Grand Forks
 (Pinger System affiliate -
 Credit Bureau Data)
11 S. 4th St.
P.O. Box 246
Suite B-2
Grand Forks, 58201
(701) 775-8165

OHIO

Akron Credit Bureau, Inc.
2641 W. Market St.
P.O. Box 5426
Akron, 44313
(216) 867-0780

Credit Bureau of Cincinnati, Inc.
309 Vine St.
P.O. Box 1239
Cincinnati, 45201
(513) 651-6200, 6208

Credit Bureau of Columbus, Inc.
 (Pinger System affiliate)
170 E. Town St.
Columbus, 43215
(614) 222-5327

Credit Bureau of Toledo, Inc.
 (Serviced by Trans Union)
626 Madison Ave., #500
Toledo, 43604
(419) 244-1991

OHIO (Continued)

Credit Bureau Services of
Northeastern Ohio
666 Euclid Ave.
Cleveland, 44114
(216) 579-3498

Trans Union Credit
 Information Co.
Dayton Division
115 E. 3rd St.
P.O. Box 698
Dayton, 45402
(513) 223-6131

OKLAHOMA

Credit Bureau of Oklahoma City
 (Serviced by Chilton)
2519 N.W. 23rd St.
Oklahoma City, 73107
(405) 947-6611

Credit Bureau of Tulsa
 (Serviced by Pinger)
615 S. Detroit
P.O. Box 3424
Tulsa, 74101
(918) 587-1261

OREGON

Credit Bureau, Inc.
Portland Regional
 Credit Reporting
921 S.W. Washingron
P.O. Box 4262
Portland, 97208
(503) 222-6463

TRW Credit Data
9570 S.W. Barbur, Suite 311
Portland, 97219
(503) 254-1352

PENNSYLVANIA

Associated Credit
 Bureau Service, Inc.
 (Independent, serviced by
 Trans Union)
739 Hamilton Mall
P.O. Box 1640
Allentown, 18105
(215) 820-6828

Credit Bureau, Inc.
 (Independent, serviced by TRW)
908 Penn Ave.
P.O. Box 596 (15230)
Pittsburgh, 15222
(412) 288-1164, 1166

Credit Bureau of Erie, Inc.
115 W. 11th St.
P.O. Box 128
Erie, 16501
(814) 454-5221

Credit Bureau of Scranton &
Lackawanna Counties
 (Independent, serviced by TRW)
420 Connell Bldg.
Scranton, 18503
(717) 344-7191

Trans Union Credit
 Information Co.
Philadelphia Division
1211 Chestnut St., 10th Fl.
Philadelphia, 19107
(215) 864-7834

RHODE ISLAND

Credit Bureau of
  Greater Providence
(Independent, serviced by
Chilton)
40 Fountain St.
P.O. Box 1366
Providence, 02901
(401) 273-7500

SOUTH CAROLINA

Credit Bureau, Inc.
Columbia Credit Reporting Center
223 Stoneridge Dr., Suite 1
Columbia, 29202
(803) 256-2206

SOUTH DAKOTA

Credit Bureau
3171/2 S. Phillips
P.O. Box 1403
Sioux Falls, 57101
(605) 336-0470

TENNESSEE

Credit Bureau, Inc.
Morristown Credit Reporting
  Center
1758 W. Andrew Johnson Hwy.
Morristown, 37814
(615) 586-5301

Credit Bureau of Chattanooga
(Independent, serviced by Chilton)
501 Cherry St.
P.O. Box 1030
Chattanooga, 37401
(615) 265-8551

Credit Bureau of Knoxville, Inc.
(Independent, serviced by Chilton)
1 Regency Square, #340
P.O. Box 830
Knoxville, 37901
(615) 546-1820

Credit Bureau of Nashville
(Independent, serviced by Chilton)
604 4th Ave., N.
P.O. Box 2563
Nashville, 37219
(615) 254-7761

Memphis Consumer Credit
Association, Inc.
#900, 2670 Union Ave., Extended
Memphis, 38112
(901) 452-6580, 5991

TEXAS

Chilton Corporation
11251 N.W. Freeway
Suite 215
Houston, 77092
(713) 956-2088

Credit Bureau of
  Greater Corpus Christi
509 Lawrence St.
P.O. Box 1269
Corpus Christi, 78403
(512) 884-2851

Credit Bureau of
  Greater Houston
2505 Fannin St.
Houston, 77002
(713) 652-3239

TEXAS (Continued)

Credit Bureau of El Paso, Inc.
1817 Wyoming
P.O. Box 942
El Paso, 79946
(915) 545-1700

Credit Bureau Services
   (Chilton)
12606 Greenville Ave.
P.O. Box 2049
Dallas, 75243
(214) 699-6111, 6381

Credit Bureau Services
   (Chilton)
102 W. Oak, Suite G
Denton, 75201
(817) 430-3221

Credit Bureau Services
   (Chilton)
3345 Winthrop St.
Ft. Worth, 76116
(817) 732-8851

Merchants & Professional Credit
Bureau, Inc.
400 E. Anderson Ln., #520
P.O. Box 1623
Austin, 78752
(512) 835-1890

San Antonio Retail
   Merchants Association
306 W. Market St.
San Antonio, 78205
(512) 225-6461

UTAH

Credit Bureau of Salt Lake City
295 Jimmy Doolittle Rd.
Salt Lake City, 84116
(801) 355-5905

VERMONT

Credit Bureau Services of
Vermont, Inc.
   (Chilton affiliate)
230 College St.
P.O. Box 56
Burlington, 05402
(802) 863-5501, 2589

VIRGINIA

Credit Bureau of Richmond, Inc.
700 E. Main St.
P.O. Box 1198
Richmond 23219
(804) 780-9345

Retail Merchants of
   Tidewater Association
   (Independent, serviced by CBI)
5755 Poplar Hall Dr.
P.O. Box 12736
Norfolk, 23502
(804) 466-1600

TRW Credit Data
20 Koger Exec. Ctr., Suite 203
Norfolk, 23502
(804) 461-4061 Norfolk
(804) 380-8992 Peninsual

WASHINGTON

Credit Bureau of Tacoma
4009 Bridgeport Way W.
Tacoma, 98466
(206) 565-6750

WASHINGTON (Continued)

Credit Bureau Services
  (Chilton)
521 W. Maxwell
P.O. Box 5393
Spokane, 99205
(509) 455-5500

Credit Northwest Corporation
P.O. Box 2088
1601 Second Avenue
Seattle, 98101
(206) 626-5500

TRW Credit Data
2037 152nd Ave., N.E.
Redmond, 98052
(206) 746-3881

WEST VIRGINIA

Credit Bureau of Charleston
P.O. Box 1707
Terminal Bldg., 2nd Fl.
Charleston, 25382
(304) 343-2182

WISCONSIN

Credit Bureau of Green Bay, Inc.
130 E. Walnut St.
P.O. Box 460
Green Bay, 54305
(414) 437-5995

Credit Bureau of Madison
  (Independent, serviced by
  Trans Union)
1400 E. Washington Ave., #233
P.O. Box 32
Madison, 53701
(608) 256-1692

Credit Bureau of Milwaukee, Inc.
  (Independent, serviced by
  Trans Union)
414 E. Mason St.
P.O. Box 1996
Milwaukee, 53201
(414) 276-6480

WYOMING

Cheyenne Credit Bureau
213 W. 18th Street
P.O. Box 346
Cheyenne, 82001
(307) 634-3511

Credit Bureau of Casper
829 Cy Ave.
P.O. Box 970
Casper, 82602
(307) 234-8901

In the following pages you'll find a list of low interest Visa and Mastercard issuers. This list was produced by Bankcard Holders of America, a nonprofit organization, after conducting a nationwide survey of banks that offer low interest credit cards.

Bankcard Holders of America has given me permission to reproduce this list; however, being things change with time, I highly recommend that you contact Bankcard Holders of America for a current updated list before contacting any sources listed herein. The cost is only $1.00.

Bankcard Holders of America has also produced several other publications including a list of approximately 20 banks who issue Visa and Mastercard with no annual fee. The other publications made available by BHA include but are not limited to:

- All That Glitters is Not Gold
- College Students and Credit
- How to Shop for a Bank Card
- Credit Cards and Seniors
- Traveling with Your Credit Card
- Credit Card Fraud
- The Wide World of Plastic
- Ten Reasons to Shop with a Credit Card

These pamphlets can be purchased by the general public for .50¢ each. The No Annual Fee List cost is $1.95. All publications are free for members of the Bankcard Holders of America.

Membership in BHA is highly recommended if you want to stay in touch and keep up with the times, as the credit system revolves and is always changing. The membership fee is only $18.00 and is billed annually.

Presently membership is over 130,000 strong and growing. Their service to American consumers is most valuable. With your membership, BHA's Consumer Action Agency will go to bat for you when you have a problem with retailers and financial institutions.

There's much more to be gained as a BHA member and I recommend you contact them for further information. The membership fee is very low for the service they provide.

Lists, publications and other information can be obtained by either calling or writing BHA at:

BHA/Publications
333 Pennsylvania Avenue, S.E.
Washington, D.C. 20003
(202) 543-5805

Note: Bankcard Holders of America cannot be held responsible for any source that changes its policy.

Northeast States:

Apple Bank for Savings
711 Stewart Ave.
Garden City, NY 11530
(516) 496-1000

card offered: Visa, interest rate: 15.8%, annual fee: $20, grace period: 30 days. Applications accepted from NY, NJ and CT residents only.

Bank of New England Old Colony
P.O. Box 788
Providence, RI 02901
(401) 431-0100

card offered: Visa, interest rate: 12%, annual fee: $20, grace period: 25 days. Applications accepted nationally.

Bank of Vermont*
P.O. Box 949
Burlington, VT 05402
(802) 658-1810

cards offered: MasterCard, Visa, interest rate: 15% on purchases (18% on cash advances), annual fee: $25, grace period: 30 days. Applications accepted nationally.
*Cards are issued through Connecticut Bank & Trust Co.

Bay Bank
Bank Card Center
88 Main Street
Waltham, MA 02154
(617) 647-5145

cards offered: MasterCard, Visa, interest rate: 16.44%, annual fee: $21, grace period: 25 days. Applications accepted nationally.

Northeast States (Continued):

Central Jersey Bank & Trust
301 Main St.
Allenhurst, NJ 07711
(201) 531-3300
card offered: MasterCard, interest rate: 14.9%, annual fee: $15,
grace period: 25 days. Applications accepted from New Jersey
residents only.

City Trust
961 Main St.
Bridgeport, CT 06601
(800) 972-9477 (toll-free in CT only)
(203) 336-7300
cards offered: MasterCard, Visa, interest rate: 15% on
purchases (18% on cash advances), annual fee: $21 ($30 for
both cards), grace period: 25 days. Applications accepted from
Connecticut residents only.

Connecticut Bank and Trust Co.
Bank Card Center
P.O. Box 41
Fairfield, CT 06430
(203) 382-6757
(800) 972-4968 (toll-free in CT only)
cards offered: MasterCard, Visa, interest rate:15% on
purchases (18% on cash advances), annual fee: $25, grace
period: 25 days. Applications accepted nationally.

Northeast States (Continued):

Connecticut National Bank
Customer Service Department
MSN 381
150 Windsor St.
Hartford, CT 06144
(203) 728-4112
(800) 842-1457 (toll-free in CT and MA only)
cards offered: MasterCard, Visa, interest rate: 11.75% on
purchases (18% on cash advances), annual fee: $25 ($40 for
premium cards), grace period: 25 days. Applications accepted
from residents of New England states and New York.

Dime Savings Bank
P.O. Box 150
Huntington Station, NY 11746
(718) 403-9600
card offered: Visa, interest rate: 14.9%, annual fee: $18, grace
period: 25 days. Applications accepted nationally.

Dime Savings Bank of New York
P.O. Box 542
Garden City, NY 11530
(516) 227-3550
card offered: Visa, interest rate: 14.9%, annual fee: $18, grace
period: 25 days. Applications accepted from NY, NJ, CT and
FL residents only.

First Jersey
P.O. Box 970

New Jersey City, NJ 07303
(201) 547-7000
cards offered: MasterCard, Visa, interest rate: 15.8%, annual fee: $15, grace period: 25 days. Applications accepted nationally.

Northeast States (Continued):

First National Bank of Toms River
P.O. Box 788
Toms River, NJ 08751
(201) 240-7918
cards offered: MasterCard, Visa, interest rate: 14.5%, annual fee: $10, grace period: 28 days. Applications accepted from New Jersey residents only.

Goldome
1 Fountain Plaza
Buffalo, NY 14203
(800) 828-1111
card offered: Visa (Costsaver), interest rate: 13.9%, annual fee: $20, grace period: none. Applications accepted from FL, NY, NJ and CT residents only.

Indian Head Bank
P.O. Box 1161
Nashua, NH 03061
(603) 880-5150
cards offered: MasterCard, Visa, interest rate: 16.5% (variable), annual fee: $18, grace period: 25 days. Applications accepted nationally.

Marine Midland
Retail Credit Department

P.O. Box 9
Buffalo, NY 14240
(800) 624-6600

cards offered: Visa, MasterCard, MasterCard Gold, interest rate: V, MC-15.27% (variable); MC Gold-14.27% (variable), annual fee: Visa, Mastercard-$25; MasterCard Gold-$45, grace period: 25 days. Applications accepted nationally.

Northeast States (Continued):

Northeast Savings
P.O. Box 351
Boston, MA 02101
(617) 847-9715

cards offered: Visa, MasterCard, interest rate: 16.5%, annual fee: $25 ($50 for premium cards), grace period: 5 days. Applications accepted nationally.

People's Bank
P.O. Box 637
Bridgeport, CT 06601
(203) 332-2222
(800) 423-3273 (toll-free in CT only)

cards offered: MasterCard, Visa, interest rate: 11.5% on purchases (15.9% on cash advances), annual fee: $20 (for one or both); ($40 for premium cards), grace period: 25 days. Applications accepted nationally.

Shawmut Bank of Boston
Credit Card Service Center
P.O. Box 1002
East Long Meadow, MA 01028
(800) 431-4011

cards offered: Visa, MasterCard, interest rate: 15.84%, annual fee: $24 ($36 for premium card), grace period: none. Applications accepted nationally.

State Street Bank
1776 Heritage Drive
Quincy, MA 02171
(617) 773-7625
(800) 543-6325
cards offered: MasterCard, Visa, interest rate: 16.5%, annual fee: $25, grace period: none. Applications accepted nationally.

Northeast States (Continued):

Society for Savings
P.O. Box 9408
Wethersfield, CT 06109
(203) 727-5760
(800) 233-8993 (toll-free in CT only)
cards offered: MasterCard, Visa, interest rate: 10.9%, annual fee: $30, grace period: none. Applications accepted from CT, RI, and NJ residents only.

Mid-Atlantic States:

Chevy Chase Savings & Loan
8401 Connecticut Ave.
Chevy Chase, MD 20815
(301) 986-7558
cards offered: MasterCard, Visa, interest rate: 14% (variable), annual fee: 1st six months free, then $18 ($30 for premium cards), grace period: 25 days. Applications accepted nationally.

Manufacturer's Hanover
P.O. Box 15147
Wilmington, DE 19885
(302) 366-8487

card offered: MasterCard, interest rate: 13.6%, annual fee: none, grace period: none. Applications accepted nationally.

Southeast States:

First Florida Bank
P.O. Box 1810
Tampa, FL 33601
(800) 282-2788 (in-state)
(800) 352-2265 (out-of-state)

cards offered: Visa, MasterCard, interest rate: 16%, annual fee: $24, grace period: 21 days. Applications accepted nationally.

Southeast States: (continued)

Republic National Bank
P.O. Box 350430
Miami, FL 33135-0430
1-(800) 441-7676

cards offered: Visa, MasterCard, MasterCard Gold, interest rate: 14% (variable), annual fee: $22 (Visa, MasterCard); $40 (MasterCard Gold), grace period: 25 days. Applications accepted nationally.

Midwest States:

Bank of Oak Brook
2021 Spring Rd.
Oak Brook, IL 60521
(312) 571-1050 Ext. 300

card offered: MasterCard Gold, interest rate: 15.6%, annual fee: $18, grace period: 25 days. Applications accepted nationally.

First National Bank of Mt. Clemens
49 Macomb St.
Mt. Clemens, MI 48043
(313) 465-2400

cards offered: MasterCard, Visa, interest rate: 15%, annual fee: $10, grace period: 15 days. Applications accepted from Michigan residents only.

First Security National Bank & Trust Co.
Bank Card Center
P.O. Box 11000
Lexington, KY 40512
(800) 432-0728 in Kentucky
(800) 821-5949 out-of-state

card offered: Premier Visa, interest rate: 12.75% (variable), annual fee: $20, grace period: 25-30 days. Applications accepted nationally.

Midwest States: (Continued)

Gem Savings Bank
P.O. Box 1826
Dayton, OH 45402
(513) 921-8000

cards offered: MasterCard, Visa, interest rate: 15% (variable), annual fee: $20grace period: 25 days. Applications accepted from Ohio, Indiana and Kentucky residents only.

Mid America Federal Savings
1144 Deblin Rd.
Columbus, OH 43215
(614) 481-4161
(800) 643-2637 (toll-free in Ohio only)

cards offered: MasterCard, Visa, interest rate: 13.9%, annual fee: $15, grace period: 25 days. Applications accepted from Ohio residents only.

National City Bank in Cleveland
P.O. Box 5570N
Cleveland, OH 44101
(216) 575-3100

cards offered: MasterCard, Visa, interest rate: 15% (variable), annual fee: $18, grace period: 25 days. Applications accepted from Ohio residents only.

Ohio Savings Bank
Visa Customer Service
P.O. Box 94712
Cleveland, OH 44114
(216) 696-2222

card offered: Visa, interest rate: 14.75% , annual fee: $18, grace period: 15 days. Applications accepted from Ohio residents only.

Midwest States: (Continued)

Security Savings Bank
301 West Michigan Ave.
Jackson, MI 49201
(517) 787-9700

cards offered: MasterCard, Visa, interest rate: 14.9% (variable), annual fee: $12, grace period: 25 days. Applications accepted nationally.

Society National Bank of Cleveland
Card Service Center

P.O. Box 6486-S
Cleveland, OH 44101
(216) 622-8863
(800) 523-7247 (toll-free in Ohio only)
cards offered: MasterCard, Visa, interest rate: 14.34%
(variable), annual fee: $20, grace period: 25 days. Applications
accepted from Ohio residents only.

State Savings
3800 W. Dublin-Granville
Dublin, OH 43107
(614) 764-1446
card offered: Visa, interest rate: 14.88%, annual fee: $18, ($45
for premium card), grace period: 25 days. Applications
accepted from Ohio residents only.

South Central States:

Banc Texas
1661 Elm St.
Dallas, TX 75201
(214) 969-6111
(800) 262-8721
cards offered: Visa, MasterCard, interest rate: 14% (variable),
annual fee: none, grace period: none. Applications accepted
from Texas residents only.

South Central States: (continued)

Broadway National Bank
P.O. Box 17001
San Antonio, TX 78286
(512) 824-0444
card offered: Visa, interest rate: 14% (variable), annual fee:
none, grace period: none. Applications accepted from residents
of San Antonio and surrounding area only.

First Commercial Bank
Credit Card Customer Service
P.O. Box 1545
Memphis, TN 38101
(901) 523-5800

cards offered: MasterCard, Visa, Premier Visa, interest rate: 10.5% (variable), annual fee: $18 ($35 for premium card), grace period: none. Applications for low-rate card accepted from Arkansas residents only.

National Bank of Ft. Sam Houston
P.O. Box 8000
San Antonio, TX 78286
(512) 223-2981

cards offered: MasterCard, Visa, interest rate: 14% (variable), annual fee: none, grace period: none. Applications accepted nationally, but applicant must have a primary bank account with them.

Simmons First National Bank
P.O. Box 6609
Pine Bluff, AR 71611
(501) 541-1000

cards offered: MasterCard, Visa, interest rate: 10.5% (variable), annual fee: $22.50, grace period: 25 days. Applications accepted nationally.

South Central States: (continued)

Texas American Bank
Bank Card Department
P.O. Box 1990

Ft. Worth, TX 76101

(817) 338-8011

cards offered: MasterCard, Visa, interest rate: 14% (variable), annual fee: none, grace period: none. Applications accepted from residents of Texas and surrounding states.

Union National Bank

P.O. Box 1541

Little Rock, AR 72203

(501) 378-4000

cards offered: MasterCard, Visa, interest rate: 10.5% (variable), annual fee: $20 ($35 for premium cards), grace period: none. Applications accepted nationally.

Pacific States:

American Savings & Loan

P.O. Box 4000

Whitter, CA 90607

(213) 947-4711

card offered: Visa, interest rate: 15% , annual fee: $15, grace period: none. Applications accepted from California residents only.

First Security Bank

P.O. Box 8105

Boise, ID 83730

(208) 338-4038

cards offered: MasterCard, Visa, interest rate: 15.7% (variable, adjusted monthly), annual fee: $20, grace period: 25 days. Applications accepted nationally.

Pacific States: (continued)

Guarantee Savings & Loan
895 W. Ashland - Suite 102
Fresno, CA 93612
(209) 438-3960

card offered: Visa, interest rate: 15% , annual fee: $13, grace period: none. Applications accepted from California residents only.

Highland Federal Savings
6301 N. Figueroa St.
Los Angeles, CA 90042
(213) 254-3424

cards offered: MasterCard, Visa, interest rate: 16% , annual fee: none, grace period: none. Applications accepted nationally.

Northwest Bank/Seattle Trust
P.O. Box 767
Seattle, WA 98111
(206) 223-2007

cards offered: Visa, MasterCard, interest rate: 15% , annual fee: $18 ($35 for MasterCard Gold), grace period: none. Applicant must be a resident of Seattle for at least one year.

People's Bank
P.O. Box 21327
Seattle, WA 98111
(206) 344-2300
(800) 426-0648 Ext. 7806

cards offered: Visa, MasterCard, interest rate: 15% on purchases; (12% on cash advances), annual fee: $18 ($30 for premium cards), grace period: 25 days. Applications accepted from residents of WA, OR and ID only.

Pacific States: (continued)

Rainier National Bank
Box C34018
Seattle, WA 98124
(206) 621-4111

card offered: Visa, interest rate: 15% , annual fee: $18 ($50 for premium card), grace period: none. Applications accepted from residents of Washington and surrounding states.

Sacramento Savings & Loan
P.O. Box 872
Sacramento, CA 95804
(916) 444-8555

cards offered: Visa, MasterCard, interest rate: 15% , annual fee: $12.50 - Visa, MasterCard, $25 - premium card, grace period: 25 days. Applications accepted from California residents only.

Seafirst Bank
P.O. Box 12920
Seattle, WA 98111
(206) 628-5720

cards offered: Visa, MasterCard, interest rate: 15%, annual fee: $18 ($36 for premium card), grace period: 21 days. Low-rate cards available to residents of Pacific Northwest only.

Valley Bank of Nevada
P.O. Box 15427
Las Vegas, NV 89114-5427
(702) 386-1000

cards offered: MasterCard, Visa, interest rate: 13.5% (variable), annual fee: $15, grace period: none. Applications accepted from Nevada residents only.

Pay special attention to those with more than one asterisk. These sources have proven to be most aggressive. They are deemed reliable but not guaranteed.

     * - Good   ** - Better   *** - Best

*   Affiliated Bank of Madison
     P.O. Box 111
     Madison, WI 53701
     (608) 252-5922

*   Alaska National
     Bank of the North
     Pouch 7010
     Anchorage, AK 99510
     (907) 278-4581

*   Albuquerque National Bank
     P.O. Box 1344
     Albuquerque, NM 87103
     (505) 765-2393

** American Express
     Applications
     Available Everywhere

*   American Federal
     Savings & Loan
     610 Grand Avenue
     Des Moines, IA 50307
     (515) 244-9131

*   American National Bank
     P.O. Box 829
     Woodward, OK 73801
     (405) 254-0243

*   American Security Bank
     P.O. Box 2000
     Honolulu, HI 96805
     (808) 525-8286

** AVCO
     17770 Cartwright Road
     Irvine, CA 92714-5852
     (800) 854-3883 - outside CA
     (800) 432-7025 - from CA only

** Bank Cal
     1700 The Alameda
     San Jose, CA 95126
     (408) 995-5455

*** Bank of America Card Center
     101 S. Marengo Avenue
     Pasadena, CA 91122
     (800) 323-1753 - from CA only

*   Bank of California, NA
     P.O. Box 45000
     San Francisco, CA 94145
     (415) 765-3324

*   Bank of Maryville
     P.O. Box 528
     Maryville, TN 37801
     (615) 977-5100

*   Bank of New Mexico
     P.O. Box 1830
     Albuquerque, NM 87103
     (505) 766-6287

*   Bank of Southwest, NA
     P.O. Box 1335
     Houston, TX 77001

** Bank of St. Louis
     P.O. Box 118
     St. Louis, MO 63166

** Bank of the West
  1590 Hamilton Ave.
  San Jose, CA 95126
  (408) 998-6677

*** Bank One
  Dept. 0553
  Columbus, OH 43271
  (614) 463-5800

** Bank One of Medina Co.
  102 Main Street
  Wadsworth, OH 44281
  (216) 334-2571

* Bankwest, NA
  P.O. Box 128
  Kadoka, SD 57543
  (605) 837-2282

** Barclays Bank of California
  60 W. Hamilton Ave.
  Campbell, CA 95008

* Bay Port State Bank
  9840 Main Street
  Bay Port, MI 48720
  (517) 656-2231

*** Beneficial National Bank
  Credit Card Center
  P.O. Box 210
  Wilmington, DE 19899
  (302) 656-5020

* Berkley Federal Savings & Loan
  555 Milburn Avenue
  Short Hills, NJ 07078
  (201) 467-2800

* Broadway National Bank
  P.O. Box 17001
  San Antonio, TX 78286
  (512) 824-0444

** Buterfield Savings & Loan
  P.O. Box 609
  Brea, CA 92622-0609

** California Canadian Bank
  340 Pine
  San Francisco, CA 94104
  (415) 981-8090

** California Federal
  Savings & Loan
  5630 Wilshire Boulevard
  Los Angeles, CA 90036

** California First Bank
  616 W. 6th Street
  Los Angeles, CA 90017
  (213) 972-5265

** Canal Bank
  P.O. Box 231
  Portland, ME 04112

* Capital Bank & Trust Company
  P.O. Box 8
  Belton, SC 29627
  (803) 338-6161

* Catalina Savings & Loan
  160 N. Stone Avenue
  Tucson, AZ 85701
  (602) 792-2222

* Central Jersey Bank &
  Trust Company
  Main & Corlies Avenue
  Allenhurst, NJ 07711
  (201) 531-3300

** Century Federal
  14441 Culver Drive
  Irvine, CA 92714-1897

** Chase Manhattan
  P.O. Box 15009
  Wilmington, DE 19850-9981
  (800) 633-0458

** Chemical Bank
  P.O. Box 2008
  Jericho, NY 11753
  (516) 937-4000

*** City Bank
P.O. Box 6062
Sioux Falls, SD 57117
(301) 797-2400

*** City Bank
P.O. Box 6000
The Lake, NV 81163

** Colorado National Bank
4930 Colorado Boulevard
Denver, CO 80206

* Colorado National
Bank of Denver
P.O. Box 5952 Terminal Annex
Denver, CO 80217
(303) 629-7755

* Commercial Bank
P.O. Box 520
Middlesboro, KY 40965

* Commonwealth Savings & Loan
P.O. Box 3398
Little Rock, AR 72203
(501) 372-1881

** Community National Bank
529 Chester Avenue
Bakersfield, CA 93301

** Continental Bank
231 S. LaSalle Street
Chicago, IL 60693

*** Credit Unions
(Lower Interest Cards)
Easy Approval

** Diner's Club
Applications Available
Everywhere

* Family Savings & Loan
124 Temple Street
New Haven, CT 06510
(203) 787-0294

* Fidelity Federal Savings
P.O. Box 989
West Palm Beach, FL 33401
(305) 659-9900

*** Fidelity Federal Savings
P.O. Box 1927
San Diego, CA 92112

* Florida Center Bank
P.O. Box 15370
Orlando, FL 32858
(305) 351-0330

* Florida National Bank
P.O. Box 11369
St. Petersburg, FL 33733
(813) 821-1111

* First Alabama Bank
of Montgomery NA
P.O. Box 511
Montgomery, AL 36101
(205) 832-8242

* First American Bank of Virginia
P.O. Box 627
McLean, VA 22101
(703) 827-8841

* First Federal Savings & Loan
P.O. Box 83009
Lincoln, NE 68501
(402) 475-0521

* First Federal Savings & Loan
110 Westminister Street
Providence, RI 02901
(401) 861-5400

* First Federal State Bank
24th & University Avenue
Des Moines, IA 50311
(515) 277-6441

* First Hawaiian Bank
P.O. Box 3200
Honolulu, HI 96847
(808) 525-7123

* First Interstate Bank
P.O. Box 30169
Salt Lake City, UT 84125
(801) 350-7760

* First Interstate Bank
P.O. Box 5757
Boise, ID 83705
(208) 383-5000

*** First Interstate Bank
Los Angeles, CA

* First National Bank
of South Carolina
P.O. Box 1457
Columbia, SC 29202
(803) 771-3737

* First National Bank & Trust
Company of Oklahoma City
P.O. Box 25189
Oklahoma City, OK 73125
(405) 272-4000

* First National Bank of Aspen
P.O. Box 3318
Aspen, CO 81611
(303) 925-1450

* First National Bank of Boston
100 Federal
Boston, MA 02241

** First National Bank of Chicago
P.O. Box 2007
Elgin, IL 60120
(800) 368-4535

* First National Bank
of Glens Falls
P.O. Box 311
Glens Falls, NY 12801
(518) 792-2165

* First National Bank of Marion
P.O. Box 609
Marion, IA 52302
(319) 377-7331

* First National Bank of Missoula
P.O. Drawer B
Missoula, MT 59806
(406) 721-4200

* First National Bank of Mobile
P.O. Box 1468
Mobile, AL 36601
(205) 438-8291

* First National Bank of Oakland
P.O. Box 273
Oakland, MD 21550
(301) 334-9471

* First National Bank of Omaha
P.O. Box 3128
Omaha, NE 68103
(402) 341-0500

* First National in Minot
P.O. Drawer 1488
Minot, ND 58701

* First National of Louisville
P.O. Box 36000
Louisville, KY 40232
(502) 581-4200

* First National of Mishawaka
P.O. Box 361
Mishawaka, IN 46344
(219) 259-3711

*** First Security Bank -
    VISA Center
    P.O. Box 30002
    Salt Lake City, UT 84130
    (801) 350-6511

* First Union National Bank
    of North Carolina
    Tower Six
    Charlotte, NC 28288
    (704) 374-6823

** First Wisconsin Bank of Mayfair
    2300 N. Mayfair Road
    Milwaukee, WI 53201

* First Wisconsin National
    Bank of Milwaukee
    P.O. Box 2066
    Milwaukee, WI 53020
    (414) 765-4354

* Fort Knox National Bank
    P.O. Box D
    Fort Knox, KY 41201
    (502) 624-2195

* Great Western Bank & Trust
    P.O. Box 146
    Phoenix, AZ 85001
    (602) 264-7441

* Guarantee Savings & Loan
    1177 Fulton Mall
    Fresno, CA 93721
    (209) 268-8111

*** Harris Trust & Savings Bank
    Charge It System
    P.O. Box 4688
    North Suburban, IL 60197-4688
    (312) 520-6500

* Heritage/Pullman Bank
    1000 E. 111th Street
    Chicago, IL 60628
    (312) 785-1000

** Highland Federal Savings
    Los Angeles, CA
    (213) 254-3424

** Home Federal Savings & Loan
    701 Broadway
    San Diego, CA 92101

* Home Savings Bank
    P.O. Box 2254
    Boston, MA 02107
    (617) 723-1600

** Household Federal
    Savings & Loan
    P.O. Box 798
    Westminster, CA 92683

** Imperial Savings
    P.O. Box 23525
    San Diego, CA 92123-9990

* Industrial National Bank
    of Rhode Island
    111 Westminister Street
    Providence, RI 02903
    (401) 278-6125

* Iowa Trust & Savings Bank
    P.O. Box 490
    Centerville, IA 52544

** Jefferson Bank
    124 S.W. Adams
    Peoria, IL 61649

** Jefferson National Bank
    10590 N. Kendall Drive
    Miami, FL 33101

* Liberty National Bank
    P.O. Box 216
    Hillsdale, NJ 07642
    (201) 666-4600

* Marine Midland Bank
  P.O. Box 1183
  Buffalo, NY 14240
  (716) 843-4487

* Mercantile Bank
  P.O. Box 509
  Louisiana, MO 63353
  (314) 754-0221

** Mercantile Bank
   P.O. Box 306
   St. Louis, MO 63166
   (314) 425-8000

* Michigan National
  Bank of Detroit
  22595 W. 8 Mile Road
  Detroit, MI 48219
  (313) 255-6400

** Mitsui-Manufacturers Bank
   9701 Wilshire Boulevard
   Beverly Hills, CA 90212

* National Bank of Alaska
  P.O. Box 600
  Anchorage, AK 99510
  (907) 276-1132

* National Bank of Commerce
  P.O. Box 2159
  Memphis, TN 38101
  (901) 523-3600

* National Bank of Commerce
  P.O. Box 6208
  Pine Bluff, AR 71611
  (501) 834-1131

* National Bank of Georgia
  P.O. Box 528
  Atlanta, GA 30301
  (404) 452-2540

* National Bank of Washington
  P.O. Box 1537
  Washington, DC 20013
  (202) 532-2000

* Nebraska State Bank
  P.O. Box 187
  Weeping Water, NE 68463
  (402) 267-2285

* Nevada Savings & Loan
  201 S. Las Vegas Boulevard
  Las Vegas, NV 89101
  (702) 385-3216

* Nevada State Bank
  P.O. Box 990
  Las Vegas, NV 89101
  (702) 383-4717

* New Orleans Federal Savings
  4948 Chestmenters Highway
  New Orleans, LA 70015
  (504) 947-0002

* Northern National Bank
  P.O. Box 1029
  Presque Isle, ME 04769
  (207) 769-2211

** Northwestern State Bank
   P.O. Box 157
   Jordan, MN 55352
   (612) 492-2666

** Olympic Savings & Loan
   Association
   926 Travel Street
   San Francisco, CA 94116

* Pacific First Federal Savings
  1126 Pacific Avenue
  Tacoma, WA 98401
  (206) 383-2511

* Pacific National Bank
of Washington
P.O. Box 160
Seattle, WA 98111

* Peoples Bank
P.O. Box 419
Ripley, MS 38663

* Peoples Bank & Trust
P.O. Box 1750
Wilmington, DE 19899

* Peoples Savings & Loan
212 W. 7th Street
Auburn, IN 46706
(219) 925-2500

* Philadelphia National Bank
P.O. Box 7618
Philaldelphia, PA 19105
(215) 629-4530

* Provident Federal Savings
P.O. Box 1460
Boise, ID 83701
(208) 343-1833

** Rainer National Bank
Box C 34212
Seattle, WA 98124

* Republic Federal Savings
P.O. Box 2458
Lafayette, LA 70502
(318) 322-3244

*** Republic National Bank
of Miami
10 N.W. 42nd Avenue
Miami, FL 33140
(305) 441-7641

* Rochester Savings Bank & Trust
22 S. Main
Rochester, NH 03867
(603) 332-4242

* Rocky Mountain Federal
Savings & Loan
P.O. Box 1167
Cheyenne, WY 82001
(307) 634-2101

* Roswell State Bank
P.O. Box 2057
Roswell, NM 88201
(505) 622-4240

** Sacramento Savings & Loan
P.O. Box 872
Sacramento, CA 95804

** San Diego Federal
Savings & Loan
P.O. Box 1000
San Diego, CA 92112

* San Jacinto Savings
P.O. Drawer 2871
Beaumont, TX 77021
(713) 838-6391

*** Sears
Any Store

*** Seafirst National Bank
601 Broadway
Seattle, WA 98122

* Security Bank of Nevada
P.O. Box 2000
Reno, NV 89520

* Security National Bank
P.O. Box 1250
Kansas City, KS 66117
(913) 281-3165

*** Security Pacific Finance Co.
(East Loans, No Cards)
3550 Wilshire Boulevard
Suite 114
Los Angeles, CA 90010
(213) 613-4787

* Security State Bank
   P.O. Box G
   Maple Lake, MN 55358
   (612) 963-3161

* Security State Bank
   P.O. Box 1127
   Starkville, MS 39759
   (601) 323-5155

* Security State Bank
   P.O. Box 129
   Harlem, MT 59526
   (406) 353-2201

** Simmons First National Bank
    P.O. Box 6609
    Pine Bluff, AR 71611
    (501) 541-1300

* Southern Savings & Loan
   P.O. Box 340
   Brownswood, TX 76801
   (915) 656-4561

* State National of Maryland
   11616 Rockville Pike
   Rockville, MD 20852
   (301) 881-7000

* State Savings & Loan
   125 S. Main
   Salt Lake City, UT 84111
   (801) 521-3210

*** State Savings & Loan (CA)
     (209) 948-1116
     (800) 422-7446

** Sterling National Bank
    540 Madison Avenue
    Manhattan, NY 10027
    (212) 826-2200

* Superior Federal
   Savings & Loan
   P.O. Box 939
   Ft. Smith, AR 72923
   (501) 782-8621

** The Arizona Bank
    Drawer A
    Douglas, AZ 85607

** The Bank of Commerce
    P.O. Box 538
    Chanute, KS 66720

* The First National Bank
   of Anchorage
   Pouch 7006
   Anchorage, AK 99510
   (907) 277-8602

** The Warren National Bank
    P.O. Box 69
    Warren, PA 16365

** Tri City National Bank
    4455 W. Bradley Road
    Milwaukee, WI 53201

*** Union National Bank
     of Little Rock
     P.O. Box 1541
     Little Rock, AR 72203
     (501) 378-4104

* Union Trust Company
   of Maryland
   11427 Georgia Avenue
   Wheaton, MD 20902
   (301) 949-7100

* United American Bank, NA
   P.O. Box 2686
   Knoxville, TN 37901
   (615) 971-2224

* United Bank of Arizona
   P.O. Box 2917
   Phoenix, AZ 85062
   (602) 248-2346

** United Bank of Boulder
    Box 299
    Boulder, CO 80306
    (303) 442-3734

* United First Federal Savings
   P.O. Box 1478
   Sarasota, FL 33578
   (813) 366-1500

** University National Bank
    P.O. Box 22355
    Denver, CO 80222
    (303) 757-7272

* Valley Bank
   P.O. Box 425
   Rosedale, MS 38769
   (601) 759-3581

* Valley Bank & Trust
   P.O. Box 1558
   Grand Forks, ND 58201
   (701) 772-5551

* Vermont National Bank
   P.O. Box 804
   Brattleboro, VT 05301
   (802) 257-7151

** Wells Fargo Bank
    P.O. Box 2808
    San Francisco, CA 94126
    (415) 396-4521

* Wheeling Dollar Savings
       Trust Company
   P.O. Box 991
   Wheeling, WV 26003
   (304) 234-9200

Check each for their requirements and process for applying for these cards. All sources are deemed reliable at the time of this writing.

Major Federal Savings
Money Bank Card Center
P.O. Box 53177
Washington, DC 20009
(800) 233-2848

Key Federal Savings & Loan
8639 Belair Road
Perry Hill, MD 21236
(301) 256-7440

Home Trust Savings
20 East Main Street
Vermillion, SD 57069
(605) 624-2608

ALABAMA

CONSUMER CREDIT
  COUNSELING SERVICE
  OF ALABAMA, INC.
217 S. Court Street, Suite 317
Montgomery, AL 36104
  Malda W. Farmer,
  Executive Director
  (205) 265-8545

ALASKA

CONSUMER CREDIT
COUNSELING SERVICE
OF ALASKA
419 Barrow, Suite A
Anchorage, AK 99501
  Myra Hollibaugh,
  Executive Director
  (907) 279-6501

ARIZONA

CONSUMER CREDIT
  COUNSELING SERVICE
  OF ARIZONA
3056 N. 33rd Avenue
Phoenix, AZ 85017
  John A. Erickson,
  Executive Director
  (602) 233-0132

Branch Office:
CCCS OF ARIZONA
  (LUKE AIR FORCE BASE)
(Appointments made by
  Base personnel; Miliary & Base
  civilians only, 1 day per week)
(602) 856-6791

TUCSON FAMILY DEBT
  COUNSELORS
5834 East Speedway
Tucson, Arizona 85712
  Raul Lopez,
    Executive Director
  (602) 747-7850

Branch Office:
  TUCSON FAMILY DEBT
  COUNSELORS
  (SOUTH TUCSON)
  (602) 882-9966

ARKANSAS

FAMILY SERVICE AGENCY
  CONSUMER CREDIT
  COUNSELING SERVICE
P.O. Box 500
North Little Rock, AR 72115
  Paul E. Blackstone, ACSW,
  Executive Director
  (510) 758-1881

CALIFORNIA

CONSUMER CREDIT
COUNSELORS
ASSOCIATION OF
CALIFORNIA
(State Administrative Office)
31 Geary Street
San Francisco, CA 94108
Frank Sperling,
President
(415) 552-8320 or 552-0665

CONSUMER CREDIT
COUNSELORS
OF KERN COUNTY
1706 Chester Avenue, Suite 320
Bakersfield, CA 93301
Nancy Johnson,
Executive Director
(805) 324-9628

CONSUMER CREDIT
COUNSELORS
OF FRESNO, INC.
2135 Fresno Street, Room 210
Fresno, CA 93721
Ray Willingham,
Executive Manager
(209) 233-6221

CONSUMER CREDIT
COUNSELORS
OF LOS ANGELES
1300 West Olympic, Room 304
Los Angeles, CA 90015
Donna Fong,
Executive Director
(213) 386-7601

Branch Offices:
Baldwin Park, CA
Canoga Park, CA
Gardena, CA
Inglewood, CA
Lakewood, CA
Lancaster, CA
Pasadena, CA
Redondo Beach, CA
(Schedule appointments through
Los Angeles office)
(213) 386-7601

CONSUMER CREDIT
COUNSELORS
TWIN CITIES
729 "D" Street
Marysville, CA 95901
Rodney N. Kennedy,
Executive Director
(916) 743-1785

CONSUMER CREDIT
COUNSELORS
OF EAST BAY (OAKLAND)
1212 Broadway, Suite 706
Oakland, CA 94612
R. F. Happ,
Manager
(415) 832-7555

Branch Offices:
Martinez, CA
Vallejo, CA
(Schedule appointments through
Oakland office)
(415) 832-7555

CALIFORNIA (Continued)

CONSUMER CREDIT
  COUNSELORS OF
  THE NORTH VALLEY
1670 Market Street
#118 Downtown Mall
P.O. Box 4044
Redding, CA 96001
  Phyllis Solberg,
  Manager
  (916) 244-9626

CONSUMER CREDIT
  COUNSELORS OF
  INLAND EMPIRE
3679 Arlington Avenue, Suite E
Riverside, CA 92506
  Anthony Fostier,
  Executive Director
  (714) 781-0114

CONSUMER CREDIT
  COUNSELORS OF
  SACRAMENTO, INC.
1815 "J" Street
Sacramento, CA 95814
  Lee A. Sweet, CCCE,
  Executive Vice
  President/Manager
  (916) 444-0740

Branch Office:
Fairfield, CA
(916) 444-0740

CONSUMER CREDIT
  COUNSELORS
  OF SAN DIEGO
861 Sixth Avenue, Room 403
P.O. Box 2131
San Diego, CA 92112
  Robert R. Osborn,
  Executive Director
  (619) 234-4118

CONSUMER CREDIT
  COUNSELORS OF
  SAN FRANCISCO AND
  THE PENINSULA
1275 Market Street, Lobby
San Francisco, CA 94103
  Kathy Pietruszewski,
  Manager
  (415) 431-0510

Branch Office:
Santa Rosa, CA
JoAnn Mithchell,
Manager
(707) 527-9221

CONSUMER CREDIT
  COUNSELORS OF
  ORANGE COUNTY, INC.
1616 E. Fourth Street, Suite 130
Santa Ana, CA 92701-5189
  Carl Lindquist,
  President
  (714) 547-8281

CALIFORNIA (Continued)

CONSUMER CREDIT
  COUNSELORS
  OF SANTA CLARA
  VALLEY, INC.
1825 De La Cruz Boulevard,
Suite 8
Santa Clara, CA 95050
  Marilynn Thain,
  Executive Director
  (408) 988-7881

CONSUMER CREDIT
  COUNSELORS OF
  STOCKTON
1325 N. Center Street, Suite 2
Stockton, CA 95202
  Irene Freeman,
  Executive Manager
  (209) 464-8319

CONSUMER CREDIT
  COUNSELORS OF
  VENTURA COUNTY
3445 Telegraph Road, Suite 105
Ventura, CA 93003
  Marlene Weatherly,
  Executive Director
  (805) 644-1500

Branch Offices:
San Luis Obispo, CA
Santa Barbara, CA
Thousand Oaks, CA
(Schedule appointments through
Ventura Office)
(805) 644-1500

COLORADO

CONSUMER CREDIT
  COUNSELING SERVICE
  OF GREATER DENVER, INC.
P.O. Box 22557, #1072
5250 Leetsdale Drive
Denver, CO 80222
  Larry Smith,
  President
  (303) 321-8988

CONNECTICUT

CONSUMER CREDIT
  COUNSELING SERVICE
  OF CONNECTICUT
36 Woodland Streeet
Hartford, CT 06105
  Beverly Tuttle,
  Executive Director
  (203) 247-9517

Branch Offices:
U.S. Submarine Base, Groton, CT
  (203) 449-3383
New Haven, CT
  (203) 247-9517

DELAWARE

No Service Reported

DISTRICT OF COLUMBIA

CONSUMER CREDIT
COUNSELING AND
EDUCATIONAL SERVICE
OF GREATER
WASHINGTON, INC.
(Branch Office of CCC & ES,
Rockville, MD)
1120 G Street, N.W. Suite 175B
Washington, D.C. 20005
James Sengstack,
Branch Director
(202) 638-6996

FLORIDA

FAMILY COUNSELING
SERVICE
(CCCS Division)
1639 Atlantic Boulevard, Suite 101
Jacksonville, FL 32207
Richard J. McCulloch,
Executive Director
(904) 396-4846

CONSUMER CREDIT
COUNSELING SERVICE
OF PINELLAS COUNTY, INC.
801 W. Bay Drive, Suite 313
S.E. Bank Building
Largo, FL 33540
Patricia Nurse,
Executive Director
(813) 585-0099

CONSUMER CREDIT
COUNSELING SERVICE
OF SOUTH FLORIDA, INC.
1190 N.E. 125th Street, Suite 11
North Miami, FL 33161
Andrew J. McGehee,
Executive Director
(305) 893-0731

Branch Offices:
Cutler Ridge, FL
Toni Langston, Manager
(305) 233-2480
Fort Lauderdale, FL
Sue Kahn, Manager
(305) 765-0502

CONSUMER CREDIT
COUNSELING SERVICE
OF CENTRAL FLORIDA, INC.
1900 N. Mills Avenue, #5
Orlando, FL 32803
George C. Reed,
Executive Director
(305) 896-2463

Branch Offices:
Lakeland, FL
(813) 686-6171
Seminole County, FL
Patricia Capsanes,
Manager/Counselor
(305) 339-6111
Volusia County, Florida
Edward Dolne,
Manager/Counselor
(904) 253-0563

FLORIDA (Continued)

CONSUMER CREDIT
  COUNSELING SERVICE
  OF WEST FLORIDA, INC.
Suite 335, Brent Building
3 West Garden Street
P.O. Box 943
Pensacola, FL 32594
  H. Ed Turner,
  Treasurer
  (904) 434-0268

CONSUMER CREDIT
  COUNSELING SERVICE
  OF BREVARD
Division of Family
  Counseling Center
220 Coral Sands Drive, Suite 1
P.O. Box 63
Rockledge, FL 32955
  Robert A. Caldwell, ACSW
  Executive Director
  Sidney T. Brooks,
  Manager
  (305) 632-5792

CONSUMER CREDIT
  COUNSELING SERVICE OF
  THE TAMPA BAY AREA,
INC.
730 S. Sterling Avenue, Suite 300
Mailing Address:
P.O. Box 18835
Tampa, FL 33679-8835
  John C. McLaughlin,
  President and
  Chief Operating Officer
  (813) 876-2749

CONSUMER CREDIT
  COUNSELING SERVICE OF
  PALM BEACH COUNTY, INC.
224 Datura Street, Suite 205
West Palm Beach, FL 33401
  Dorothy G. Kunze,
  Executive Director
  (305) 655-0885

Branch Offices:
Boca Raton East, FL
  (305) 391-2402
Boca Raton West, FL
  (305) 482-0269
Port St. Lucie, FL
  (305) 878-8000

GEORGIA

CONSUMER CREDIT
  COUNSELING SERVICE OF
  GREATER ATLANTA, INC.
100 Edgewood Avenue,
  N.E. Suite 810
Atlanta, GA 30303
  Fred R. Tonney,
  President
  (404) 659-4391

Branch Office:
Cobb County, GA
James O. Wood, Jr.,
  Senior Counselor
  (404) 422-5291

GEORGIA (Continued)

CONSUMER CREDIT
COUNSELING SERVICE OF
MIDDLE GEORGIA, INC.
654 First Street, Suite 5
P. O. Box 31
Macon, GA 31202
William P. Boisclair,
Executive Director
(912) 745-6197

CONSUMER CREDIT
COUNSELING SERVICE OF
THE SAVANNAH AREA, INC.
15 East Montgomery Crossroads
Suites A and B
Savannah, GA 31499
W. Otis Beasley,
Executive Director
(912) 927-HELP

HAWAII

CONSUMER CREDIT
COUNSELING SERVICE
OF HAWAII
1125 N. King Street, Suite 204
Honolulu, HI 96817
Peggy Young,
Director
(808) 841-7516

IDAHO

CONSUMER CREDIT
COUNSELING SERVICE
OF IDAHO, INC.
P.O. Box 9264
6068 Emerald
Boise, ID 83703
B. Jan Brockett,
Executive Director
(208) 375-8140

Branch Offices:
Nampa, ID
(208) 467-2927
Twin Falls, ID
(208) 733-0586

CONSUMER CREDIT
COUNSELING SERVICE OF
NORTHERN IDAHO, INC.
307 Weisburger Building
Lewiston, ID 83501
Lydia Hosmer,
Director
(208) 746-0127

CONSUMER CREDIT
COUNSELING SERVICE
OF SOUTHEASTERN
IDAHO, INC.
P.O. Box 112
343 W. Lewis
Pocatello, ID 83204-0112
Lola Harmison,
Executive Director
(208) 233-7640

ILLINOIS

FAMILY COUNSELING
  SERVICE
122 W. Downer Place
Aurora, IL 60506
  Karl Flodstrom,
  Director
  (312) 844-6820

FAMILY COUNSELING
  CENTER
201 E. Grove, Suite 200
Bloomington, Illinois 61701
  Jo Stephen Major,
  Executive Director
  (309) 828-4343

UNITED CHARITIES
  OF CHICAGO
14 E. Jackson Boulevard
Chicago, IL 60604
  Sue Pape,
  Director of Family Service
  (312) 461-0800

Branch Offices:
Calumet Family Center, IL
(312) 264-3010
Loop Family Center, IL
(312) 939-1300
Parkside Family Center, IL
(312) 282-9535

Family and Mental
  Health Services
  of Southwest Cook County, IL
(312) 448-5700

FAMILY SERVICE
  ASSOCIATION OF
  GREATER ELGIN AREA
Financial Counseling Service
22 S. Spring Street
Elgin, IL 60120
  Catherine M. Williams,
  Program Director
  (312) 695-3680

CENTRAL ILLINOIS CREDIT
  COUNSELING SERVICE, INC.
505 First National Bank Building
Peoria, IL 61602
  James P. Carr,
  Executive Director
  (309) 676-2941

CONSUMER CREDIT
  COUNSELING SERVICE
  OF SPRINGFIELD
1021 S. Fourth Street
Springfield, IL 62703
  Ron Peters,
  Director
  (217) 523-3621

FAMILY SERVICE
  ASSOCIATION OF DUPAGE
  COUNTY - BUDGET
  COUNSELING/DEBT
  MANAGEMENT
402 W. Liberty Drive
Wheaton, IL 60187
  Ferdinand O. Pauls,
  Director
  (312) 682-1802

ILLINOIS (Continued)

CONSUMER CREDIT
    COUNSELING SERVICE
    OF McHENRY COUNTY, INC.
P.O. Box 746
Woodstock, IL 60098
    Don Price,
    Executive Director
    (815) 338-5757

INDIANA

CONSUMER CREDIT
    COUNSELING SERVICE
    OF TRI-STATE, INC.
715 First Avenue, Suite 37
P.O. Box 4783
Evansville, IN 47711
    Connie O. Russell,
    Executive Director
    (812) 422-1108

CONSUMER CREDIT
    COUNSELING SERVICE OF
    NORTHEASTERN INDIANA
345 W. Wayne Street
P.O. Box 11403
Fort Wayne, IN 46858
    Thomas E. Hufford,
    Executive Director
    (219) 422-3806

Branch Office:
    Warsaw, IN
    (Appointments on Tuesdays)
    (800) 552-3650 (In Indiana)
    (219) 422-3806 (All Others)

CONSUMER CREDIT
    COUNSELING SERVICE OF
    NORTHWEST INDIANA, INC.
3660 Grant Street, Suite 5
Gary, IN 46408
    Barbara L. Bibb,
    Executive Director
    (219) 980-4800

CONSUMER CREDIT
    COUNSELING SERVICE OF
    CENTRAL INDIANA, INC.
615 N. Alabama Street
Indianapolis, IN 46204
    Clyde Green,
    Executive Director
    (317) 632-4501

Branch Office:
Muncie, IN
(317) 632-4501
(800) 382-2227 (Indiana Only)

FAMILY & CHILDREN'S
    CENTER, INC.
CCCS Division
1411 Lincoln Way West
Mishawaka, IN 46544
    Mary Bryant,
    Program Manager
    (219) 259-5666

IOWA

FINANCIAL MANAGEMENT
   SERVICE
(Family Service Agency)
400 Third Avenue, S.E.
Cedar Rapids, IA 52401-1623
   Scott Shook,
   Executive Director
   (319) 398-3574

CONSUMER CREDIT
   COUNSELING SERVICE
A.I.D. Center
206 6th Street
Sioux City, IA 51101
   Mike Ford,
   Counselor
   (712) 252-1861

KANSAS

CONSUMER CREDIT
   COUNSELING
   SERVICE, INC.
227 N. Sante Fe, #207
Salina, KS 67401
   Ruth Self,
   Counselor
   (913) 827-6731

TOPEKA HOUSING
   INFORMATION CENTER
Consumer Credit
   Counseling Services
1195 S.W. Buchanan, Suite 203
Topeka, KS 66604
   Karen Hiller,
   Executive Director
   Roberta Lindburg,
   Program Director
   (913) 234-0217

KENTUCKY

No Service Reported

LOUISIANA

CONSUMER CREDIT
   COUNSELING SERVICE
   OF GREATER NEW
   ORLEANS, INC.
1539 Jackson Avenue, Room 201
New Orleans, LA 70130
   Vern Svendson,
   President and
   Chief Executive Officer
   (504) 529-2396

MAINE

CREDIT COUNSELING
CENTERS, INC.
175 Lancaster Street
P.O. Box 1021
Portland, ME 04101
G. D. (Rick) Dobson, Jr.
Executive Director
(207) 774-6278
(800) 882-CCCS

Branch Office:
Bangor, ME
William Gradie, Manager
(800) 882-CCCS

MARYLAND

CONSUMER CREDIT
COUNSELING SERVICE
OF MARYLAND, INC.
Bradford Federal Building,
2nd Floor
Fayette Street & Luzerne Avenue
Baltimore, MD 21224
Victor L. Boehm,
President
(301) 732-3604

Branch Offices:
Bel Air, MD
Matthew A. Keller, Manager
(301) 838-6112
Hagerstown, MD
John Cable, Manager
(301) 733-5810
Laurel, MD
Joan Wolter, Manager
(301) 498-9400
Salisbury, MD
Wayne Ensor, Manager
(301) 742-4422

CONSUMER CREDIT
COUNSELING SERVICE
OF SOUTHEAST
MARYLAND, INC.
9418 Annapolis Road
Lanham, MD 20706
Laurine C. Gibson,
Executive Director
(301) 459-8766

Branch Office:
Temple Hills, MD
Joan P. Kelly, Manager
(301) 423-6902

CONSUMER CREDIT
COUNSELING AND
EDUCATIONAL SERVICE
OF GREATER
WASHINGTON, INC.
11426 Rockville Pike
Suite 105
Rockville, MD 20852
Joanne Kerstetter,
Executive Director
(301) 231-5833

MASSACHUSETTS

CONSUMER CREDIT
COUNSELING SERVICE
OF EASTERN
MASSACHUSETTS, INC.
8 Winter Street, Suite 1210
Boston, MA 02108
Mel R. Stiller,
Executive Director
(617) 426-6644

Branch Offices:
Brockton, MA
(617) 426-6644
Worcester, MA
(617) 795-1444

PIONEER VALLEY CONSUMER
CREDIT COUNSELING
SERVICE, INC.
293 Bridge Street, Suite 221
P.O. Box 171
Springfield, MA 01101
Robin Walker,
Executive Director
(413) 788-6106

Branch Offices:
Northampton, MA
Southbridge, MA
(Schedule appointments through
Springfield office)
(413) 788-6106

MICHIGAN

No Service Reported

MINNESOTA

FAMILY SERVICE OF
DULUTH, INC.
600 Ordean Building
424 W. Superior Street
Duluth, MN 55802
Elizabeth George,
Program Coordinator
(218) 726-4826

CONSUMER CREDIT
COUNSELING SERVICE
OF MINNESOTA, INC.
600 1st Avenue, N., Suite 790
Minneapolis, MN 55403
Wayne B. Wensley,
President
(612) 339-1485

Branch Office:
St. Paul, MN
(612) 293-9197

MISSISSIPPI

No Service Reported

MISSOURI

CONSUMER CREDIT
COUNSELING SERVICE
OF GREATER
KANSAS CITY, INC.
3435 Broadway, Suite 203
Kansas City, MO 64111
Jerry W. Lewis,
Executive Director
(816) 753-0535

CONSUMER CREDIT
COUNSELING SERVICE
OF METROPOLITAN
ST. LOUIS, INC.
3833 Gravois
St. Louis, MO 63116
Virginia M. Nagel,
Executive Vice President
and Director
(314) 773-3660

Branch Office:
St. Charles, MO
Carol Bello,
Counselor
(314) 773-3660

SPRINGFIELD AREA FAMILY
DEBT COUNSELORS
950 St. Louis Street
Springfield, MO 65806
Wendell T. Gregory,
Director
(417) 862-5139

MONTANA

CONSUMER CREDIT
COUNSELING SERVICE
OF BILLINGS, MONTANA
2160 Central, Suite #4
Billings, MT 59102
Kathy Ruegamer,
Manager
(406) 656-3172

CONSUMER CREDIT
COUNSELING SERVICE
OF GALLATIN VALLEY, INC.
Martel Financial Center
220 W. Lamme, Suite C
Bozeman, MT 59715
Marsha Brann,
Executive Director
(406) 586-7653 (message only)
(406) 586-2328

CONSUMER CREDIT
COUNSELING SERVICE
OF CASCADE COUNTY
600 6th Street, N.W., #8
P.O. Box 2343
Great Falls, MT 59403
Duane Delphy,
Manager
(406) 761-8721

NEBRASKA

CONSUMER CREDIT
  COUNSELING SERVICE
  OF NEBRASKA, INC.
P.O. Box 31002
Omaha, NE 68131
  Donald A. Leu, Jr.,
  President
  (402) 345-3110

Branch Office:
Lincoln, NE
Sheree Atwood,
Manager
(402) 474-6127

NEVADA

CONSUMER CREDIT
  COUNSELING SERVICE
  OF LAS VEGAS
3305 Spring Mountain Road,
  Suite 60
Las Vegas, NV 89102
  Melanie Crews,
  Executive Secretary
  (702) 364-0344

NEW HAMPSHIRE

FAMILY FINANCIAL
  COUNSELING SERVICE
Administrative Office
8 Union Street
P.O. Box 676
Concord, NH 03301
  Patricia Muzzey,
  Executive Director
  (603) 224-6593

Branch Offices:
Keene, NH
Laconia, NH
Manchester, NH
Nashua, NH
Peterborough, NH
  (Schedule appointments
  throughConcord office)
  (800) 852-3385

NEW JERSEY

CONSUMER CREDIT
  COUNSELING SERVICE
  OF NEW JERSEY, INC.
76 Mount Kemble Avenue
Morristown, NJ 07960
Mailing Address:
P.O. Box 97C
Convent Station, NJ 07961
  Ruth K. Volger,
  Executive Director
  (201) 267-4324

Branch Office:
Newark, NJ
(201) 267-4324

NEW MEXICO

CONSUMER CREDIT
  COUNSELING SERVICE
  OF ALBUQUERQUE, INC.
5318 Menaul, N.E.
Albuquerque, NM 87110-3195
  Helen Casey,
  Executive Director
  (505) 884-6601

NEW YORK

CONSUMER CREDIT
  COUNSELING SERVICE
  OF BUFFALO, INC.
730 Convention Tower
43 Court Street
Buffalo, NY 14202
  John Y. Pax,
  Executive Director
  (716) 854-1710

FAMILY SERVICE
  ASSOCIATION OF
  NASSAU COUNTY
129 Jackson Street
Hempstead, NY 11550
  Lawrence Gumbs,
  Director of Family
  Financial Counseling
  (516) 485-4600

BUDGET & CREDIT
  COUNSELING
  SERVICES, INC.
44 E. 23rd Street, Suite 304
New York, NY 10010
  Luther R. Gatling,
  President
  (212) 677-3066

CONSUMER CREDIT
  COUNSELING SERVICE
  OF ROCHESTER, INC.
50 Chestnut Plaza, Suite 410
Rochester, NY 14604
  Charles Foster,
  Executive Director
  (716) 546-3440

CONSUMER CREDIT
  COUNSELING SERVICE OF
  CENTRAL NEW YORK, INC.
351 S. Warren Street, #304
Syracuse, NY 13202
  Sharon Patchett,
  Executive Director
  (315) 474-6026

Branch Offices:
Binghamton, NY
  (607) 722-1251
Cortland, NY
  (607) 753-9301
Fulton, NY
  (315) 598-3980

Griffis Air Force Base, NY
(315) 330-1110, X3121
Utica, NY
  Patricia Manley,
  Counselor
  (315) 797-5366

NORTH CAROLINA

CONSUMER CREDIT
COUNSELING SERVICE
OF WESTERN NORTH
CAROLINA, INC.
50 S. French Broad
Plateau Building
P.O. Box 2192
Asheville, NC 28802
Lee Dawes,
Executive Director
(704) 255-5166

CONSUMER CREDIT
COUNSELING SERVICE
(A division of United
Family Services)
301 S. Brevard Street
Charlotte, NC 28202
William M. Pickens,
Division Director
(704) 332-4191

Branch Office:
Union County, NC
(704) 283-1539

CONSUMER CREDIT
COUNSELING SERVICE
OF FAYETTEVILLE
118 Gillespie Street
P.O. Box 272
Fayetteville, NC 28302
Kenneth G. Smith,
Executive Director
(919) 323-3192

FAMILY COUNSELING
SERVICE, INC. OF
GASTON COUNTY
318 South Street
Gastonia, NC 28052
Phil DeLuca,
Acting Director
(704) 864-7704

CONSUMER CREDIT
COUNSELING SERVICE
(A division of Family and
Children's Services of
Greater Greensboro, Inc.)
1301 N. Elm Street
Greensboro, NC 27401
M. Edward Roach,
Program Director
(919) 373-1511

CONSUMER CREDIT
COUNSELING SERVICE
#17 Highway 64-70, S.E.
Hickory, NC 28601
Floyd J. Tucker,
Program Director
(704) 322-7161

CONSUMER CREDIT
COUNSELING
(A division of Family Services
of Wake County, Inc.)
3803 Computer Drive, Suite 101A
Raleigh, NC 27609
DeFrancia L. Scott,
Director
(919) 781-9307

NORTH CAROLINA (Continued)

CONSUMER CREDIT
  COUNSELING SERVICE
  FAMILY SERVICES
2841 Carolina Beach Road
P.O. Box 944
Wilmington, NC 28402
  Teresa Morgan,
  Counselor
  (919) 392-7051

CONSUMER CREDIT
  COUNSELING SERVICE
  OF FORSYTH COUNTY, INC.
440 First Union National
  Bank Building
Winston-Salem, NC 27101
  Z. Gray Jackson,
  Executive Director
  (919) 725-1958

NORTH DAKOTA

THE VILLAGE FAMILY
  SERVICE CENTER
1721 S. University Drive
Fargo, ND 58103
  Mark Carman, CCC,
  Director
  (701) 235-3328

Branch Offices:
Bismarck, ND
  Susan Wefald, Counselor
  (701) 255-3328
Grand Forks, ND
Sig Meier, Counselor
  (701) 746-4584
Minot, ND
Jim Bailey, Counselor
  (701) 852-3328
Williston, ND
  Jan Holmen, Counselor
  (800) 732-4475

OHIO

FAMILY SERVICES OF SUMMIT
  COUNTY CCCS DIVISION
212 E. Exchange Street
Akron, OH 44304

Robert P. Labbe, ACSW
  Executive Director
Sue Lillis,
Director, CCCS
(216) 376-9494
(216) 376-9351 - TTY for Deaf

CONSUMER CREDIT
  COUNSELING SERVICE
  OF STARK COUNTY, INC.
618 Second Street, N.W.
Canton, OH 44703
  Suzanne DeHoff,
  Executive Director
  (216) 455-8118

OHIO (Continued)

FAMILY CREDIT COUNSELING
  SERVICE
(A Division of Family Service of
  the Cincinnati Area)
205 West 4th Street
Cincinnati, OH 45202
  Bernard Kaiser,
  Program Director
  (513) 381-6300

CONSUMER CREDIT
  COUNSELING SERVICE
  OF NORTHEASTERN OHIO
423 Euclid Avenue
Cleveland, OH 44114
  William De Vries,
  President/Director
  (216) 781-8624 (in Cleveland)
  (800) 621-8261 (all others)

Branch Offices:
Cuyahoga County, OH
Geauga County, OH
Lake County, OH
Loraine County, OH
  (Schedule all appointments
  through Cleveland Office)
  (800) 621-8261

CONSUMER CREDIT
  COUNSELING SERVICE
  OF CENTRAL OHIO, INC.
697 Broad Street
Columbus, OH 43215
  Paul B. Eberts,
  President/Executive Director
  (614) 464-2227

Branch Offices:
Chillicothe, OH
  (614) 464-2227
Delaware, OH
  (614) 464-2227
Lancaster, OH
  (614) 464-2227
Mansfield, OH
  (419) 524-0733
Marion, OH
  (614) 464-2227

LUTHERAN SOCIAL SERVICES
CCCS Department
P.O. Box 506
3304 N. Main Street
Dayton, OH 45405
  Robert F. Libecap,
  Program Manger
  (513) 278-9617

Branch Office:
Sidney, OH
  (513) 492-1953

CONSUMER CREDIT
  COUNSELING SERVICE
  FAMILY SERVICE OF
  BUTLER COUNTY
111 Buckeye Street
Hamilton, OH 45011
  Irma Sandage,
  Executive Director
  (513) 868-9220

CONSUMER CREDIT
  COUNSELING SERVICE
  OF PORTAGE COUNTY
302 North Depeyster
Kent, OH 44240
  Mary Sites,
  Coordinator
  (216) 678-4782

OHIO (Continued)

CONSUMER CREDIT
  COUNSELING SERVICE
  OF COLUMBIANA COUNTY
964 N. Market Street
P.O. Box 413
Lisbon, OH 44432
  John A. Hudak,
  Executive Director
  (216) 424-9509

CONSUMER CREDIT
  COUNSELING SERVICE
  FAMILY COUNSELING
  SERVICE
126 W. Church Street
Newark, OH 43055
  Dorothy Higgins,
  Program Manager
  (614) 349-7051

Branch Office:
Mt. Vernon, OH
(614) 349-7066

CHILDREN'S AND FAMILY
  SERVICE ASSOCIATION
  CCCS OF THE UPPER
  OHIO VALLEY
(Branch of Children's and
  Family Service Association,
  Wheeling, West Virginia)
Steubenville, OH
  Lonnie Williams,
  Executive Vice President
  (614) 283-4763

CONSUMER CREDIT
  COUNSELING PROGRAM
1704 North Road, S.E.
Heaton Square
Warren, OH 44484
  Nancy Gray, Coordinator
  (216) 856-2907

CHILDREN'S & FAMILY
  SERVICE CCCS DIVISION
535 Marmion Avenue
Youngstown, OH 44502
  Kathy Virgallito,
  Program Director
  (216) 782-5664

CONSUMER CREDIT
  COUNSELING SERVICE
  OF MUSKINGUM VALLEY
721 Market Street
Zanesville, OH 43701
  Rebecca Donne,
  Executive Director
  Rebecca Bee,
  Program Manager
  (614) 454-6872

Branch Office:
New Lexington, OH
(614) 342-1063

OKLAHOMA

CONSUMER CREDIT
COUNSELING SERVICE OF
CENTRAL OKLAHOMA, INC.
2519 Northwest 23rd
P.O. Box 75405
Oklahoma City, OK 73147
Gloria E. Kelley,
Executive Director
(405) 947-6631

CREDIT COUNSELING
CENTERS OF
OKLAHOMA, INC.
2140 South Harvard
P.O. Box 4450
Tulsa, OK 74159
Victor R. Schock,
Director
(918) 744-5611

OREGON

CONSUMER CREDIT
COUNSELING SERVICE
OF LINN-BENTON, INC.
201 West First
P.O. Box 1006
Albany, OR 97321
Jan Amling,
Executive Director
(503) 926-5843

CONSUMER CREDIT
COUNSELING SERVICE
OF CENTRAL OREGON, INC.
2115 N.E. Division, Suite A
Bend, OR 97701-3599
Dee Foss,
Executive Director
(503) 389-6181

CONSUMER CREDIT
COUNSELING SERVICE
OF LANE COUNTY, INC.
1601 - B, Oak Street
Eugene, OR 97401
Evelyn L. Smith,
Executive Director
(503) 342-4459

CONSUMER CREDIT
COUNSELING SERVICE
OF SOUTHERN
OREGON, INC.
33 N. Central, #300
Medford, OR 97501
Jan Safely,
Office Manager
(503) 779-2273

Branch Office:
Klamath Falls, OR
(503) 884-5193

COOS-CURRY CONSUMER
CREDIT COUNSELING
SERVICE
Pony Village Mall
North Bend, OR 97459
Deborah L. Graham,
Executive Director
(503) 756-4008

OREGON (Continued)

CONSUMER CREDIT
COUNSELING SERVICE
OF OREGON, INC.
3420 S.E. Powell Boulevard
P.O. Box 42155
Portland, OR 97242
    Lawrence Winthrop,
    President
    (503) 232-8139

DOUGLAS CONSUMER CREDIT
COUNSELING SERVICE
P.O. Box 1011
Roseburg, OR 97470
    Jan Phelps,
    Executive Director
    (503) 673-3104

CONSUMER CREDIT
COUNSELING SERVICE
OF MID-WILLIAMETTE
VALLEY, INC.
665 Cottage, N.E.
Salem, OR 97301
    Frank Lackey,
    Executive Director
    (503) 581-7301

PENNSYLVANIA

CONSUMER CREDIT
COUNSELING SERVICE
OF LEHIGH VALLEY, INC.
1031 Linden Street
Allentown, PA 18102
    Albert J. Kotch,
    Executive Director
    (215) 821-4011

Branch Office:
Reading, PA
Slate Belt Medical Center, PA
(Schedule appointments through
Allentown Office)
(215) 821-4011

CONSUMER CREDIT
COUNSELING DIVISION
FAMILY SERVICES
110 W. 10th Street, Room 208
Erie, PA 16501
    David C. Shiel,
    ACSW
    (814) 454-6478

CONSUMER CREDIT
COUNSELING SERVICE
OF DELAWARE VALLEY
(Also serving southern New Jersey
and Delaware)
1211 Chestnut Street, Suite 411
Philadelphia, PA 19107
    Thomas A. O'Neill,
    Executive Director
    (215) 563-5665 or 563-5694

Branch Office:
West Chester, PA
(215) 563-5665

CONSUMER CREDIT
COUNSELING SERVICE
OF WESTERN
PENNSYLVANIA, INC.
309 Smithfield Street, Suite 5000
Pittsburgh, PA 15222
    Carl J. Eidenmuller,
    President
    (412) 471-7584

PENNSYLVANIA (Continued)

Branch Offices:
Blair County, PA
Diane Karikas,
Counselor
(814) 696-3546
Greensburg, PA
Edward Graszl,
Counselor
(412) 838-1290
New Castle, PA
Mary Ellen Sotus,
Counselor
(412) 652-8074

CONSUMER CREDIT
COUNSELING SERVICE
OF NORTHEASTERN
PENNSYLVANIA, INC.
402 Connell Building
P.O. Box 168
Scranton, PA 18501
Michael A. Elick,
Executive Director
(717) 342-1072 or 655-9527

RHODE ISLAND

CONSUMER CREDIT
COUNSELING DIVISION
RHODE ISLAND
CONSUMERS' COUNCIL
365 Broadway
Providence, RI 02909
Paul F. McHale,
Administrator
(401) 277-2764

SOUTH CAROLINA

CONSUMER CREDIT
COUNSELING SERVICE
OF GREATER
CHARLESTON, S.C.
3005 W. Montague, Suite C
Charleston, SC 29418
Donald Buckland,
Director
(803) 747-3616

FAMILY SERVICE CENTER
1800 Main Street
P.O. Box 7876
Columbia, SC 29202
L. Russell Rawls, Jr.,
Executive Dirctor
M. Susie Irvine,
Coordinator, CCCS
(803) 733-5450

Branch Office:
ACS Fort Jackson, SC
William M. Meares, Counselor
(803) 751-5256

FAMILY SERVICE
GREENVILLE
844 E. Washington Street
P.O. Box 10306, Federal Station
Greenville, SC 29603
Amelia K. Croft, ACSW
Executive Director
(803) 232-2434 or 232-6266

SOUTH DAKOTA

CONSUMER CREDIT
  COUNSELING SERVICE
  OF THE BLACK HILLS
P.O. Box 14
7th and Kansas City Streets
Rapid City, SD 57709
  Flo A. Brenton,
  Director
  (605) 348-4550

LUTHERAN SOCIAL SERVICES
  OF SOUTH DAKOTA
CCCS Division
600 W. 12th Street
Sioux Falls, SD 57104
  Judy Reinke,
  Program Director
  (605) 336-3387

TENNESSEE

FAMILY & CHILDREN'S
  SERVICES OF
  CHATTANOOGA
CCCS Division
323 High Street
Chattanooga, TN 37403
  Sharon Cabeen,
  Supervisor
  (615) 755-2860

CONSUMER CREDIT
  COUNSELING SERVICE OF
  GREATER KNOXVILLE, INC.
Suite 200, 705 Broadway
P.O. Box 3343
Knoxville, TN 37927-3343
  Sue L. Brown,
  Director
  (615) 522-2661 or 522-7151

CONSUMER CREDIT
  COUNSELING SERVICE
  OF METROPOLITAN
  NASHVILLE, INC.
250 Venture Circle, Suite 205
Nashville, TN 37228-1604
  Marvin N. Wright,
  Executive Director
  (615) 244-5184 or 244-5185

TEXAS

CHILD AND FAMILY SERVICE
  CCCS Division
2001 Chicon Street
Austin, TX 78722
  Bob Bowman,
  Executive Director
  Lonnie Williams,
  CCCS Division Director
  (512) 478-1648

MONEY MANAGEMENT
  COUNSELING & SERVICES
1721 S. Brownlee Boulevard
Corpus Christi, TX 78404
  David C. Melton,
  Executive Director
  (512) 882-1791

TEXAS (Continued)

CONSUMER CREDIT
COUNSELING SERVICE
OF GREATER DALLAS, INC.
5415 Maple Avenue, Suite 205
Dallas, TX 75235-7490
David H. Dugan,
Executive Director
(214) 634-1560

Branch Office:
Richardson, TX
Nancy Fernandez,
Counselor
(214) 437-6252

CONSUMER CREDIT
COUNSELING SERVICE
Y.W.C.A.
1600 N. Brown Street
El Paso, TX 79902
Darlene Gade,
Executive Director
(915) 533-7475 X42

CONSUMER CREDIT
COUNSELING SERVICE
OF GREATER
FORT WORTH, INC.
807 Texas Street, Suite 104
Fort Worth, TX 76102
Warren E. Coggins,
Executive Director
(817) 334-0151

CONSUMER CREDIT
COUNSELING SERVICE OF
HOUSTON AND THE
GULF COAST AREA, INC.
4203 Fannin Street
Houston, TX 77004
Terry M. Blaney,
President
(713) 520-0742

Branch Offices:
Fannin, TX
Jean Law, Director
(713) 520-0742
Fort Bend County, TX
Bayla Abrams, Director
(713) 520-0742 or 499-5681
Montgomery County, TX
Louise Rochford, Director
(713) 520-0742 or 363-4364
Pasadena, TX
Nancy Koretz, Director
(713) 520-0742

CONSUMER CREDIT
COUNSELING OF NORTH
CENTRAL TEXAS, INC.
1006 W. University Drive
McKinney, TX 75069
Pamela Gray,
Executive Director
(214) 542-0257

Branch Offices:
Denton, TX
(817) 382-0331
Greenville, TX
(214) 455-3987
Plano, TX
(214) 542-0257
Sherman, TX
(214) 892-6927

TEXAS (Continued)

CONSUMER CREDIT
COUNSELING SERVICE
OF GREATER SAN
ANTONIO, INC.
4203 Woodcock, Suite 251
San Antonio, TX 78228
Ruby Bainum,
Director
(512) 734-8112

UTAH

COMMUNITY CONSUMER
CREDIT COUNSELING
SERVICE OF NORTHERN
UTAH, INC.
295 30th Street, P.O. Box 547
Ogden, Utah 84402
Brent Littlefield,
President
(801) 394-7759

CONSUMER CREDIT
COUNSELING SERVICE
OF UTAH, INC.
220 E. 3900 South, Suite 1
Salt Lake City, UT 84107
Dale G. Taylor,
Executive Director
(801) 266-0064

VERMONT

FAMILY FINANCIAL
COUNSELING SERVICE
(BRATTLEBORO, VT)
(Branch of FFCS, Concord, NH)
(603) 244-6593, call collect

FAMILY FINANCIAL
COUNSELING SERVICE
(BENNINGTON, VT)
(Branch of FFCS, Concord, NH)
(603) 224-6593, call collect

VIRGINIA

CONSUMER CREDIT
COUNSELING AND
EDUCATIONAL SERVICE
OF NORTHERN VIRGINIA
(Branch of CCC & ES OF
GREATERWASHINGTON)
300 Montgomery Street
Alexandria, VA 22314
Marilyn Morgan,
Branch Director
(703) 836-8772

CONSUMER CREDIT
COUNSELING AND
EDUCATIONAL SERVICE
OF NORTHERN VIRGINIA
(Branch of CCC & ES OF
GREATER WASHINGTON)
3541 Chain Bridge Road, Suite 3A
Fairfax, VA 22030
Judy McCoid,
Branch Director
(703) 591-9020

VIRGINIA (Continued)

PENINSULA FAMILY SERVICE
    AND TRAVELLERS AID, INC.
CCCS Division
1520 Aberdeen Road
P.O. Box 7315
Hampton, VA 23666
    Edwin Cotten,
    Executive Director
    (804) 827-8344

Branch Office:
    Williamsburg, VA
    Edwin Cotten,
    Executive Director
    (804) 874-6580

CONSUMER CREDIT
    COUNSELING SERVICE
    OF TIDEWATER
(Division of Family Services)
222 Nineteenth Street West
Norfolk, VA 23517
    Sharon Brooks,
    Program Coordinator
    (804) 622-7017

CONSUMER CREDIT
    COUNSELING SERVICE
    OF VIRGINIA, INC.
6 N. Sixth Street, Suite 200
Richmond, VA 23219
    Robert E. Bryan,
    Executive Director
    (804) 780-9042

Branch Offices:
Fredericksburg, VA
Dale Leite, Manager
(703) 371-7575
Petersburg, VA
Vicki Lynn,
Manager
(804) 862-4300

CONSUMER CREDIT
    COUNSELING SERVICE OF
    ROANOKE VALLEY, INC.
104 W. Campbell Ave.
State and City Building, Suite 703
Roanoke, VA 24011
    Virginia H. Gayle,
    Executive Director
    (703) 342-3724

WASHINGTON

CONSUMER CREDIT
    COUNSELING SERVICE
    OF THE TRI-CITIES
113 W. Kennewick Avenue
P.O. Box 6551
Kennewick, WA 99336
    Thelma Flanagan,
    Executive Director
    (509) 586-2181

CONSUMER CREDIT
    COUNSELING SERVICE
    OF SEATTLE
2326 Sixth Avenue, Suite 206
Seattle, WA 98121
    S. F. Williams,
    President
    (206) 441-3291

WASHINGTON (Continued)

Branch Offices:
Everett, WA
(206) 441-3291
Naval Air Station/Whidby Island
Betty Justus,
Counselor/Area Representative
(206) 679-2545
Oak Harbor, WA
(204) 679-5076

CONSUMER CREDIT
COUNSELING SERVICE
OF TACOMA-PIERCE
11300 Bridgeport Way, S.W.
Suite D
Tacoma, WA 98499
Laura G. Johnson,
Executive Director
(206) 588-1858

CONSUMER CREDIT
COUNSELING SERVICE
OF YAKIMA VALLEY
1218 W. Lincoln
Yakima, WA 98902
Georgia W. Norcott,
Executive Director
(509) 248-5270

WEST VIRGINIA

CONSUMER CREDIT
COUNSELING SERVICE
OF SOUTHERN WEST
VIRGINIA, INC.
Room A-117,
Pinecrest Office Complex
P.O. Box 2129
Beckley, WV 25802
Raymond L. Coleman,
Executive Director
(304) 255-2499

CONSUMER CREDIT
COUNSELING SERVICE
OF THE KANAWHA VALLEY
503 Terminal Building
8 Capitol Street
Charleston, WV 25301
Geraldine Allen,
Manager
(304) 344-3843

CONSUMER CREDIT
COUNSELING SERVICE
OF NORTH CENTRAL
WEST VIRGINIA
CRISS-CROSS, INC.
166 Washington Avenue
P.O. Box 1831
Clarksburg, WV 26302-1831
Edward J. Welp, MSW,
Executive Director
(304) 623-0921

WEST VIRGINIA (Continued)

CONSUMER CREDIT
COUNSELING OF
FAMILY SERVICE, INC.
1007 Fifth Avenue
Huntington, WV 25701
Jane M. Chafin,
Executive Director
(304) 522-4321

CONSUMER CREDIT
COUNSELING SERVICE
OF THE MID-OHIO
VALLEY, INC.
4101/2 Market Street
P.O. Box 454
Parkersburg, WV 26102
June Shelene,
Manager
(304) 485-3141 or 485-6280

CHILDREN AND FAMILY
SERVICE ASSOCIATION
CCCS OF THE UPPER
OHIO VALLEY
51 11th Street
Wheeling, WV 26003
Lonnie Wineman,
Executive Vice President
(304) 232-6733

Branch Office:
CHILDREN AND FAMILY
SERVICE ASSOCIATION
(Steubenville, OH)
Lonnie Wineman,
ExecutiveVice President
(614) 283-4763

WISCONSIN

No Service Reported

WYOMING

No Service Reported

CANADIAN AGENCIES
Affiliated with the National
Foundation for Consumer Credit

CREDIT COUNSELLING
SERVICE OF
METROPOLITAN TORONTO
100 Lombard Street, Suite 301
Toronto, Ontario M5C 1M3
Beulam "Sam" Hastings
Executive Director
(416) 366-5251

For further information on Canadian
counseling locations contact:

THE ONTARIO ASSOCIATION
OF CREDIT COUNSELLING
SERVICE3
297 Lakeshore Road, East, Suite 5
P.O. Box 248
Oakville, Ontario, Canada L6J 5A2
Ronald M. Mason,
Executive Director
(416) 845 2423

FEDERAL TRADE COMMISSION

INDIVIDUAL COMPLAINT FORM - PLEASE PRINT

YOUR NAME	TELEPHONE NUMBER (*Include Area Code*)		
	DAY EVE,		

STREET ADDRESS	CITY	STATE	ZIP CODE

I wish to file a complaint against the company or firm named below. I understand that the Federal Trade Commission does not represent private citizens seeking the return of their money or other personal remedies. I am, however, filing this complaint to notify your office of the activities of this company., I understand that if this matter is not within the scope of the Federal Trade Commission's regulatory activities, it will be referred to another agency, federal, state, or local, if possible.

NAME OF COMPANY COMPLAINED ABOUT

COMPANY ADDRESS	CITY	STATE	ZIP CODE

DATE OF TRANSACTION	TYPE OF PRODUCT	COST OF PRODUCT	DID YOU SIGN A CONTRACT? ☐ NO ☐ YES

HAVE YOU COMPLAINED TO THE COMPANY? ☐ NO   ☐ YES
IF YES, WHAT WAS THE RESULT OF YOUR COMPLAINT?

PLEASE STATE YOUR COMPLAINT

_____

_____

_____

_____

_____

_____

_____

_____

_____

_____

_____

_____

_____

_____

NOTE: If you enclose additional information, please provide two (2) copies.

         I hereby certify that I have read the information contained in this complaint and that all of the information which I have given herein is true, correct, and complete to the best of my knowledge, information and belief.

I DO ____ DO NOT _____ authorize the use of my name in contacting or investigating the company complained about and in referring my complaint to other regulatory or law enforcement agencies.

SIGNATURE	DATE SIGNED

FTC Form 360-LA (12/84)

APPENDIX 153-A

Synopsis

Sec.

The Fair Credit Reporting Act (FCRA) covers all reporting on individuals as consumers, whether in connections with obtaining credit, insurance, or employment. Credit or other reports on business firms, or the business activities of individuals, are specifically excluded from the coverage of the act.

The FCRA creates the following consumer rights:

(1) To be told the reasons for adverse action on an application for credit, insurance, or employment when a credit report was a factor, and to be given the name and address of the credit reporting agency.

(2) To be informed of the nature and substance of all information in one's credit file by the credit reporting agency.

(3) To have another person present at the credit reporting agency when one's credit file is discussed.

(4) To be told who has received credit reports during the preceding six months for credit or insurance purposes, and during the preceding two years for employment purposes.

(5) To have inaccurate or unverifiable information deleted from the file.

(6) To have the information in the file reinvestigated whenever its accuracy is disputed.

(7) To have the right to file a brief explanatory statement in connection with disputed items, and to have that statement included in subsequent reports.

(8) To have the information in the file kept confidential and used only for legitimate business purposes.

(9) To have personal information in the file kept from governmental agencies unless otherwise ordered by a court.

(10) To be informed when adverse public record information is reported for employment purposes, or to have this information kept current.

(11) To have adverse information deleted from the file after seven years, or after ten years in the case of bankruptcy.

(12) To be informed of the scope and nature of investigative reports on one's personal life.

(13) To have adverse information contained in investigative reports reverified before it can be used again.

(14) To collect actual damages in civil actions against negligent credit reporting agencies, and punitive damages where the agency was willful in reporting inaccurate information.

Requirements for Consumer Reporting Agencies

Consumer reporting agency may furnish consumer reports only for permissible purposes including use in credit extensions or reviews and collections of accounts as well as responses to court orders or written consumer instructions; credit information must be current and accurate, and consumer can obtain contents of his file; agency must reinvestigate if information challenged, and disclose consumer's assertions if consumer supplies them; adverse information in investigative consumer reports must be reinvestigated every three months; government agencies can obtain only identifying information if request not for permissible purpose.

[I] Permissible Purpose

A consumer reporting agency may furnish consumer reports only for prescribed reasons, referred to as "permissible purposes." These purposes are

(1) in response to an order of a court having jurisdiction to issue the order;

(2) in response to written instructions from the consumer to whom the report relates;

(3) for use by a person in connection with a credit transaction and involving the extension of credit to, or review or collection of an account of, the consumer to whom the report relates;

(4) for use by a person in connection with an employment decision;

(5) for use by a person in determining a consumer's eligibility for a license or other benefit granted by a governmental instrumentality required by law to consider an applicant's financial responsibility or status; and

(6) for use by a person with a legitimate business need for the information in connection with a business transaction involving the consumer.

§　602 Findings and purpose

(a) The Congress makes the following findings:

(1) The banking system is dependent upon fair and accurate credit reporting. Inaccurate credit reports directly impair the efficiency of the banking system, and unfair credit reporting methods undermine the public confidence which is essential to the continued functioning of the banking system.

(2) An elaborate mechanism has been developed for investigating and evaluating the credit worthiness, credit standing, credit capacity, character, and general reputation of consumers.

(3) Consumer reporting agencies have assumed a vital role in assembling and evaluating consumer credit and other information on consumers.

(4) There is a need to insure that consumer reporting agencies exercise their grave responsibilities with fairness, impartiality, and a respect for the consumer's right of privacy.

(b) It is the purpose of this title to require that consumer reporting agencies adopt reasonable procedures for meeting the needs of commerce for consumer credit, personnel, insurance, and other information in a manner which is fair and equitable to the consumer, with regard to the confidentiality, accuracy, relevancy, and proper utilization of such information in accordance with the requirements of this title.

[15 U.S.C. 1681. Pub. L. 90-321, 602, as added by Act of Oct. 26, 1970, Pub. L. 91-508, 601, 84 Stat. 1128.]

§ 603 Definitions and rules of construction

(a) Definitions and rules of construction set forth in this section are applicable for the purposes of this title.

(b) The term "person" means any individual, partnership, corporation, trust, estate, cooperative, association, government or governmental subdivision or agency, or other entity.

(c) The term "consumer" means an individual.

(d) The term "consumer report" means any written, oral, or other communication of any information by a consumer reporting agency bearing on a consumer's credit worthiness, credit standing, credit capacity, character, general reputation, personal characteristics, or mode of living which is used or expected to be used or collected in whole or in part for the purpose of serving as a factor in establishing the consumer's eligibility for (1) credit or insurance to be used primarily for personal, family, or household purposes, or (2) employment purposes, or (3) other purposes authorized under section 1681b of this title. The term does not include (A) any report containing information solely as to transactions or experiences between the consumer and the person making the report; (B) any authorization or approval of a specific extension of credit directly or indirectly by the issuer of a credit card or similar device; or (C) any report in which a person who has been requested by a third party to make a specific extension of credit directly or indirectly to a consumer conveys his decision with respect to such request, if the third party advises the consumer of the name and address of the person to whom the request was made and such person makes the disclosures to the consumer required under section 1681m of this title.

(e) The term "investigative consumer report" means a consumer report or portion thereof in which information on a consumer's character, general reputation, personal characteristics, or mode of living is obtained through personal interviews with neighbors, friends, or associates of the consumer reported on or with others with whom he is acquainted or who may have knowledge concerning any such items of information. However, such information shall not include specific factual information on a consumer's credit record obtained directly from a creditor of the consumer or from a consumer reporting agency when such information was obtained directly from a creditor of the consumer or from the consumer.

(f) The term "consumer reporting agency" means any person which, for monetary fees, dues, or on a cooperative nonprofit basis, regularly engages in whole or in part in the practice of assembling or evaluating consumer credit information or other information on consumers for the purpose of furnishing consumer reports to third parties, and which uses any means or facility of interstate commerce for the purpose of preparing or furnishing consumer reports.

(g) The term "file," when used in connection with information on any consumer, means all of the information on that consumer recorded and retained by a consumer reporting agency regardless of how the information is stored.

(h) The term "employment purposes" when used in connection with a consumer report means a report used for the purpose of evaluating a consumer for employment, promotion, reassignment or retention as an employee.

(i) The term "medical information" means information or records obtained, with the consent of the individual to whom it relates, from licensed physicians or medical practitioners, hospitals, clinics, or other medical or medically related facilities.

[15 U.S.C. 1681a. Pub. L. 90-321, 603, as added by Act of Oct. 26, 1970, Pub. L. 91-508, 601, 84 Stat. 1128.]

§   604 Permissible purpose of reports.

A consumer reporting agency may furnish a consumer report under the following circumstances and no other:

(1) In response to the order of a court having jurisdiction to issue such an order.

(2) In accordance with the written instructions of the consumer to whom it relates.

(3) To a person which it has reason to believe -

(A) intends to use the information in connection with a credit transaction involving the consumer on whom the information is to be furnished and involving the extension of credit to, or review or collection of an account of, the consumer; or

(B) intends to use the information for employment purposes; or

(C) intends to use the information in connection with the under-writing of insurance involving the consumer; or

(D) intends to use the information in connection with a determination of the consumer's eligibility for a license or other benefit granted by a governmental instrumentality required by law to consider an applicant's financial responsibility or status; or

(E) otherwise has a legitimate business need for the information in connection with a business transaction involving the consumer.

[15 U.S.C. 1681b. Pub. L. 90-321, 604, as added by Act of Oct. 26, 1970, Pub. L. 91-508, 601, 84 Stat. 1129.]

§   605 Obsolete information

(a) Except as authorized under subsection (b), no consumer reporting agency may make any consumer report containing any of the following items of information.

(1) Bankruptcies which, from date of adjudication of most recent bankruptcy, antedate the report by more than ten years.

(2) Suits and judgments which, from date of entry, antedate the report by more than seven years or until the governing statute of limitations has expired, whichever is the longer period.

(3) Paid tax liens which, from day of payment, antedate the report by more than seven years.

(4) Accounts placed for collection or charged to profit and loss which antedate the report by more than seven years.

(5) Records of arrest, indictment, or conviction of crime which, from date of disposition, release, or parole, antedate the report by more than seven years.

(6) Any other adverse item of information which antedates the report by more than seven years.

(b) The provisions of subsection (a) are not applicable in the case of any consumer credit report to be used in connection with -

(1) a credit transaction involving, or which may reasonably be expected to involve, a principal amount of $50,000 or more;

(2) the underwriting of life insurance involving, or which may reasonably be expected to involve, a face amount of $50,000 or more; or

(3) the employment of any individual at an annual salary which equals, or which may reasonably be expected to equal $20,000, or more.

[15 U.S.C. 1681c. Pub. L. 90-321, 605, as added by Act of Oct. 26, 1970, Pub. L. 91-508, 601, 84 Stat. 1129. Amended by Act of Nov. 6, 1978, Pub. L. 95-598, 312(b), 92 Stat. 2676.]

§   606 Disclosure of investigative consumer reports

(a) A person may not procure or cause to be prepared an inves-tigative consumer report on any consumer unless-

(1) it is clearly and accurately disclosed to the consumer that an investigative consumer report including information as to his character, general reputation, personal characteristics, and mode of living, whichever are applicable, may be made, and such disclosure (A) is made in a writing mailed, or otherwise delivered, to the consumer, not later than three days after the date on which the report was first requested, and (B) includes a statement informing the consumer of his right to request the additional disclosures provided for under subsection (b) of this section; or

(2) the report is to be used for employment purposes for which the consumer has not specifically applied.

(b) Any person who procures or causes to be prepared an investigative consumer report on any consumer shall, upon written request made by the consumer within a reasonable period of time after the receipt by him of the disclosure required by subsection (a)(1), make a complete and accurate disclosure of the nature and scope of the investigation requested. This disclosure shall be made in a writing mailed, or otherwise delivered, to the consumer not later than five days after the date on which the request for such disclosure was received from the consumer or such report was first requested, whichever is the later.

(c) No person may be held liable for any violation of subsection (a) or (b) of this section if he shows by a preponderance of the evidence that at the time of the violation he maintained reasonable procedures to assure compliance with subsection (a) or (b).

[15 U.S.C. 1681d. Pub. L. 90-321, 606, as added by Act of Oct. 26, 1970, Pub. L. 91-508, 601, 84 Stat. 1130.]

§   607 Compliance procedures

(a) Every consumer reporting agency shall maintain reasonable procedures designed to avoid violations of section 1681c of this title and to limit the furnishing of consumer reports to the purposes listed under section 1681b of this title. These procedures shall require that prospective users of the information identify themselves, certify the purposes for which the information is sought, and certify that the information will be used for no other purpose. Every consumer reporting agency shall make a reasonable effort to verify the identity of a new prospective user and the uses certified by such prospective user prior to furnishing such user a consumer report. No consumer reporting agency may furnish a consumer report to any person if it has reasonable grounds for believing that the consumer report will not be used for a purpose listed in section 1681b of this title.

(b) Whenever a consumer reporting agency prepares a consumer report it shall follow reasonable procedures to assure maximum possible accuracy of the information concerning the individual about whom the report relates.

[15 U.S.C. 1681e. Pub. L. 90-321, 607, as added by Act of Oct. 26, 1970, Pub. L. 91-508, 601, 84 Stat. 1130.]

§ 608 Disclosures to governmental agencies

Notwithstanding the provisions of section 1681b of this title, a consumer reporting agency may furnish identifying information respecting any consumer, limited to his name, address, former addresses, places of employment, or former places of employment, to a governmental agency.

[15 U.S.C. A 1681f. Pub. L. 90-321, 608, as added by Act of Oct. 26, 1970, Pub. L. 91-508, 601, 84 Stat. 1131.]

§ 609 Disclosures to consumers

(a) Every consumer reporting agency shall, upon request and proper identification of any consumer, clearly and accurately disclose to the consumer:

(1) The nature and substance of all information (except medical information) in its files on the consumer at the time of the request.

(2) The sources of the information; except that the sources of information acquired solely for use in preparing an investigative con sumer report and actually used for no other purpose need not be dis closed: Provided, That in the event an action is brought under this title, such sources shall be available to the plaintiff under appropri ate discovery procedures in the court in which the action is brought.

(3) The recipients of any consumer report on the consumer which it has furnished -

(A) for employment purposes within the two-year period preced ing the request, and

(B) for any other purpose within the six-month period preceding the request.

(b) The requirements of subsection (a) respecting the disclosure of sources of information and the recipients of consumer reports do not apply to information received or consumer reports furnished prior to the effective date of this title except to the extent that the matter involved is contained in the files of the consumer reporting agency on that date.

[15 U.S.C. 1681g. Pub. L. 90-321, 609, as added by Act of Oct. 26, 1970, Pub. L. 91-508, 601, 84 Stat. 1131.]

§   610 Conditions of disclosure to consumers

(a) A consumer reporting agency shall make the disclosures required under section 1681g of this title during normal business hours and on reasonable notice.

(b) The disclosures required under section 1681g of this title shall be made to the consumer -

(1) in person if he appears in person and furnishes proper identification; or

(2) by telephone if he has made a written request, with proper identification, for telephone disclosure and the toll charge, if any, for the telephone call is prepaid by or charged directly to the con sumer.

(c) Any consumer reporting agency shall provide trained person nel to explain to the consumer any information furnished to him pur suant to section 1681g of this title.

(d) The consumer shall be permitted to be accompanied by one other person of his choosing, who shall furnish reasonable identifica tion. A consumer reporting agency may require the consumer to fur nish a written statement granting permission to the consumer report ing agency to discuss the consumer's file in such person's presence.

(e) Except as provided in sections 1681o and 1681p of this title, no consumer may bring any action or proceeding in the nature of defamation, invasion of privacy, or negligence with respect to the reporting of information against any consumer reporting agency, any user of information, or any person who furnishes information to a consumer reporting agency, based on information disclosed pursuant to section 1681g, 1681h, 1681m of this title, except as to false infor mation furnished with malice or willful intent to injure such consumer.

[15 U.S.C. 1681h. Pub. L. 90-321, 610, as added by Act of Oct. 26, 1970, Pub. L. 91-508, 601, 84 Stat. 1131.]

§   611 Procedure in case of disputed accuracy

(a) If the completeness or accuracy of any item of information contained in his file is disputed by a consumer, and such dispute is directly conveyed to the consumer reporting agency by the consumer, the consumer reporting agency shall within a reasonable period of time reinvestigate and record the current status of that information unless it has reasonable grounds to believe that the dispute by the consumer is frivolous or irrelevant. If after such reinvestigation such information is found to be inaccurate or can no longer be verified, the consumer reporting agency shall promptly delete such information. The presence of contradictory information in the consumer's file does not in and of itself constitute reasonable grounds for believing the dispute is frivolous or irrelevant.

(b) If the reinvestigation does not resolve the dispute, the consumer may file a brief statement setting forth the nature of the dispute. The consumer reporting agency may limit such statements to not more than one hundred words if it provides the consumer with assistance in writing a clear summary of the dispute.

(c) Whenever a statement of a dispute is filed, unless there is reasonable grounds to believe that it is frivolous or irrelevant, the consumer reporting agency shall, in any subsequent consumer report containing the information in question, clearly note that it is disputed by the consumer and provide either the consumer's statement or a clear and accurate codification or summary thereof.

(d) Following any deletion of information which is found to be inaccurate or whose accuracy can no longer be verified or any notation as to disputed information, the consumer reporting agency shall, at the request of the consumer, furnish notification that the item has been deleted or the statement, codification or summary pursuant to subsection (b) or (c) to any person specifically designated by the consumer who has within two years prior thereto received a consumer report for employment purposes, or within six months prior thereto received a consumer report for any other purpose, which contained the deleted or disputed information. The consumer reporting agency shall clearly and conspicuously disclose to the consumer his rights to make such a request. Such disclosure shall be made at or prior to the time the information is deleted or the consumer's statement regarding the disputed information is received.

[15 U.S.C. 1681i. Pub. L. 90-321, 611, as added by Act of Oct. 26, 1970, Pub. L. 91-508, 601, 84 Stat. 1132.]

§ 612 Charges for certain disclosures

A consumer reporting agency shall make all disclosures pursuant to section 1681g of this title and furnish all consumer reports pursuant to section 1681i(d) of this title without charge to the consumer if within thirty days after receipt by such consumer of a notification pursuant to section 1681m of this title or notification from a debt collection agency affiliated with such consumer reporting agency stating that the consumer's credit rating may be or has been adversely af fected, the consumer makes a request under section 1681g or 1681i(d) of this title. Otherwise, the consumer reporting agency may impose a reasonable charge on the consumer for making disclosure to such con sumer pursuant to section 1681g of this title, the charge for which shall be indicated to the consumer prior to making disclosure; and for furnishing notifications, statements, summaries, or codifications to persons designated by the consumer pursuant to section 1681i(d) of this title, the charge for which shall be indicated to the consumer prior to furnishing such information and shall not exceed the charge that the consumer reporting agency would impose on each designated recipient for a consumer report except that no charge may be made for notifying such persons of the deletion of information which is found to be inaccurate or which can no longer be verified. [15 U.S.C. 1681j. Pub. L. 90-321, 612, as added by Act of Oct. 26, 1970, Pub. L. 91-508, 601, 84 Stat. 1132.]

§ 613 Public record information for employment purposes

A consumer reporting agency which furnishes a consumer report for employment purposes and which for that purpose compiles and re ports items of information on consumers which are matters of public record and are likely to have an adverse effect upon a consumer's ability to obtain employment shall -

(1) at the time such public record information is reported to the user of such consumer report, notify the consumer of the fact that public record information is being reported by the consumer reporting agency, together with the name and address of the person to whom such information is being reported; or

(2) maintain strict procedures designed to insure that whenever public record information which is likely to have an adverse effect on a consumer's ability to obtain employment is reported it is complete and up to date. For purposes of this paragraph, items of public re cord relating to arrests, indictments, convictions, suits, tax liens, and outstanding judgments shall be considered up to date if the cur rent public record status of the item at the time of the report is re ported.

[15 U.S.C. 1681k. Pub. L. 90-321, 613, as added by Act of Oct. 26, 1970, Pub. L. 91-508, 601, 84 Stat. 1133.]

§   614 Restrictions on investigative consumer reports

Whenever a consumer reporting agency prepares an investigative consumer report, no adverse information in the consumer report (oth er than information which is a matter of public record) may be included in a subsequent consumer report unless such adverse infor mation has been verified in the process of making such subsequent consumer report, or the adverse information was received within the threemonth period preceding the date the subsequent report is fur nished.

[15 U.S.C. 1681l. Pub. L. 90-321, 614, as added by Act of Oct. 26, 1970. Pub. L. 91-508, 601, 84 Stat. 1133.]

§   615 Requirements on users of consumer reports

(a) Whenever credit or insurance for personal, family, or house hold purposes, or employment involving a consumer is denied or the charge for such credit or insurance is increased either wholly or partly because of information contained in a consumer report from a consumer reporting agency, the user of the consumer report shall so advise the consumer against whom such adverse action has been taken and supply the name and address of the consumer reporting agency making the report.

(b) Whenever credit for personal, family, or household purposes involving a consumer is denied or the charge for such credit is in creased either wholly or partly because of information obtained from a person other than a consumer reporting agency bearing upon the con sumer's credit worthiness, credit standing, credit capacity, charac ter, general reputation, personal characteristics, or mode of living, the user of such information shall, within a reasonable period of time, upon the consumer's written request for the reasons for such adverse action received within sixty days after learning of such adverse action, disclose the nature of the information to the consumer. The user of such information shall clearly and accurately disclose to the consumer his right to make such written request at the time such ad verse action is communicated to the consumer.

(c) No person shall be held liable for any violation of this sec tion if he shows by a preponderance of the evidence that at the time of the alleged violation he maintained reasonable procedures to assure compliance with the provisions of subsections (a) and (b).

[15 U.S.C. 1681m. Pub. L. 90-321, 615, as added by Act of Oct. 26, 1970, Pub. L. 91-508, 601, 84 Stat. 1133.]

§ 616 Civil liability for willful noncompliance

Any consumer reporting agency or user of information which will fully fails to comply with any requirement imposed under this title with respect to any consumer is liable to that consumer in an amount equal to the sum of -

(1) any actual damages sustained by the consumer as a result of the failure;

(2) such amount of punitive damages as the court may allow; and

(3) in the case of any successful action to enforce any liability under this section, the costs of the action together with reasonable attorney's fees as determined by the court.

[15 U.S.C. 1681n. Pub. L. 90-321, 616, as added by Act of October 26, 1970, Pub. L. 91-508, 601, 84 Stat. 1134.]

§ 617 Civil liability for negligent noncompliance

Any consumer reporting agency or user of information which is negligent in failing to comply with any requirement imposed under this title with respect to any consumer is liable to that consumer in an amount equal to the sum of -

(1) any actual damages sustained by the consumer as a result of the failure;

(2) in the case of any successful action to enforce any liability under this section, the costs of the action together with reasonable attorney's fees as determined by the court.

[15 U.S.C. 1681o. Pub. L. 90-321, 617, as added by Act of Oct. 26, 1970, Pub. L. 91-508, 601, 84 Stat. 1134.]

§ 618 Jurisdiction of courts; limitation of actions

An action to enforce any liability created under this title may be brought in any appropriate United States district court without regard to the amount in controversy, or in any other court of compe tent jurisdiction, within two years from the date on which the liability arises, except that where a defendant has materially and willfully mis represented any information required under this title to be disclosed to an individual and the information so misrepresented is material to the establishment of the defendant's liability to that individual under this title, the action may be brought at any time within two years after discovery by the individual of the misrepresentation.

[15 U.S.C. 1681p. Pub. L. 90-321, 618, as added by Act of Oct. 26, 1970, Pub. L. 91-508, 601, 84 Stat. 1134.]

§ 619 Obtaining information under false pretenses

Any person who knowingly and willfully obtains information on a consumer from a consumer reporting agency under false pretenses shall be fined not more than $5,000 or imprisoned not more than one year, or both.

[15 U.S.C. 1681q. Pub. L. 90-321, 619, as added by Act of Oct. 26, 1970, Pub. L. 91-508, 601, 84 Stat. 1134.]

§ 620 Unauthorized disclosures by officers or employees

Any officer or employee of a consumer reporting agency who knowingly and willfully provides information concerning an individual from the agency's files to a person not authorized to receive that information shall be fined not more than $5,000 or imprisoned not more than one year, or both.

[15 U.S.C. 1681r. Pub. L. 90-321, 620, as added by Act of Oct. 26, 1970, Pub. L. 91-508, 601, 84 Stat. 1134.]

§ 621 Administrative enforcement

(a) Compliance with the requirements imposed under this title shall be enforced under the Federal Trade Commission Act by the Federal Trade Commission with respect to consumer reporting agencies and all other persons subject thereto, except to the extent that enforcement of the requirements imposed under this title is specifical ly committed to some other government agency under subsection (b) hereof. For the purpose of the exercise by the Federal Trade Com mission of its functions and powers under the Federal Trade Commis sion Act, a violation of any requirement or prohibition imposed under this title shall constitute an unfair or deceptive act or practice in commerce in violation of section 5(a) of the Federal Trade Commission Act and shall be subject to enforcement by the Federal Trade Commis sion under section 5(b) thereof with respect to any consumer report ing agency or person subject to enforcement by the Federal Trade Commission pursuant to this subsection, irrespective of whether that person is engaged in commerce or meets any other jurisdictional tests in the Federal Trade Commission Act. The Federal Trade Commission shall have such procedural, investigative, and enforcement powers, including the power to issue procedural rules in enforcing compliance with the requirements imposed under this title and to require the fil ing of reports, the production of documents, and the appearance of witnesses as though the applicable terms and conditions of the Federal Trade Commission Act were part of this title. Any person violating any of the provisions of this title shall be subject to the penalties and entitled to the privileges and immunities provided in the Federal Trade Commission Act as though the applicable terms and provisions thereof were part of this title.

(b) Compliance with the requirements imposed under this title with respect to consumer reporting agencies and persons who use consumer reports from such agencies shall be enforced under -

(1) section 8 of the Federal Deposit Insurance Act, in the case of:

(A) national banks, by the Comptroller of the Currency;

(B) member banks of the Federal Reserve System (other than na tional banks), by the Federal Reserve Board; and

(C) banks insured by the Federal Deposit Insurance Corporation (other than members of the Federal Reserve System), by the Board of   Directors of the Federal Deposit Insurance Corporation.

(2) section 5(d) of the Home Owners Loan Act of 1933, sec tion 407 of the National Housing Act, and sections 6(i) and 17 of the Federal Home Loan Bank Act, by the Federal Home Loan Bank Board (acting directly or through the Federal Savings and Loan Insurance Corporation), in the case of any institution subject to any of those provisions;

(3) the Federal Credit Union Act, by the Administrator of the National Credit Union Administration with respect to any Federal credit union;

(4) the Acts to regulate commerce, by the Interstate Commerce Commission with respect to any common carrier subject to those Acts;

(5) the Federal Aviation Act of 1958, by the Secretary of Transportation with respect to any air carrier or foreign air carrier subject to that Act; and

(6) the Packers and Stockyards Act, 1921 (except as provided in section 406 of the Act), by the Secretary of Agriculture with respect to any activities subject to that Act.

(c) For the purpose of the exercise by any agency referred to in subsection (b) of its powers under any Act referred to in that subsection, a violation of any requirement imposed under this title shall be deemed to be a violation of a requirement imposed under that Act. In addition to its powers under any provision of law specifically referred to in subsection (b), each of the agencies referred to in that subsection may exercise, for the purpose of enforcing compliance with any requirement imposed under this title any other authority conferred on it by law.

[15 U.S.C. 1681s. Pub. L. 90-321, 621, as added by Act of Oct. 26, 1970, Pub. L. 91-508, 601, 84 Stat. 1134; Oct. 3, 1984, Pub. L. 98-443, 98 Stat 1708.]

§   622 Relation to State laws

This title does not annul, alter, affect, or exempt any person subject to the provisions of this title from complying with the laws of any State with respect to the collection, distribution, or use of any information on consumers, except to the extent that those laws are inconsistent with any provision of this title, and then only to the extent of the inconsistency.

[15 U.S.C. 1681t Pub. L. 90-321, 622, as added by Act of Oct. 26, 1970, Pub. L. 91-508, 601, 84 Stat. 1136.]

Has the department store's computer ever billed you for merchandise you returned to the store or never received? Or has a credit card company ever charged you twice for the same item or failed to properly credit a payment made on your account? Credit billing errors do occur, but they are easy to resolve if you know how to use the Fair Credit Billing Act (FCBA). Congress passed this law in 1975 to help consumers resolve disputes with creditors and to ensure fair handling of credit accounts.

Which Credit Transactions Are Covered?

The FCBA generally applies only to "open end" credit accounts. Open end accounts include credit cards, revolving charge accounts (such as department store accounts), and overdraft checking. The periodic bills, or billing statements, you receive (usually monthly) for such accounts are covered by the FCBA. The Act does not apply to a loan or credit sale which is paid according to a fixed schedule until the entire amount is paid back.

What Types of Disputes Are Covered?

The FCBA settlement procedure applies only to disputes over "billing errors" on periodic statements, such as the following:

Charges not made by you or anyone authorized to use your account.

Charges which are incorrectly identified or for which the wrong amount or date is shown.

Charges for goods or services you did not accept or which were not delivered as agreed.

Computational or similar errors.

Failure to properly reflect payments or other credits, such as returns.

Not mailing or delivering bills to your current address (provided you give a change of address at least 20 days before the billing period ends).

Charges for which you request an explanation or written proof of purchase.

How to Use the Settlement Procedure
When many consumers find a mistake on their bill, they pick up the phone and call the company to correct the problem. You can do this if you wish, but phoning does not trigger the legal safeguards provided under the FCBA.

To be protected under the law, you must send a separate written billing error notice to the creditor. Your notice must reach the creditor within 60 days after the first bill containing the error was mailed to you. Send the notice to the address provided on the bill for billing error notices (and not, for example, directly to the store, unless the bill says that's where it should be sent). In your letter, you must include the following information:

Your name and account number.

A statement that you believe the bill contains a billing error and the dollar amount involved.

The reasons why you believe there is a mistake.

It's a good idea to send it by certified mail, with a return receipt requested. That way you'll have proof of the dates of mailing and receipt. If you wish, send photocopies of sales slips or other documents, but keep the originals for your records.

What Must The Creditor Do?
Your letter claiming a billing error must be acknowledged by the creditor in writing within 30 days after it is received, unless the problem is resolved within that period. In any case, within two billing cycles (but not more than 90 days), the creditor must

conduct a reasonable investigation and either correct the mistake or explain why the bill is believed to be correct.

What Happens While A Bill Is Being Disputed?
You may withhold payment of the amount in dispute, including the affected portions of minimum payments and finance charges, until the dispute is resolved. You are still required to pay any part of the bill which is not disputed, including finance and other charges on undisputed amounts.

While the FCBA dispute settlement procedure is going on, the creditor may not take any legal or other action to collect the amount in dispute. Your account may not be closed or restricted in any way, except that the disputed amount may be applied against your credit limit.

What About Your Credit Rating?
While a bill is being disputed, the creditor may not threaten to damage your credit rating or report you as delinquent to anyone. However, the creditor is permitted to report that you are disputing your bill.

Another federal law, the Equal Credit Opportunity Act, prohibits creditors from discriminating against credit applicants who, in good faith, exercise their rights under the FCBA. You cannot be denied credit merely because you have disputed a bill.

If The Creditor Makes A Mistake
If your bill is found to contain a billing error, the creditor must write you explaining the corrections to be made on your account. In addition to crediting your account with the amount not owed, the creditor must remove all finance charges, late fees, or other charges relating to that amount. If the creditor concludes that you owe part of the disputed amount, this must be explained in writing. You also have the right to request copies of documents proving you owe the money.

If The Bill Is Correct
If the creditor investigates and still believes the bill is correct, you must be told promptly in writing how much you owe and why.

You may ask for copies of relevant documents. At this point, you will owe the disputed amount, plus any finance charges that accumulated while it was disputed. You may also have to pay the minimum payment amount missed because of the dispute.

If You Still Disagree

Even after the FCBA dispute settlement procedure has ended, you may still feel the bill is wrong. If this happens, write the creditor within 10 days after receiving the explanation and say you still refuse to pay the disputed amount. At this point, the creditor may begin collection procedures. However, if the creditor reports you to a credit bureau as delinquent, he must also state that you don't think you owe the money. Also, you must be told who receives such reports.

If The Creditor Doesn't Follow The Procedures

Any creditor who fails to follow the FCBA dispute settlement procedure may not collect the amount in dispute, or any finance charges on it, up to $50, even if the bill turns out to be correct. For example, this penalty would apply if a creditor acknowledges your complaint in 45 days (15 days too late) or takes more than two billing cycles to resolve a dispute. It also applies if a creditor threatens to report - or goes ahead and improperly reports - your nonpayments to anyone. You also have the right, as more fully described below, to sue a creditor for any violation of the FCBA.

Complaints About Quality

Disputes about the quality of goods and services are not necessarily "billing errors," so the dispute procedure may not apply. However, if you purchase unsatisfactory goods or services with a credit card, the FCBA allows you to take the same legal actions against the credit card issuer as you could take under state law against the seller. If your state law permits you to withhold payment to a seller for defective merchandise, or pay and sue for a refund, you might also be able to withhold payment to your credit card issuer. Because state laws on your right to stop payment vary, it is best to get legal advice before you do so.

However, before you take legal action, you must give the seller a chance to remedy the problem. Also, unless the seller is also the card issuer (such as a company that issued you a gasoline credit card), you must have bought the item in your home state or within 100 miles of your current mailing address, and the amount charged must have been more than $50.

Other Billing Rights For Consumers

The FCBA also requires "open end" creditors to do the following for their customers:

Give you a written notice when you open a new account, and at other specified times, describing your right to dispute billing errors.

Provide a statement for each billing period in which you owe - or they owe you - more than $1.00.

Mail or deliver your bill to you at least 14 days before the payment is due, if you are given a time period within which to pay the bill without incurring additional finance or other charges.

Credit all payments to your account as of the date they are received, unless not doing so would not result in extra charges.

Promptly credit or refund overpayments.

You Can Also Sue

You can sue a creditor who violates any FCBA provisions. If you win, you may be awarded damages resulting from the violation, plus twice the amount of any finance charges (not less than $100 or more than $1,000). The court may also order the creditor to pay your attorney's fees and costs. If possible, retain a private attorney who is willing to accept whatever fee the court awards as the entire fee for representing you. Some lawyers may not be willing to accept your case unless you agree to pay their fee - win or lose - or if you will add to a fee awarded by the court but which they believe is too low. Be sure you get a full explanation of what it could cost before you go to court.

Where To Report FCBA Violations
The Federal Trade Commission enforces the FCBA for almost all creditors except banks. While the Commission does not represent individuals in private disputes, information from consumers as to their experiences and concerns is vital to the enforcement of the Act. Questions or complaints may be addressed to the nearest Federal Trade Commission Regional Office. If they concern national creditors, write: Federal Trade Commission, Fair Credit Billing, Washington, D.C. 20580.

915 Second Avenue
SEATTLE, WA 98174
(206) 442-4655

150 Causeway Street
BOSTON, MA 02114
(617) 223-6621

26 Federal Plaza
NEW YORK, NY 10278
(212) 264-1207

118 St. Clair Avenue
CLEVELAND, OH 44114
(216) 522-4207

450 Golden Gate Avenue
SAN FRANCISCO, CA 94102
(415) 556-1270

55 East Monroe Street
CHICAGO, IL 60603
(312) 353-4423

1405 Curtis Street
DENVER, CO 80202
(303) 837-2271

2001 Bryan Street
DALLAS, TX 75201
(214) 767-0032

11000 Wilshire Boulevard
LOS ANGELES, CA 90024
(213) 824-7575

1718 Peachtree Street, N.W.
ATLANTA, GA 30367
(404) 881-4836

CENTRAL OFFICE:
6th St. & Pennsylvania Ave., N.W.
WASHINGTON, D.C. 20580
(202) 724-1139

FDIC OFFICES

Director
Office of Consumer Affairs & Civil Rights
Federal Deposit Insurance Corporation
Washington, D.C. 20429
(202) 389-4427

ATLANTA REGION
Regional Director   Alabama
Federal Deposit Insurance Corporation   Florida
233 Peachtree Street, N.E., Suite 2400   Georgia
Atlanta, GA 30303
(404) 221-6631

BOSTON REGION
Regional Director   Connecticut
Federal Deposit Insurance Corporation   Maine
60 State Street, 17th Floor   Massachusetts
Boston, MA 02109   New Hampshire
(617) 223-6420   Rhode Island
                                               Vermont

CHICAGO REGION
Regional Director   Illinois
Federal Deposit Insurance Corporation   Indiana
233 S. Wacker Drive, Suite 6116
Chicago, IL 60606
(312) 353-2600

COLUMBUS REGION
Regional Director   Kentucky
Federal Deposit Insurance Corporation   Ohio
1 Nationwide Plaza, Suite 2600   West Virginia
Columbus, OH 43215
(614) 469-7301

DALLAS REGION
Regional Director   Colorado
Federal Deposit Insurance Corporation   New Mexico
300 North Ervay Street, Suite 3300   Oklahoma
Dallas, TX 75201   Texas
(214) 754-0098

KANSAS CITY REGION
Regional Director   Kansas
Federal Deposit Insurance Corporation   Missouri
2345 Grand Avenue, Suite 1500
Kansas City, MO 64108
(816) 374-2851

MADISON REGION
Regional Director   Michigan
Federal Deposit Insurance Corporation   Wisconsin
1 South Pinckney Street, Room 813
Madison, WI 53703
(608) 252-5226

MEMPHIS REGION
Regional Director   Arkansas
Federal Deposit Insurance Corporation   Louisiana
1 Commerce Square, Suite 1800   Mississippi
Memphis, TN 38103   Tennessee
(901) 521-3872

MINNEAPOLIS REGION
Regional Director   Minnesota
Federal Deposit Insurance Corporation   Montana
730 Second Avenue South, Suite 266   North Dakota
Minneapolis, MN 55402   South Dakota
(612) 725-2046   Wyoming

NEW YORK REGION
Regional Director
Federal Deposit Insurance Corporation
345 Park Avenue, 21st Floor
New York, NY 10022
(212) 826-4762

New Jersey
New York
Puerto Rico
Virgin Islands

OMAHA REGION
Regional Director
Federal Deposit Insurance Corporation
1700 Farham Street, Suite 1200
Omaha, NE 68102
(402) 221-3366

Iowa
Nebraska

PHILADELPHIA REGION
Regional Director
Federal Deposit Insurance Corporation
5 Penn Center Plaza, Suite 2901
Philadelphia, PA
(215) 597-2295

Delaware
Maryland
Pennsylvania

RICHMOND REGION
Regional Director
Federal Deposit Insurance Corporation
Eighth and Main Building
707 East Main Street, Suite 2000
Richmond, VA 23219
(804) 782-2395/782-2401

District of Columbia
North Carolina
South Carolina
Virginia

SAN FRANCISCO REGION
Regional Director
Federal Deposit Insurance Corporation
44 Montgomery Street, Suite 3600
San Francisco, CA 94104
(415) 556-2736

Alaska,Arizona
California,Guam
Hawaii,Idaho
Nevada,Oregon
Utah,Washington

FEDERAL ENFORCEMENT AGENCIES

National Banks
> Comptroller of the Currency
> Consumer Affairs Division
> Washington, D.C. 20219

State Member Banks
> Federal Reserve Bank serving the area in which the
> State member bank is located.

State Nonmember Banks
> FDIC Regional Director for the Region in which the
> nonmember insured bank is located or the Office of
> Consumer Affairs and Civil Rights in Washington,
> D.C. The addresses of these offices are listed in this
> appendix.

Savings Institutions Insured by the FSLIC and Members of the
FHLB System (except for Savings Banks insured by FDIC)
> The FHLBB's Supervisory Agent in the Federal
> Home Loan Bank District in which the institution is
> located.

Federal Credit Unions
> Regional Office of the National Credit Union
> Administration, serving the area in which the
> Federal Credit Union is located.

Creditors Subject to Civil Aeronautics Board
Director, Bureau of Enforcement
> Civil Aeronautics Board
> 1825 Connecticut Avenue, N.W.
> Washington, D.C. 20428

Creditors Subject to Packers and Stockyards Act
>   Nearest Packers and Stockyards Administration area supervisor.

Federal Land Banks, Federal Land Bank Associations, Federal Intermediate Credit Banks, and Production Credit Associations
>   Farm Credit Association
>   490 L'Enfant Plaza West
>   Washington, D.C. 20578

Retail Department Stores, Consumer Finance Companies, All Other Creditors, and All Nonbank Credit Card Issuers
>   Truth in Lending
>   Federal Trade Commission
>   Washington, D.C. 20580

If you use credit cards, owe money on a loan, or are paying off a home mortgage, you are a "debtor." Most Americans are.

You may never come in contact with a debt collector. But if you do, you should know that there is a law to make sure you are treated fairly. The Fair Debt Collection Practices Act was passed by Congress in 1978 to prohibit certain methods of debt collection. Of course, the law does not erase any legitimate debt you owe.

Here are answers to some questions you may have about your rights under the Debt Collection Act:

What debts are covered?

Personal, family, and household debts are covered under the Act. This includes money owed for the purchase of a car, for medical care, or for charge accounts.

Who is a debt collector?

A debt collector is anyone, other than the creditor or the creditor's attorney, who regularly collects debts for others.

How may a debt collector contact you?

A debt collector may contact you in person, by mail, telephone, or telegram. However, a debt collector may not contact you at inconvenient or unusual times or places, such as before 8 a.m. or after 9 p.m. unless you agree. A debt collector may not contact you at work if your employer disapproves.

Can you stop a debt collector from contacting you?

You may stop a debt collector from contacting you by writing a letter to the collection agency telling them to stop. Once they receive this letter, they may not contact you again except to say there will be no further contact. The debt collector is allowed to notify you that some specific action may be taken, but only if the debt collector or the creditor usually takes such action.

May a debt collector contact any other person concerning your debt?

If you have an attorney, the collector may not contact anyone but the attorney. If you do not have an attorney, a debt collector may contact other people, but only to find out where you live or work.

The collector is not allowed to tell anyone other than you or your attorney that you owe money. In most cases, collectors are prohibited from contacting any person more than once.

What is the debt collector required to tell you about the debt?

Within 5 days after you are first contacted, the debt collector must send you a written notice telling you the amount of money you owe; the name of the creditor to whom you owe the money; and what to do if you feel you do not owe the money.

If you believe you do not owe the money, may a debt collector continue to contact you?

The debt collector may not contact you if you send the collector a letter within 30 days after you are first contacted saying you do not owe the money. However, a debt collector can begin collection activities again if you are sent proof of the debt, such as a copy of the bill.

What types of debt collection practices are prohibited?

Harassment. Debt collectors may not harass, oppress or abuse any person. For example, debt collectors may not:

- Use threats of violence or harm to property or reputation.
- Publish a list of consumers who refuse to pay their debts (except to a credit bureau).
- Use obscene or profane language.
- Repeatedly use the telephone to annoy someone.
- Telephone people without identifying themselves.
- Advertise your debt.

False Statements. Debt collectors may not use any false statements when collecting a debt. For example, debt collectors may not:

- Falsely imply that they are an attorney or government representative.
- Falsely imply that you have committed a crime.

- Falsely represent that they operate or work for a credit bureau.

- Misrepresent the amount of the debt.

- Indicate that papers being sent are legal forms when they are not.

- Indicate that papers being sent are not legal forms when they are.

Also, debt collectors may not say that:

- You'll be arrested if you do not pay your debt.

- They will seize, garnish, attach, or sell your property or wages, unless the collection agency or the creditor intends to do so, and it is legal.

- Actions will be taken against you which legally may not be taken.

Debt collectors may not:

- Give false credit information about you to anyone.

- Send you anything that looks like an official document which might be sent by any court or agency of the United States or any state or local government.

- Use any false name.

Unfair Practices. Debt collectors may not engage in unfair practices in attempting to collect a debt. For example, debt collectors may not:

- Collect any amount greater than your debt, unless allowed by law.

- Deposit a post-dated check before the date on the check.

- Make you accept collect calls or pay for telegrams.

- Take or threaten to take your property unless this can be done legally.

- Contact you by postcard.

- Put anything on an envelope other than the debt collector's address and name. Even the name can't be used if it shows that the communication is about the collection of a debt.

What control do you have over specific debts?

If you owe several debts, any payment you make must be applied to the debt you choose. A debt collector may not apply a payment to any debt you feel you do not owe.

What can you do if the debt collector breaks the law?

You have the right to sue a debt collector in a State or Federal court within one year from the date the law was violated. If you win, you may recover money for the damage you suffered. Court costs and attorney's fees also can be recovered. A group of people may sue a debt collector and recover money for damages up to $500,000.

Who can you tell if the debt collector breaks the law?

In addition to this Federal law, many states have their own debt collection laws. Check with your state Attorney General's office to determine your rights under state law. Federal agencies rely on consumer complaints to decide which companies to investigate. You can assist these enforcement efforts by contacting the appropriate government office.

If a retail store, department store, small loan and finance company, oil company, public utility company, state credit union, government lending program, or travel and expense credit card company is involved, contact the Federal Trade Commission office nearest you:

6th and Pennsylvania, N.W.
WASHINGTON, D.C. 20580
(202) 523-3598

55 East Monroe Street
CHICAGO, IL 60603
(312) 353-4423

150 Causeway Street
BOSTON, MA 02114
(617) 223-6621

1405 Curtis Street
DENVER, CO 80202
(303) 837-2271

26 Federal Plaza	2001 Bryan Street
NEW YORK, NY 10278	DALLAS, TX 75201
(212) 264-1207	(214) 767-0032
118 St. Clair Avenue	11000 Wilshire Boulevard
CLEVELAND, OH 44114	LOS ANGELES, CA 90024
(216) 522-4207	(213) 824-7575
1718 Peachtree Street, N.W.	450 Golden Gate Avenue
ATLANTA, GA 30367	SAN FRANCISCO, CA 94102
(404) 881-4836	(415) 556-1270

If your complaint concerns a nationally-chartered bank (National or N.A. will be part of the name), write to:
> Comptroller of the Currency
> Consumer Affairs Division,
> Washington, D.C. 20219

If your complaint concerns a state-chartered bank that is a member of the Federal Reserve System, write to:
> Board of Governors of the Federal Reserve System
> Consumer Affairs Division,
> Washington, D.C. 20551

If your complaint concerns a bank that is state-chartered and insured by the Federal Deposit Insurance Corporation, but is not a member of the Federal Reserve System, write to:
> FDIC
> Consumer Affairs Division,
> Washington, D.C. 20429

If your complaint concerns a federally-chartered or federally-insured savings and loan association, write to:
> Federal Home Loan Bank Board
> Washington, D.C. 20552

If your complaint concerns a federally-chartered credit union, write to:
> National Credit Union Administration
> Consumer Affairs Division,
> Washington, D.C. 20456

If you still think only of credit cards when you hear the word "credit," think again. Credit is used by millions of consumers for a variety of purposes: to finance educations, remodel homes, obtain small business loans, and pay for home mortgages.

A law passed by Congress ensures that all consumers will be given an equal chance to receive credit. The Equal Credit Opportunity Act says it is illegal for creditors to discriminate against applicants on the basis of their sex, race, marital status, national origin, religion, age, or because they get public assistance income. This doesn't mean all consumers who apply for credit will get it. Creditors can still use factors such as income, expenses, debts, and credit history to judge applicants.

The law protects you when dealing with any creditor who regularly extends credit, including: banks, small loan and finance companies, retail and department stores, credit card companies, and credit unions. Anyone participating in the decision to grant credit, such as a real estate broker who arranges financing, is covered by the law. Businesses applying for credit are protected by the law, too.

Consumers have equal rights in every phase of the credit application process. Here is a checklist of important rights to remember when you request credit:

When You Apply For Credit, A Creditor May Not...

Discourage you from applying because of your sex, marital status, age, religion, race, national origin, or because you receive public assistance income.

Ask you to reveal your sex, race, national origin, or religion. A creditor may ask you to voluntarily disclose this information if you are applying for a real estate loan. This information helps federal agencies enforce anti-discrimination laws. A creditor may ask what your residence or immigration status is.

Ask whether you are divorced or widowed.

Ask what your marital status is if you are applying for a separate, unsecured account. A creditor may ask you to reveal this information if you live in Arizona, California, Idaho, Louisiana, Nevada, New Mexico, Texas, and Washington - the "community property" states. In any state, a creditor may ask for this information if you apply for a joint account or any account secured by property.

Ask you for information about your husband or wife. A creditor may ask about your spouse if: your spouse is applying with you; your spouse will be allowed to use the account; you are relying on your spouse's income or on alimony or child support income from a former spouse; or if you reside in a community property state (listed above).

Ask about your plans for having or raising children.

Ask if you receive alimony, child support, or separate maintenance payments. A creditor may ask for this information if you are first told that you don't have to reveal it if you won't rely on it to get credit. A creditor may ask if you have to pay alimony child support, or separate maintenance payments.

When Deciding To Give You Credit, A Creditor May Not...

Consider your sex, marital status, race, national origin, or religion.

Consider whether you have a telephone listing in your name. A creditor may consider whether there is a phone in your home.

Consider the race of the people who live in the neighborhood where you want to buy or improve a house with borrowed money.

Consider your age, with certain exceptions:

- if you are too young to sign contracts. Generally, this applies to those 18 and under.

- if you are 62 or over, and the creditor will favor you because of your age.

- if it is used to determine the meaning of other factors which are important to credit-worthiness. (For example, a creditor could use your age to see if your income might be reduced because you are about to retire.)

- if it is used in a scoring system which favors applicants age 62 and over. A credit-scoring system assigns different points to your answers to application questions. (For example, owning a home might be worth 10 points, while renting might be worth 5.) The total number of points helps the creditor to decide if you are credit-worthy.

When Evaluating Your Income, A Creditor May Not...

Refuse to consider reliable public assistance income in the same manner as other income.

Discount income because of your sex or marital status. (For example, a creditor cannot count a man's salary at 100% and a woman's at 75%.) A creditor may not assume a woman of child-bearing age will stop work to have or raise children.

Discount or refuse to consider income because it is derived from part-time employment or from pension, annuity, or retirement benefit programs.

Refuse to consider consistently-received alimony, child support, or separate maintenance payments. A creditor may ask you for proof that this income has been received consistently.

You Also Have The Right...

To have credit in your maiden name (Mary Smith), your first name and your husband's last name (Mary Jones), or your first name and a combined last name (Mary Smith-Jones).

To get credit without a co-signer, if you meet the creditor's standards.

To have a co-signer other than your husband or wife, if one is necessary.

To keep your own accounts after you change your name, marital status, reach a certain age, or retire, unless the creditor has evidence that you are unable or unwilling to pay.

To know whether your application was accepted or rejected within 30 days of filing it.

To know why your application was rejected. The creditor must either immediately give you the specific reasons for your rejection or tell you of your right to learn the reasons if you ask them within 60 days. (Examples of reasons are: "Your income was too low," or "You haven't been employed at your job long enough." Examples of unacceptable reasons are: "You didn't meet our minimum standards," or "You didn't receive enough points on our credit-scoring system.") Indefinite and vague reasons are illegal____ask for specifics.

To learn the specific reasons why you were offered less favorable terms than you applied for. (Examples of less favorable terms include higher finance charges or less money than you requested). This does not hold if you accept the less favorable terms.

To know the specific reasons why your account was closed or why the terms of the account were made less favorable to you. This does not hold if these actions were taken because your account was delinquent or because you have not used the account for some time.

A Special Note To Women

A good credit history, or record of how you paid past bills is often necessary to obtain credit. Unfortunately, this hurts many married, separated, divorced, and widowed women. There are two common reasons women do not have credit histories in their own names: they lost their credit histories when they married and changed their name, and creditors reported accounts shared by married couples in the husband's name only.

The law says that when creditors report histories to credit bureaus or to other creditors they must report information on accounts shared by married couples in both names. This is true only for accounts opened after June 1, 1977. If you and your spouse opened an account before that time, you should ask the creditor to use both names.

If you are married, divorced, separated, or widowed, you should make a special point to call or visit your local credit bureau(s) to ensure that all relevant information is in a file under your own name. To learn more about building your credit file, write for a free brochure, "Women and Credit Histories," from any of the FTC offices listed below.

What You Can Do If You Suspect Discrimination...

Complain to the creditor. Make it known that you are aware of the law. The creditor may reverse the decision or detect an error.

Many states have their own equal credit opportunity laws. Check with your state's Attorney General's office to see if the creditor violated state laws. Your state may decide to take the creditor to court.

Bring a case in Federal district court. If you win, you can recover actual damages and be awarded a penalty. You can also recover reasonable attorney's fees and court costs. An attorney can advise you on how to proceed.

Join with others to file a class action suit. You may recover punitive damages for the class of up to $500,000 or 1% of the creditor's net worth, whichever is less.

Report violations to the appropriate government agency. If you are denied credit, the creditor must give you the name and address of the agency to contact. While the agencies do not resolve individual complaints, they do use consumer comments to decide which companies to investigate.

Where to Send Complaints and Questions

If a retail store, department store, small loan and finance company, oil company, public utility company, state credit union, government lending program, or travel and expense credit card company is involved, contact the Federal Trade Commission office nearest you:

915 Second Avenue
SEATTLE, WA 98174
(206) 442-4655

55 East Monroe Street
CHICAGO, IL 60603
(312) 353-4423

150 Causeway Street
BOSTON, MA 02114
(617) 223-6621

1405 Curtis Street
DENVER, CO 80202
(303) 837-2271

26 Federal Plaza
NEW YORK, NY 10278
(212) 264-1207

8303 Elmbrook Drive
DALLAS, TX 75247
(214) 767-7050

118 St. Clair Avenue
CLEVELAND, OH 44114
(216) 522-4207

11000 Wilshire Boulevard
LOS ANGELES, CA 90024
(213) 209-7575

450 Golden Gate Avenue
SAN FRANCISCO, CA 94102
(415) 556-1270

1718 Peachtree Street, N.W.
ATLANTA, GA 30367
(404) 881-4836

CENTRAL OFFICE:
6th St. and Washington Ave., N.W.
WASHINGTON, D.C. 20580
(202) 523-3598

If your complaint concerns a nationally-chartered bank (National or N.A. will be part of the name), write to:
Comptroller of the Currency
Consumer Affairs Division,
Washington, D.C. 20219

If your complaint concerns a state-chartered bank that is a member of the Federal Reserve System, write to:
Board of Governors of the Federal Reserve System
Consumer Affairs Division,
Washington, D.C. 20551

If your complaint concerns a bank that is state-chartered and insured by the Federal Deposit Insurance Corporation, but is not a member of the Federal Reserve System, write to:
FDIC
Consumer Affairs Division,
Washington, D.C. 20429

If your complaint concerns a federally-chartered or federally-insured savings and loan association, write to:
Federal Home Loan Bank Board
Equal Credit Opportunity,
Washington, D.C. 20552

If your complaint concerns a federally-chartered credit union, write to:

> National Credit Union Administration
> Consumer Affairs Division,
> Washington, D.C. 20456

Complaints against all kinds of creditors can be referred to:

> Department of Justice
> Civil Rights Division,
> Washington, D.C. 20530